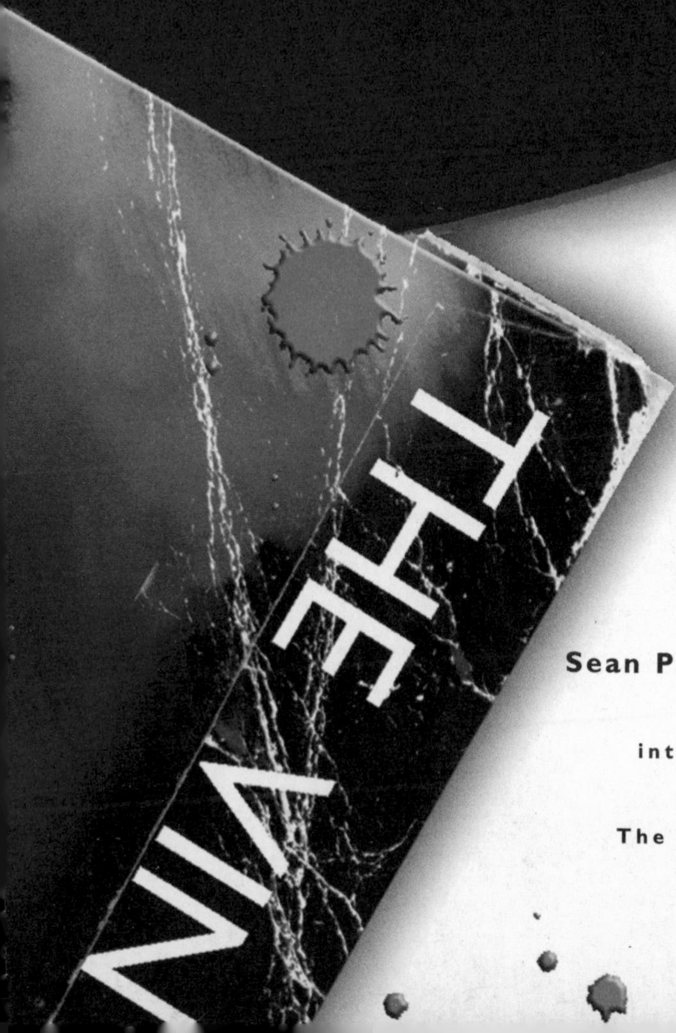
THE VIN

Si Spencer writer

Simon Gane penciller

Cameron Stewart inker

Guy Major colorist

Jared K. Fletcher letterer

Sean Phillips original series covers

introduction by **David Lapham**

The Vinyl Underground created by
Spencer & Gane

KAREN BERGER Senior VP-Executive Editor   SHELLY BOND Editor-original series
ANGELA RUFINO Assistant Editor-original series   BOB HARRAS Editor-collected edition
ROBBIN BROSTERMAN Senior Art Director   PAUL LEVITZ President & Publisher
GEORG BREWER VP-Design & DC Direct Creative   RICHARD BRUNING Senior VP-Creative Director
PATRICK CALDON Executive VP-Finance & Operations   CHRIS CARAMALIS VP-Finance
JOHN CUNNINGHAM VP-Marketing   TERRI CUNNINGHAM VP-Managing Editor
ALISON GILL VP-Manufacturing   DAVID HYDE VP-Publicity   HANK KANALZ VP-General Manager, WildStorm
JIM LEE Editorial Director-WildStorm   PAULA LOWITT Senior VP-Business & Legal Affairs
MARYELLEN MCLAUGHLIN VP-Advertising & Custom Publishing   JOHN NEE Senior VP-Business Development
GREGORY NOVECK Senior VP-Creative Affairs   SUE POHJA VP-Book Trade Sales
STEVE ROTTERDAM Senior VP-Sales & Marketing   CHERYL RUBIN Senior VP-Brand Management
JEFF TROJAN VP-Business Development, DC Direct   BOB WAYNE VP-Sales

Cover illustration by Sean Phillips   Publication design by Amelia Grohman

THE VINYL UNDERGROUND: WATCHING THE DETECTIVES

Published by DC Comics. Cover, introduction and compilation Copyright © 2008 DC Comics. All Rights Reserved.
Originally published in single magazine form as THE VINYL UNDERGROUND 1-5 Copyright © 2007, 2008
Si Spencer and Simon Gane. All Rights Reserved. VERTIGO and all characters, their distinctive likenesses and
related elements featured in this publication are trademarks of DC Comics. The stories, characters and incidents
featured in this publication are entirely fictional. DC Comics does not read or accept unsolicited submissions
of ideas, stories or artwork.

DC Comics, 1700 Broadway, New York, NY 10019. A Warner Bros. Entertainment Company.
Printed in Canada. First Printing. ISBN 13: 978-1-4012-1812-6

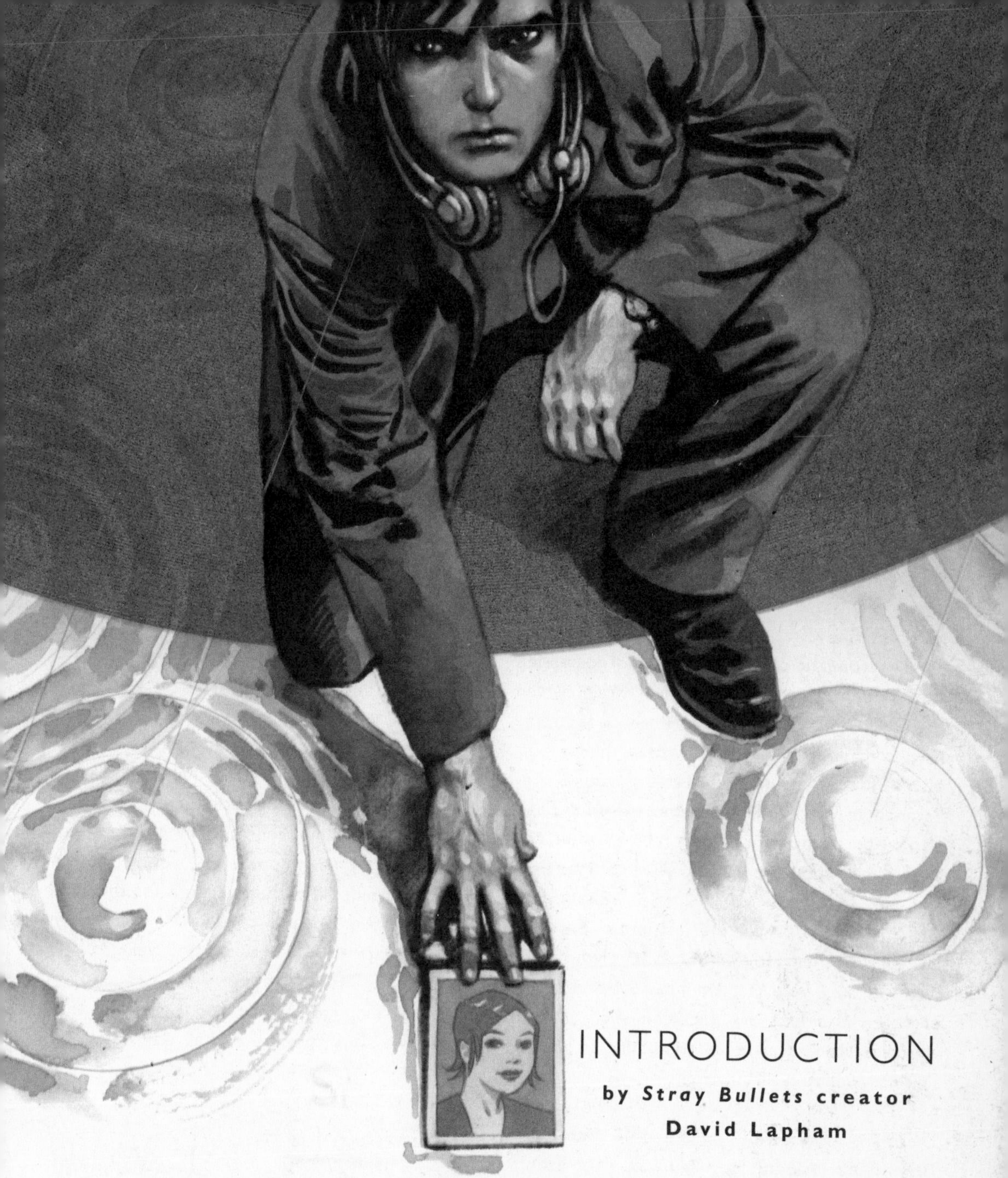

INTRODUCTION

by *Stray Bullets* creator David Lapham

I WAS IN LONDON once many years ago, and all I can tell you is two things: The first is that, unlike New York, the cab drivers know where they're going, and the second is that there's this overwhelming feeling there—a vague, creepy feeling—that Jack the Ripper or Professor Moriarty or Margaret Thatcher is lurking around the next corner, smiling broadly and holding the biggest knife you've ever seen...that every alley contains a drug den or a cult of wizards eviscerating some prostitute. Londoners must get a kick out of all this, or...or they'd be Americans like me and worry about normal psychos, like twelve-year-olds with guns.

The UK has always been a land where magic and legend are so mixed with fact that they're really inseparable. Who is King Richard? He's the noble monarch whose honor Robin and his Merry Men fought for, right? What do we know about William Shakespeare other than that he supposedly wrote a few plays? Nothing. Maybe he's fiction. And Sherlock Holmes seems more real to me than, say, Lord Byron, who always seemed sort of suspect.

Well, when they dig up these VINYL UNDERGROUND books a few thousand years after the apocalypse, Moz and his occult hunters are going to be every bit as real as such factual or fictional icons as Dr. Jekyll, Dorian Grey, and Winston Churchill. That's because writer Si Spencer mixes up his well-conceived but imaginary cast with cold hard fact.

And style. Let me tell you, this book's got style.

Our main player, Morrison "Moz" Shepherd, is the pretty boy, orphaned son of a soccer star, a D-list tabloid darling, and soul-spinning DJ. He's also a rehabbing drug-addicted ex-con, and the leader of a tightly knit group of occult crime detectives whose HQ is in a way cool converted underground tube station. Then there's Perv, a psychic/asthmatic/convicted child pornographer. And a...um...an arsonist/porn star/virgin named Leah, aka "Juicy Lou," who will go to extreme lengths to get the job done. I mean things-your-mama-never-warned-you-about-because-she-never-thought-they-were-possible extreme. She's also pretty handy with an uppercut, a lighter and a can of hair spray. And finally, we've got Moz's ex, Abi, an African Tribal Princess/Architectural Historian. Not since the infamous Butthole Surfers moshed together album titles like *Psychic...Powerless...Another Man's Sac* and *Locust Abortion Technician* have we seen such random wordplay used to make up something so utterly senseless yet so brilliantly right.

These are some seriously f%#ked up characters. They don't do anything halfway, this group. Despite their unorthodox approach to life, for all the bickering and arguing, they're all in it for their leader, Morrison Shepherd; they love this man. They're a family, and not a dysfunctional one either. Individually, they're severely dysfunctional, but as a group, they're solid. Maybe every Tom, Dick, and Edmund on the street is like this in London (where these little nightmares take place); maybe this is the norm for a person of the British persuasion. How would I know? I'm an American, and it all seems pretty messed up to me.

And, oh by the by, that's a very good thing.

The streets of London hide a deep history running red with murder, and Mr. Spencer knows where the bodies are buried. He knows this city like the back of his hand. Its secrets mirror those of our characters. Though we're just getting started here, you can see the tapestry begin to form. The story of Morrison Shepherd is part of the city and the more we learn about him the deeper we travel into London's dark heart. And it's not just in the words. Along with Spencer's detailed travelogue, Simon Gane and Cameron Stewart's artwork brings the architecture of London alive. They merge the old and the new, keeping the cast slick and modern while never forgetting the ancient pile of rot they inhabit.

A great rule of thumb I go by when reading a new book is to ask myself a few questions: Did it leave me wanting more? Was the artist drawing with more style and conviction on the last page than on the first? Was the writer hitting his zone and pulling out deeper mysteries to mire his characters in? Is it worth coming back to peel the layers and see what's hidden beneath? The answer to all of these is, of course, yes, yes, yes, which, of course, is a nine-letter Americanism for the simple three-letter British word "yes," which oddly translates back to American as "Hell, yeah!"

So sit back and enjoy your guided tour of London. It ain't always pretty, but that's the way we like it.

Lapham

DAVID LAPHAM
In Safe and Sunny California
March 2008

David Lapham is an Eisner Award-winning comic book writer and artist, best known for his work on the independent comic book STRAY BULLETS. He writes and draws the monthly series YOUNG LIARS for Vertigo.

M NCB

delity

(66-10127)

OHIBITED

SNOGGING FOR ENGLAND

①

THE VIN

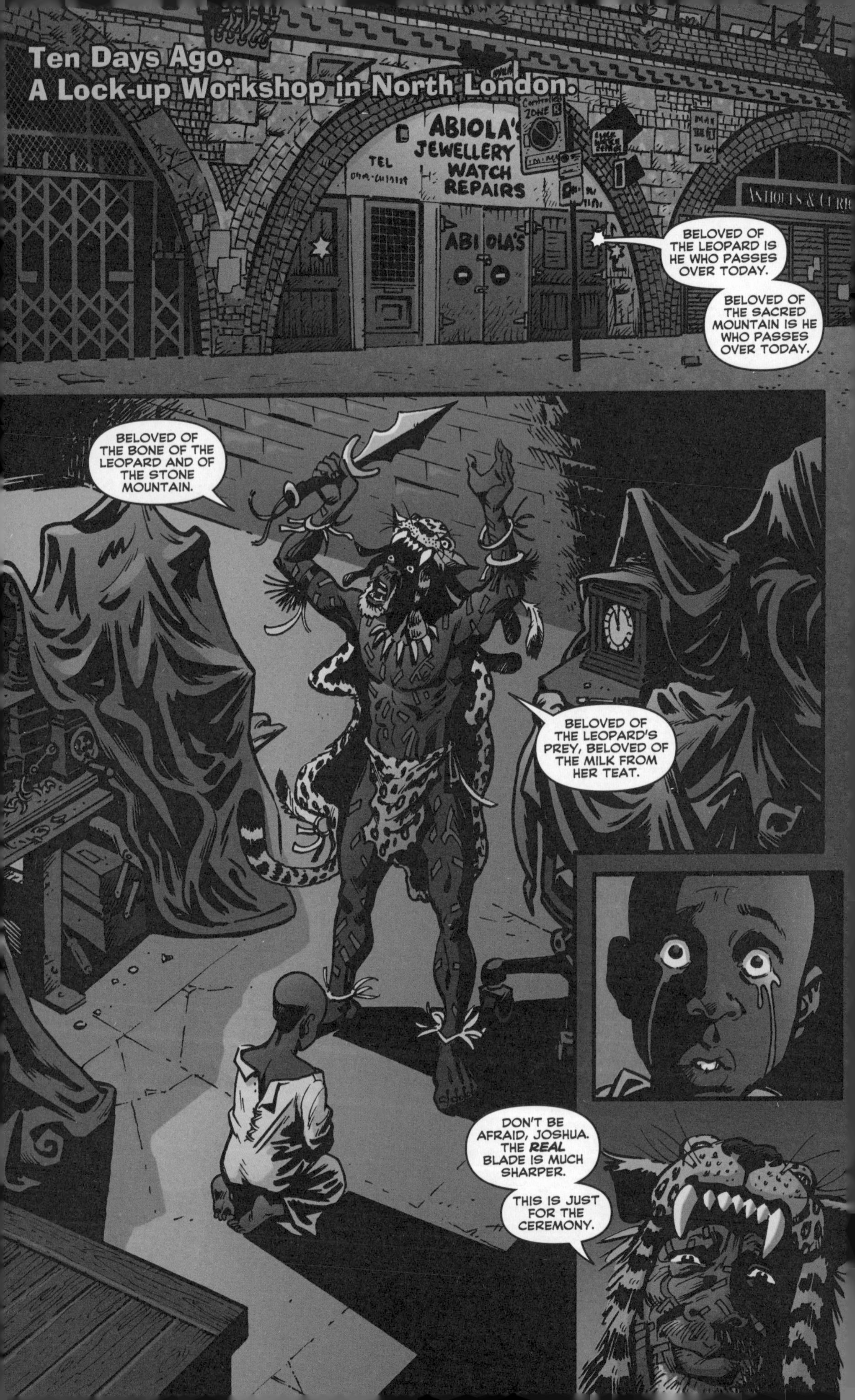
Ten Days Ago.
A Lock-up Workshop in North London.
ABIOLA'S JEWELLERY WATCH REPAIRS
TEL
ABI OLA'S
ANTIQUES & CURIO
BELOVED OF THE LEOPARD IS HE WHO PASSES OVER TODAY.
BELOVED OF THE SACRED MOUNTAIN IS HE WHO PASSES OVER TODAY.
BELOVED OF THE BONE OF THE LEOPARD AND OF THE STONE MOUNTAIN.
BELOVED OF THE LEOPARD'S PREY, BELOVED OF THE MILK FROM HER TEAT.
DON'T BE AFRAID, JOSHUA. THE *REAL* BLADE IS MUCH SHARPER.
THIS IS JUST FOR THE CEREMONY.

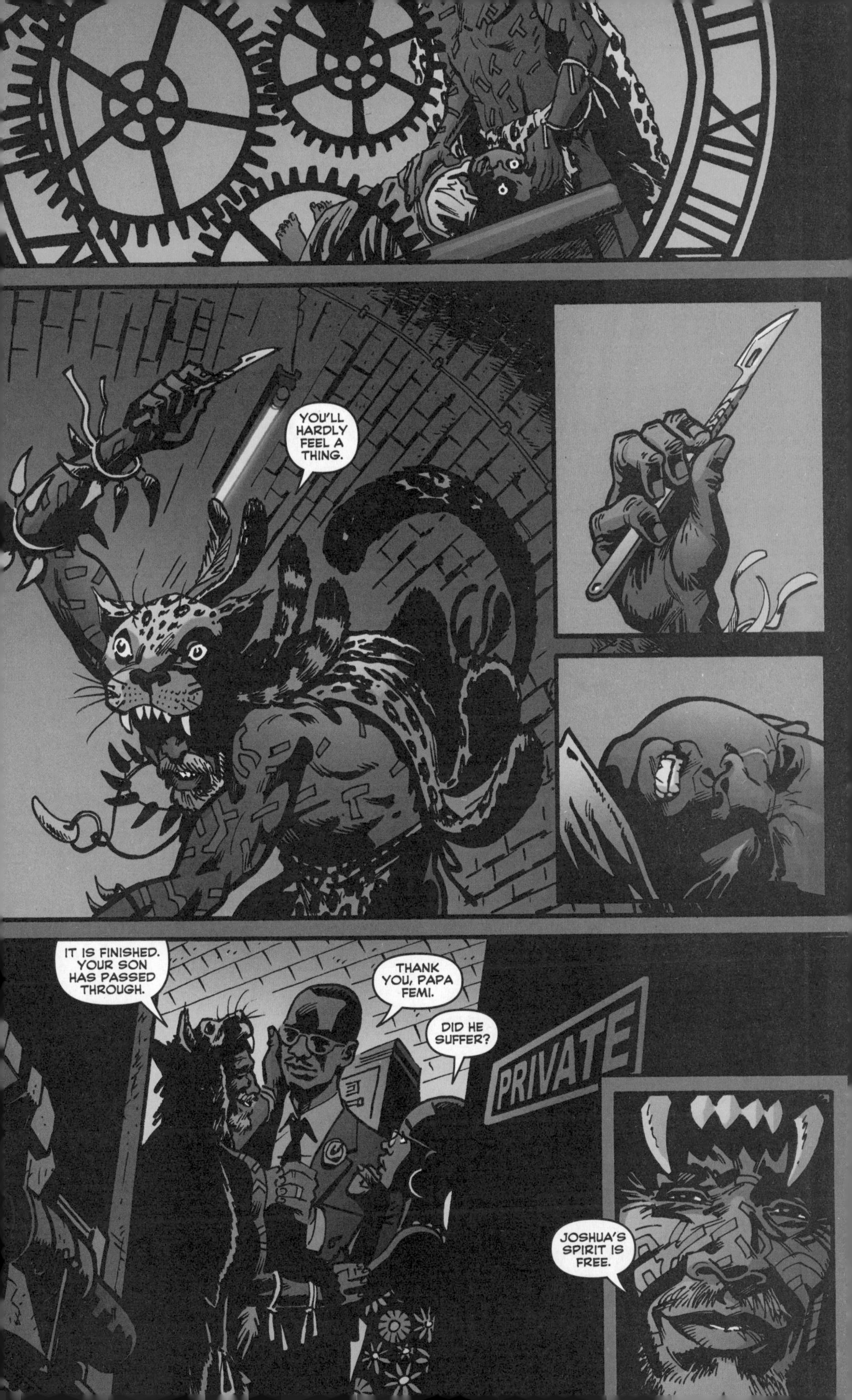
YOU'LL HARDLY FEEL A THING.
IT IS FINISHED. YOUR SON HAS PASSED THROUGH.
THANK YOU, PAPA FEMI.
DID HE SUFFER?
PRIVATE
JOSHUA'S SPIRIT IS FREE.

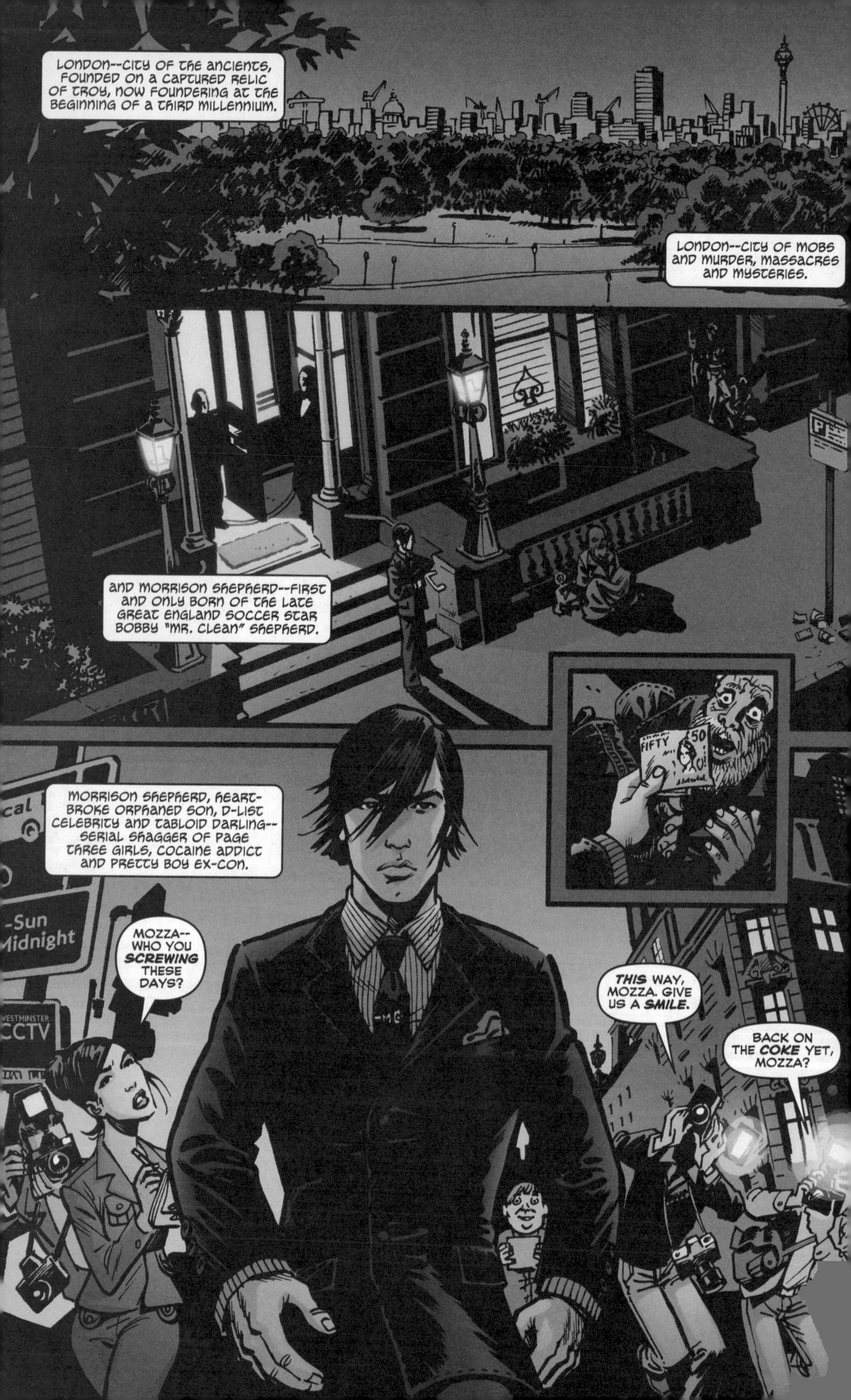
LONDON--CITY OF THE ANCIENTS, FOUNDED ON A CAPTURED RELIC OF TROY, NOW FOUNDERING AT THE BEGINNING OF A THIRD MILLENNIUM.
LONDON--CITY OF MOBS AND MURDER, MASSACRES AND MYSTERIES.
AND MORRISON SHEPHERD--FIRST AND ONLY BORN OF THE LATE GREAT ENGLAND SOCCER STAR BOBBY "MR. CLEAN" SHEPHERD.
FIFTY
50
MORRISON SHEPHERD, HEART-BROKE ORPHANED SON, D-LIST CELEBRITY AND TABLOID DARLING--SERIAL SHAGGER OF PAGE THREE GIRLS, COCAINE ADDICT AND PRETTY BOY EX-CON.
-Sun
Midnight
WESTMINSTER
CCTV
MOZZA--WHO YOU SCREWING THESE DAYS?
THIS WAY, MOZZA. GIVE US A SMILE.
BACK ON THE COKE YET, MOZZA?

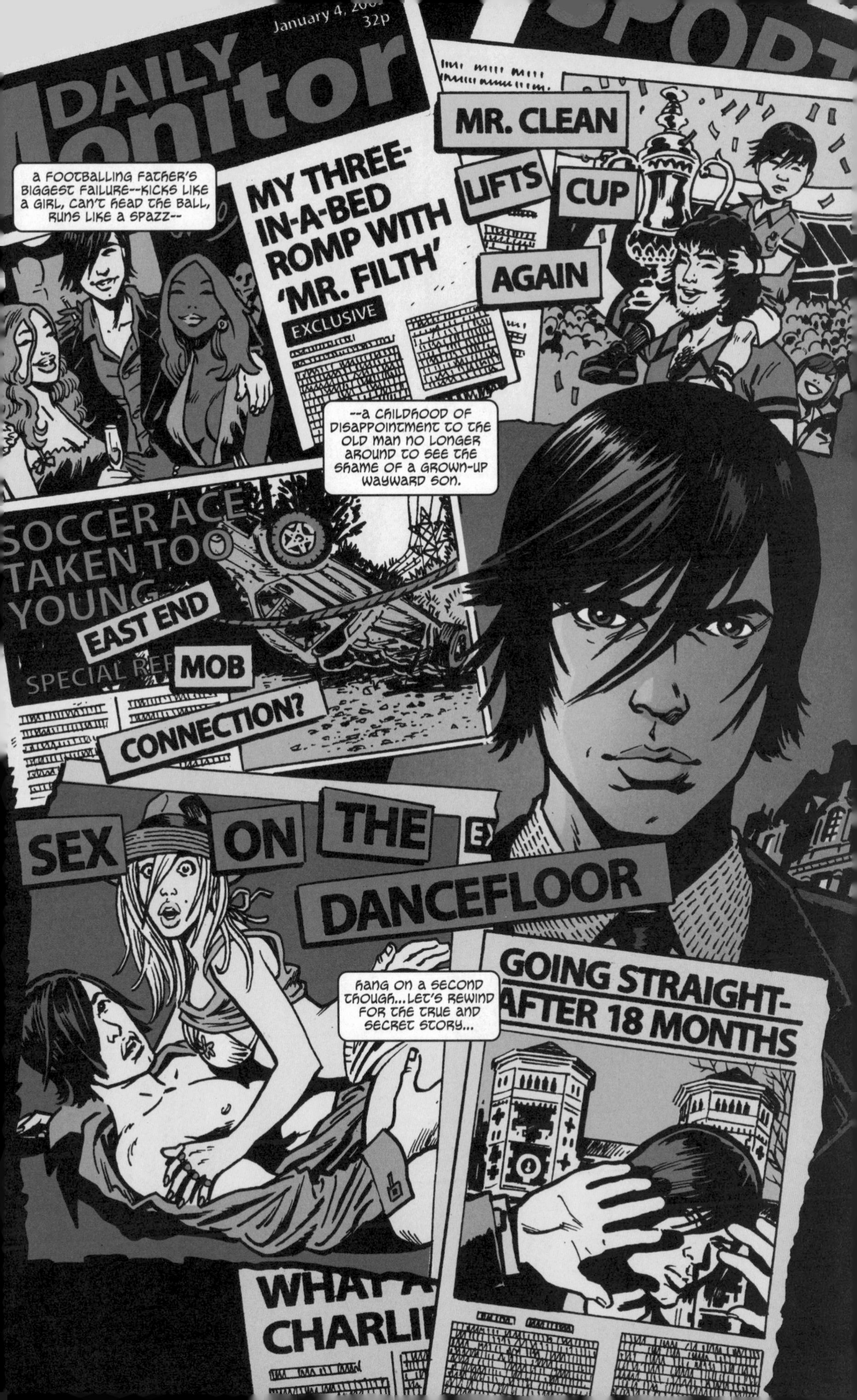
January 4, 200
32p
DAILY
Monitor
A FOOTBALLING FATHER'S BIGGEST FAILURE--KICKS LIKE A GIRL, CAN'T HEAD THE BALL, RUNS LIKE A SPAZZ--
MY THREE-IN-A-BED ROMP WITH 'MR. FILTH'
EXCLUSIVE
MR. CLEAN
LIFTS
CUP
AGAIN
--A CHILDHOOD OF DISAPPOINTMENT TO THE OLD MAN NO LONGER AROUND TO SEE THE SHAME OF A GROWN-UP WAYWARD SON.
SOCCER ACE TAKEN TOO YOUNG
EAST END
MOB
CONNECTION?
SPECIAL RE
SEX
ON
THE
DANCEFLOOR
GOING STRAIGHT-AFTER 18 MONTHS
HANG ON A SECOND THOUGH...LET'S REWIND FOR THE TRUE AND SECRET STORY...
WHAT A
CHARLI

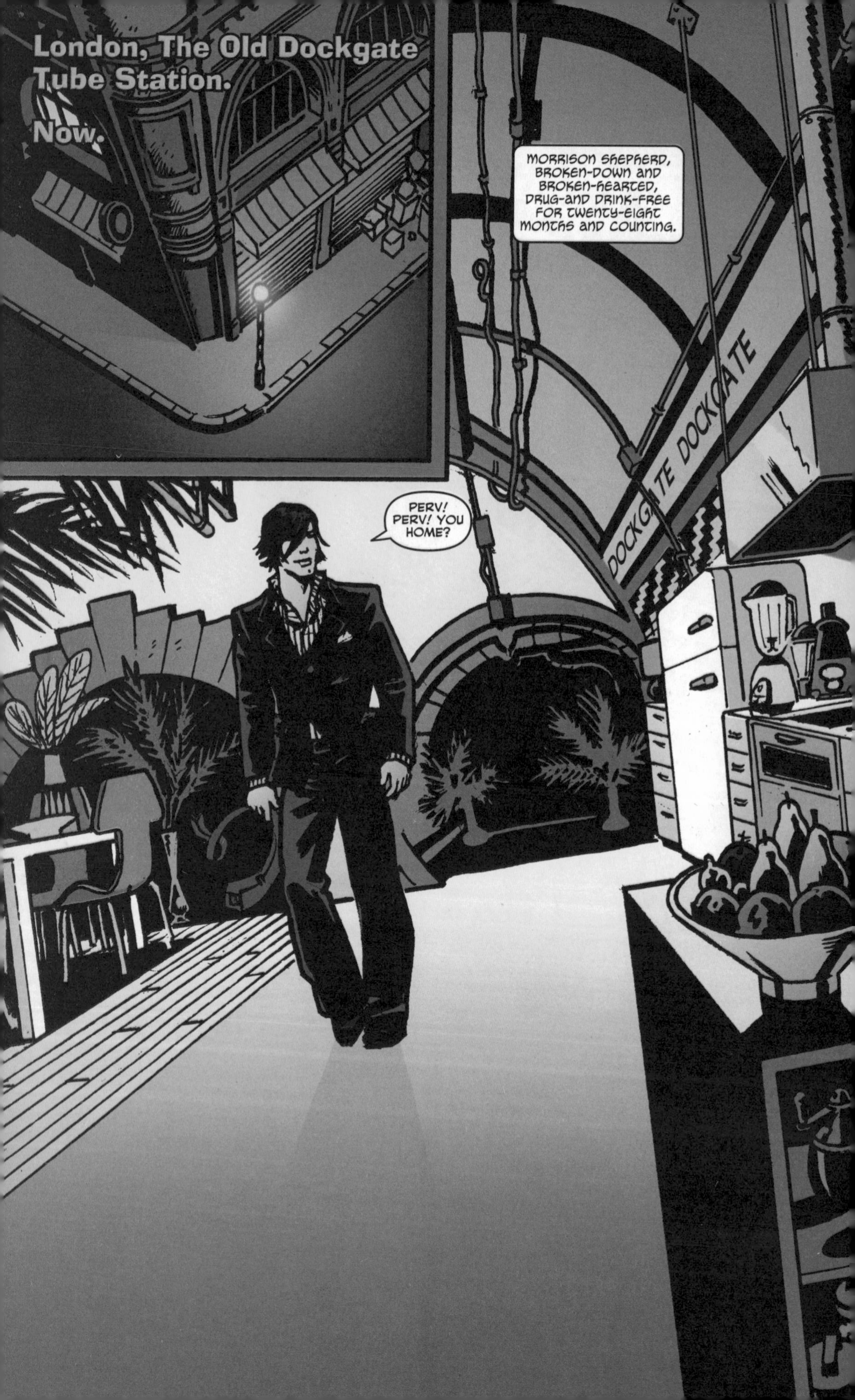
London, The Old Dockgate Tube Station.
Now.
MORRISON SHEPHERD, BROKEN-DOWN AND BROKEN-HEARTED, DRUG-AND DRINK-FREE FOR TWENTY-EIGHT MONTHS AND COUNTING.
PERV! PERV! YOU HOME?
DOCKGATE DOCKGATE

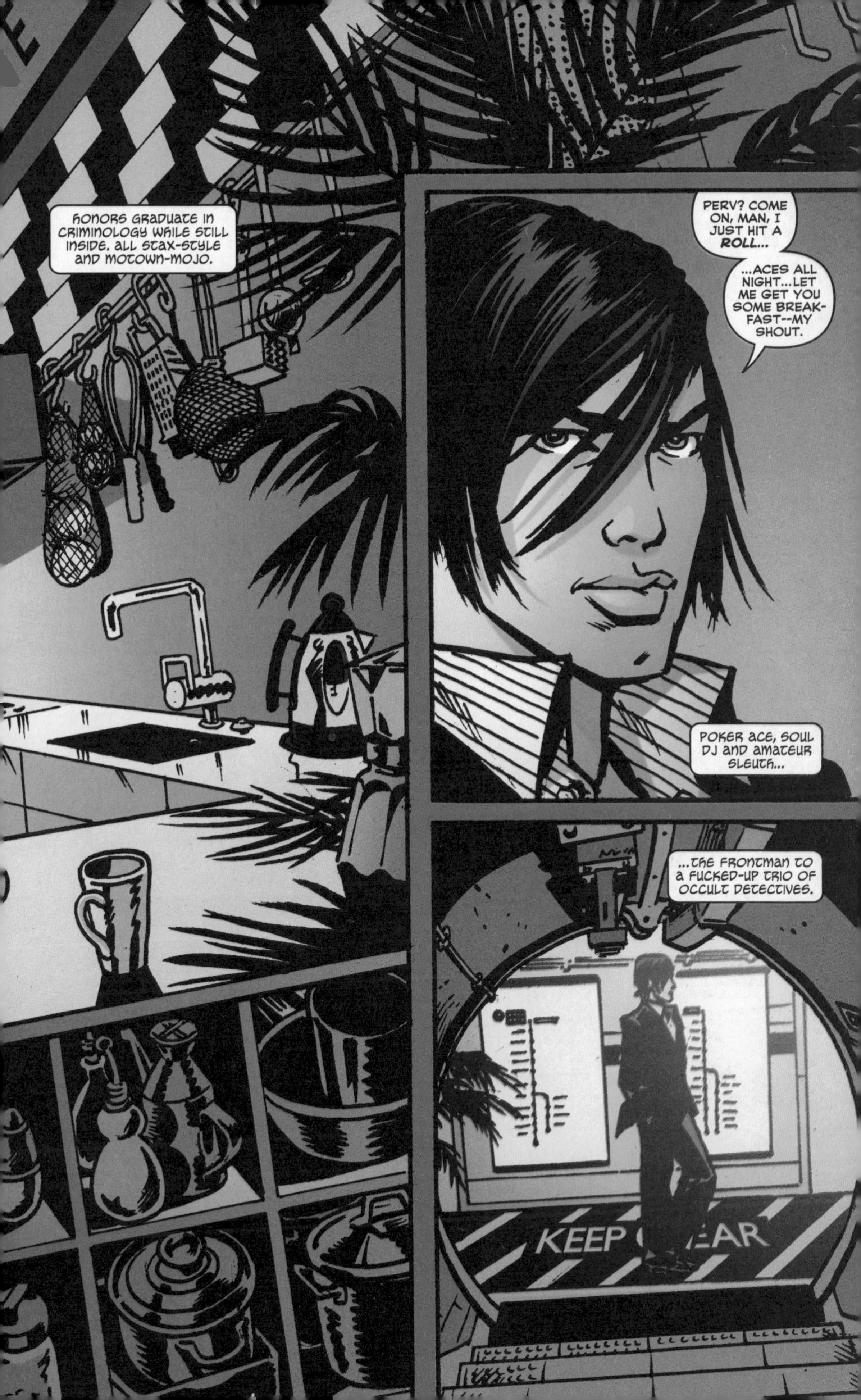
HONORS GRADUATE IN CRIMINOLOGY WHILE STILL INSIDE. ALL STAX-STYLE AND MOTOWN-MOJO.
PERV? COME ON, MAN, I JUST HIT A ROLL...
...ACES ALL NIGHT...LET ME GET YOU SOME BREAK-FAST--MY SHOUT.
POKER ACE, SOUL DJ AND AMATEUR SLEUTH...
...THE FRONTMAN TO A FUCKED-UP TRIO OF OCCULT DETECTIVES.

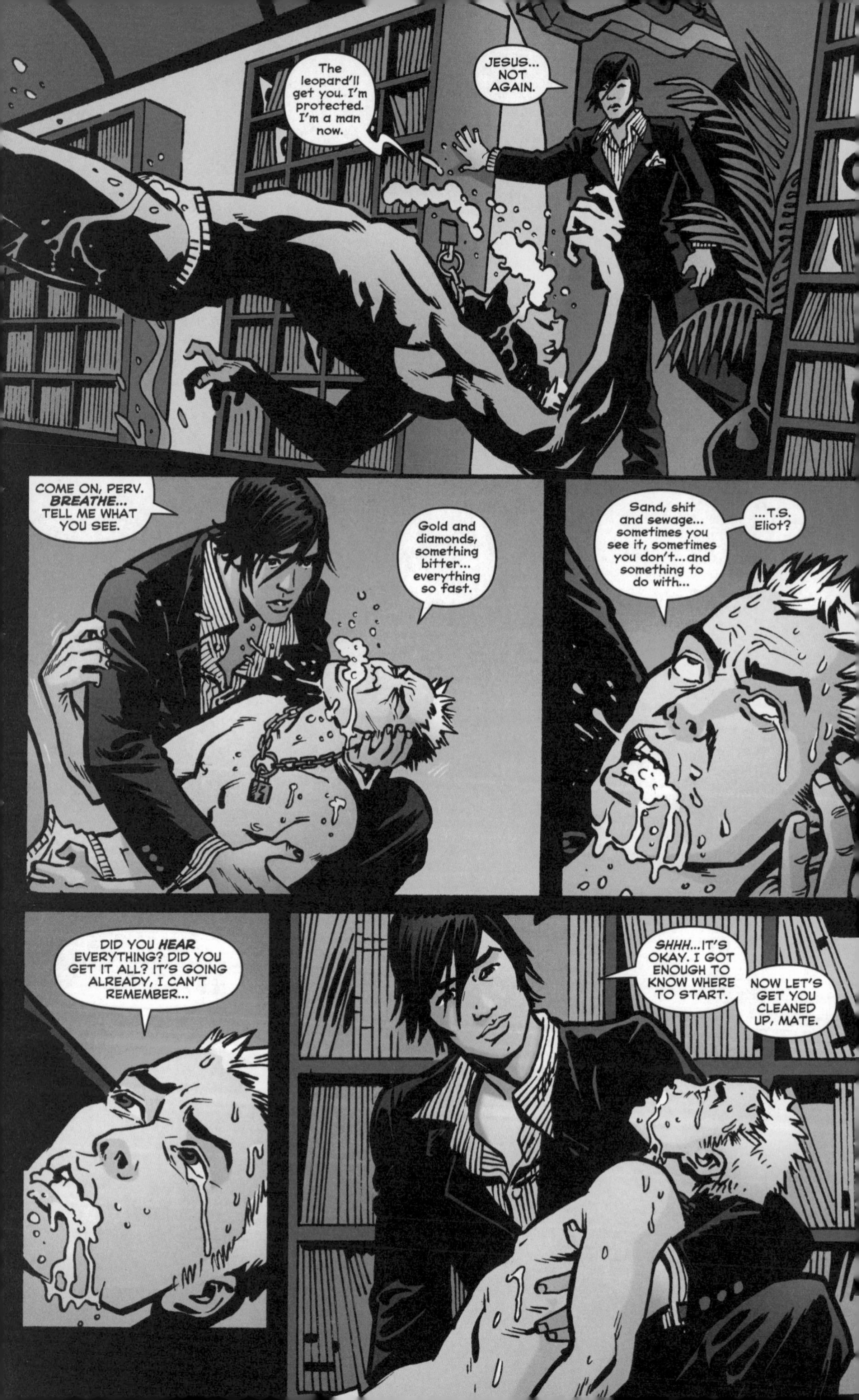
The leopard'll get you. I'm protected. I'm a man now.
JESUS... NOT AGAIN.
COME ON, PERV. BREATHE... TELL ME WHAT YOU SEE.
Gold and diamonds, something bitter... everything so fast.
Sand, shit and sewage... sometimes you see it, sometimes you don't...and something to do with...
...T.S. Eliot?
DID YOU HEAR EVERYTHING? DID YOU GET IT ALL? IT'S GOING ALREADY, I CAN'T REMEMBER...
SHHH...IT'S OKAY. I GOT ENOUGH TO KNOW WHERE TO START.
NOW LET'S GET YOU CLEANED UP, MATE.

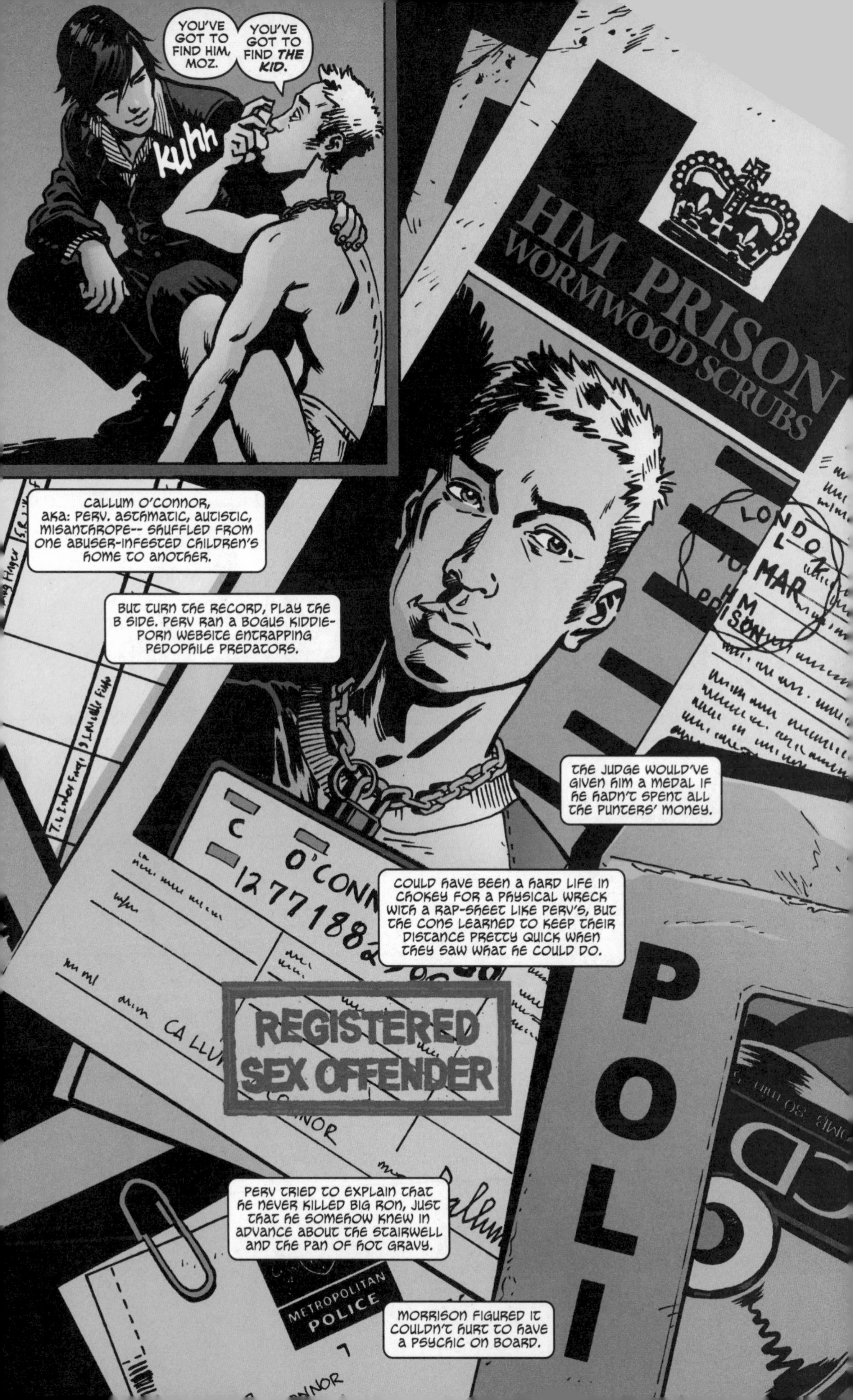
YOU'VE GOT TO FIND HIM, MOZ.
YOU'VE GOT TO FIND THE KID.
kuhh
HM PRISON
WORMWOOD SCRUBS
CALLUM O'CONNOR, AKA: PERV. ASTHMATIC, AUTISTIC, MISANTHROPE-- SHUFFLED FROM ONE ABUSER-INFESTED CHILDREN'S HOME TO ANOTHER.
BUT TURN THE RECORD, PLAY THE B SIDE. PERV RAN A BOGUS KIDDIE-PORN WEBSITE ENTRAPPING PEDOPHILE PREDATORS.
LONDON
MAR
HM PRISON
THE JUDGE WOULD'VE GIVEN HIM A MEDAL IF HE HADN'T SPENT ALL THE PUNTERS' MONEY.
C O'CONN
12771882
COULD HAVE BEEN A HARD LIFE IN CHOKEY FOR A PHYSICAL WRECK WITH A RAP-SHEET LIKE PERV'S, BUT THE CONS LEARNED TO KEEP THEIR DISTANCE PRETTY QUICK WHEN THEY SAW WHAT HE COULD DO.
REGISTERED SEX OFFENDER
CALLUM
POLI
PERV TRIED TO EXPLAIN THAT HE NEVER KILLED BIG RON, JUST THAT HE SOMEHOW KNEW IN ADVANCE ABOUT THE STAIRWELL AND THE PAN OF HOT GRAVY.
METROPOLITAN POLICE
MORRISON FIGURED IT COULDN'T HURT TO HAVE A PSYCHIC ON BOARD.

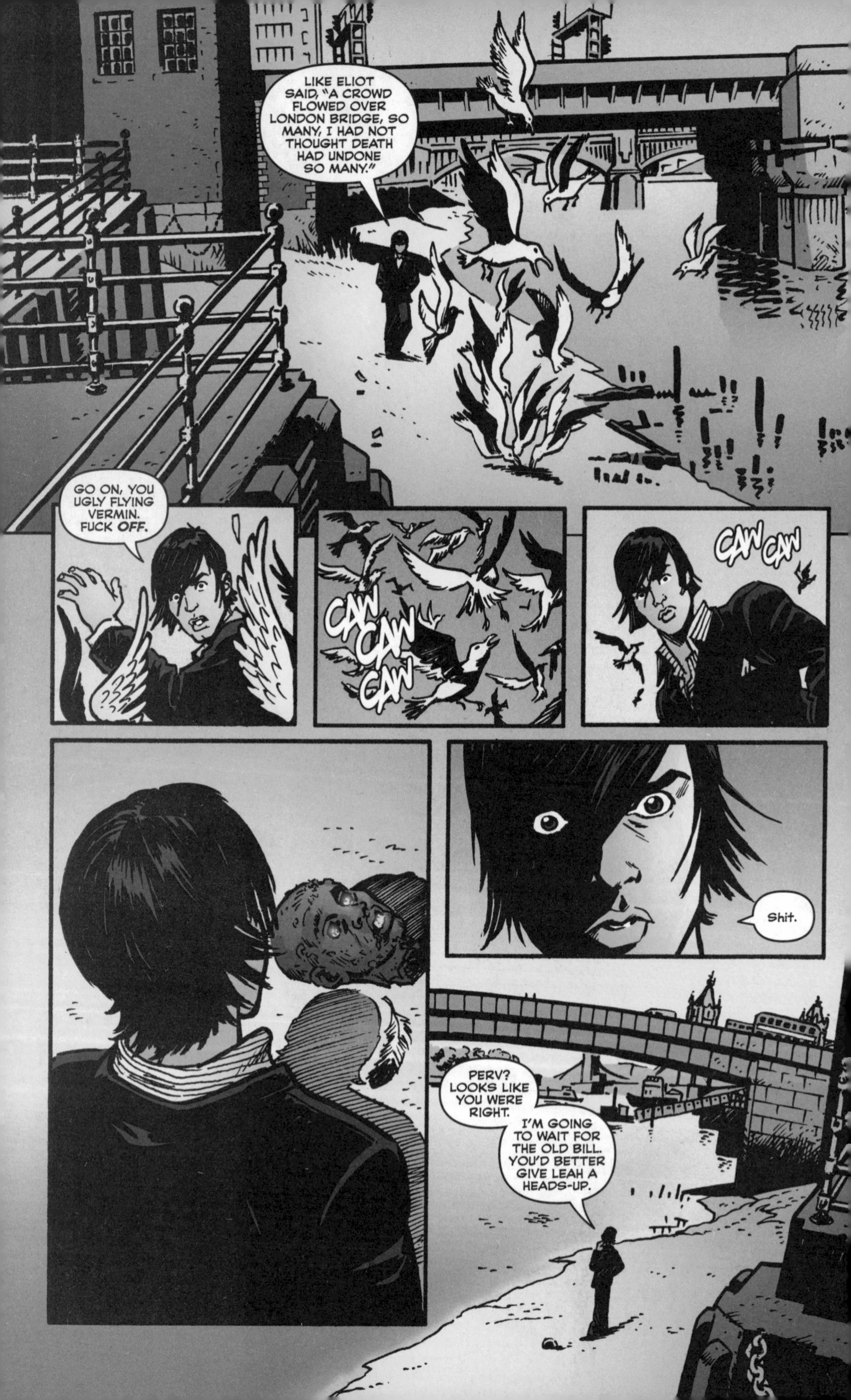
LIKE ELIOT SAID, "A CROWD FLOWED OVER LONDON BRIDGE, SO MANY, I HAD NOT THOUGHT DEATH HAD UNDONE SO MANY."
GO ON, YOU UGLY FLYING VERMIN. FUCK OFF.
CAW CAW CAW
CAW CAW
Shit.
PERV? LOOKS LIKE YOU WERE RIGHT.
I'M GOING TO WAIT FOR THE OLD BILL. YOU'D BETTER GIVE LEAH A HEADS-UP.

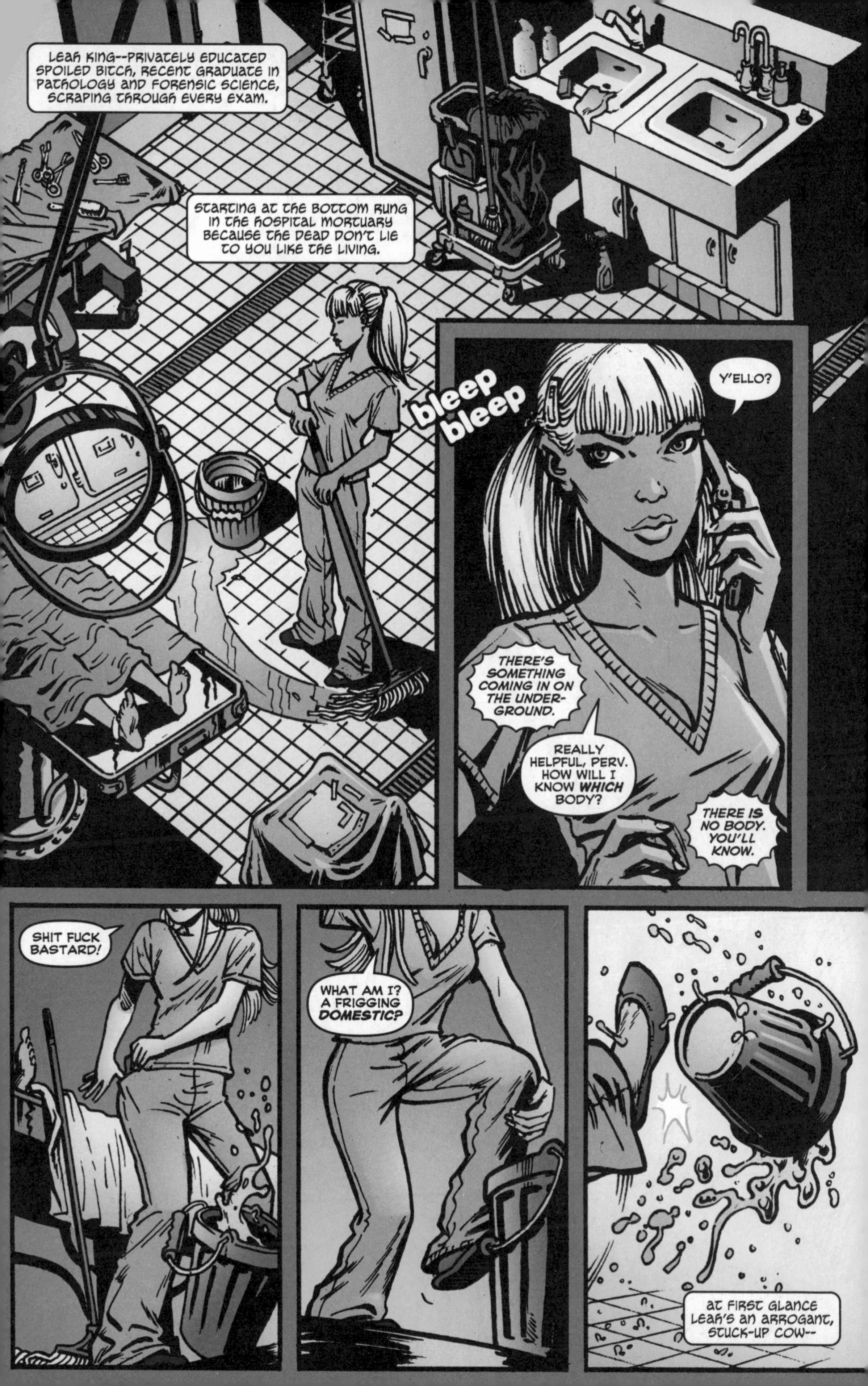
LEAH KING--PRIVATELY EDUCATED SPOILED BITCH, RECENT GRADUATE IN PATHOLOGY AND FORENSIC SCIENCE, SCRAPING THROUGH EVERY EXAM.
STARTING AT THE BOTTOM RUNG IN THE HOSPITAL MORTUARY BECAUSE THE DEAD DON'T LIE TO YOU LIKE THE LIVING.
bleep bleep
Y'ELLO?
THERE'S SOMETHING COMING IN ON THE UNDER-GROUND.
REALLY HELPFUL, PERV. HOW WILL I KNOW WHICH BODY?
THERE IS NO BODY. YOU'LL KNOW.
SHIT FUCK BASTARD!
WHAT AM I? A FRIGGING DOMESTIC?
AT FIRST GLANCE LEAH'S AN ARROGANT, STUCK-UP COW--

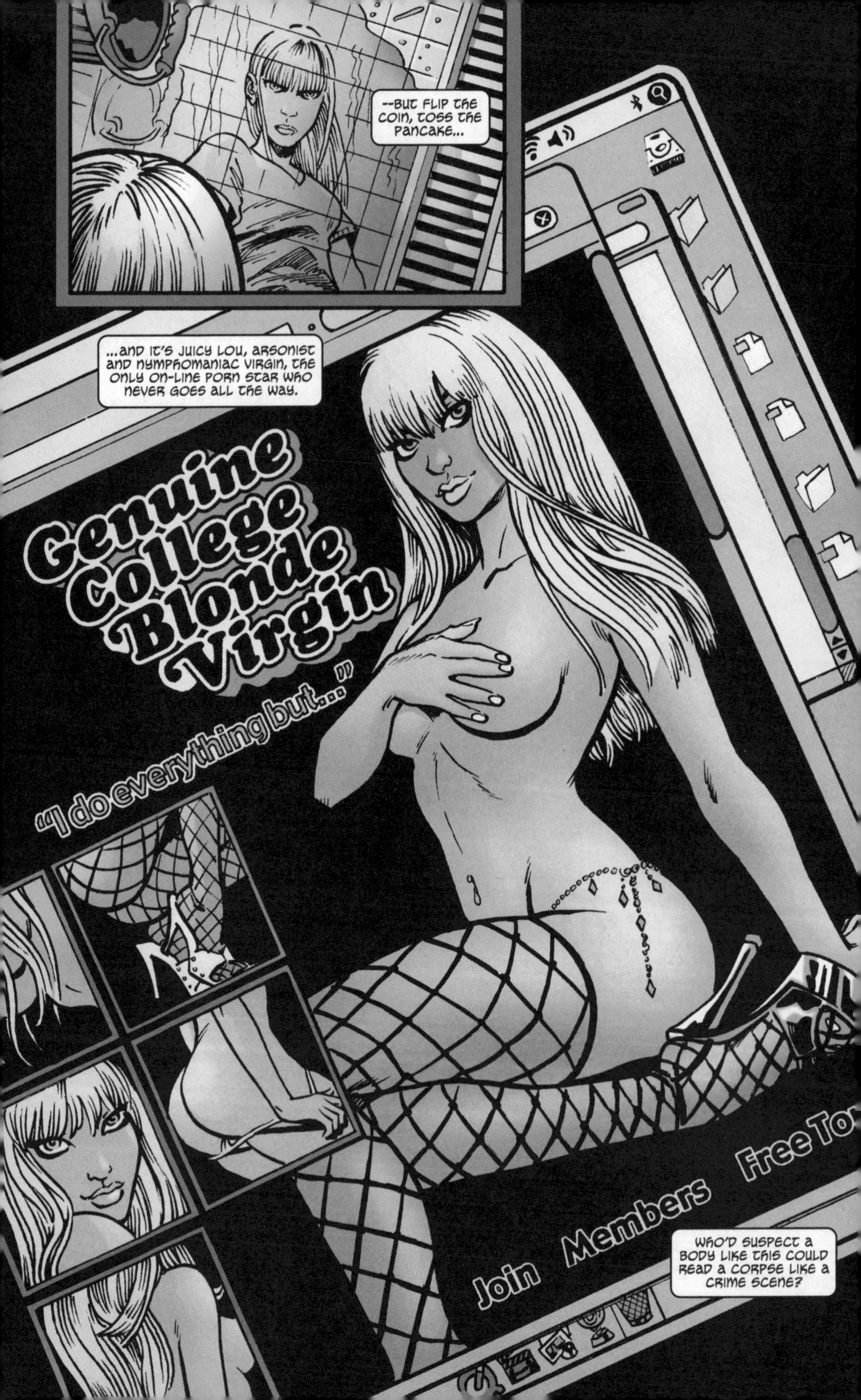
--BUT FLIP THE COIN, TOSS THE PANCAKE...
...AND IT'S JUICY LOU, ARSONIST AND NYMPHOMANIAC VIRGIN, THE ONLY ON-LINE PORN STAR WHO NEVER GOES ALL THE WAY.
Genuine College Blonde Virgin
"I do everything but..."
Join
Members
Free To
WHO'D SUSPECT A BODY LIKE THIS COULD READ A CORPSE LIKE A CRIME SCENE?

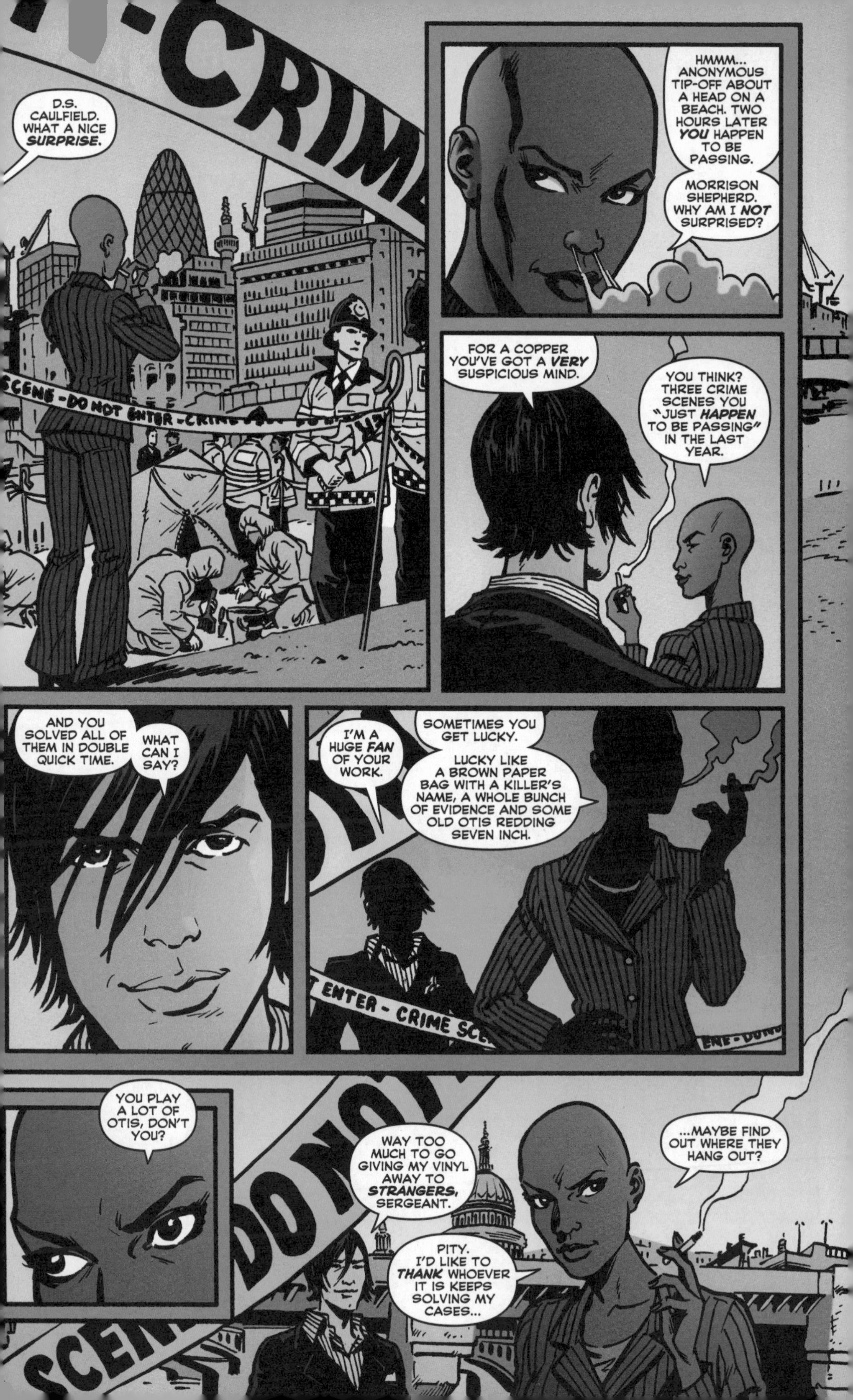

CRIME
D.S. CAULFIELD. WHAT A NICE SURPRISE.
SCENE - DO NOT ENTER - CRIME
HMMM... ANONYMOUS TIP-OFF ABOUT A HEAD ON A BEACH. TWO HOURS LATER YOU HAPPEN TO BE PASSING.
MORRISON SHEPHERD. WHY AM I NOT SURPRISED?
FOR A COPPER YOU'VE GOT A VERY SUSPICIOUS MIND.
YOU THINK? THREE CRIME SCENES YOU "JUST HAPPEN TO BE PASSING" IN THE LAST YEAR.
AND YOU SOLVED ALL OF THEM IN DOUBLE QUICK TIME.
WHAT CAN I SAY?
I'M A HUGE FAN OF YOUR WORK.
SOMETIMES YOU GET LUCKY.
LUCKY LIKE A BROWN PAPER BAG WITH A KILLER'S NAME, A WHOLE BUNCH OF EVIDENCE AND SOME OLD OTIS REDDING SEVEN INCH.
ENTER - CRIME SCE
YOU PLAY A LOT OF OTIS, DON'T YOU?
WAY TOO MUCH TO GO GIVING MY VINYL AWAY TO STRANGERS, SERGEANT.
PITY. I'D LIKE TO THANK WHOEVER IT IS KEEPS SOLVING MY CASES...
...MAYBE FIND OUT WHERE THEY HANG OUT?
DO NO
SCEN

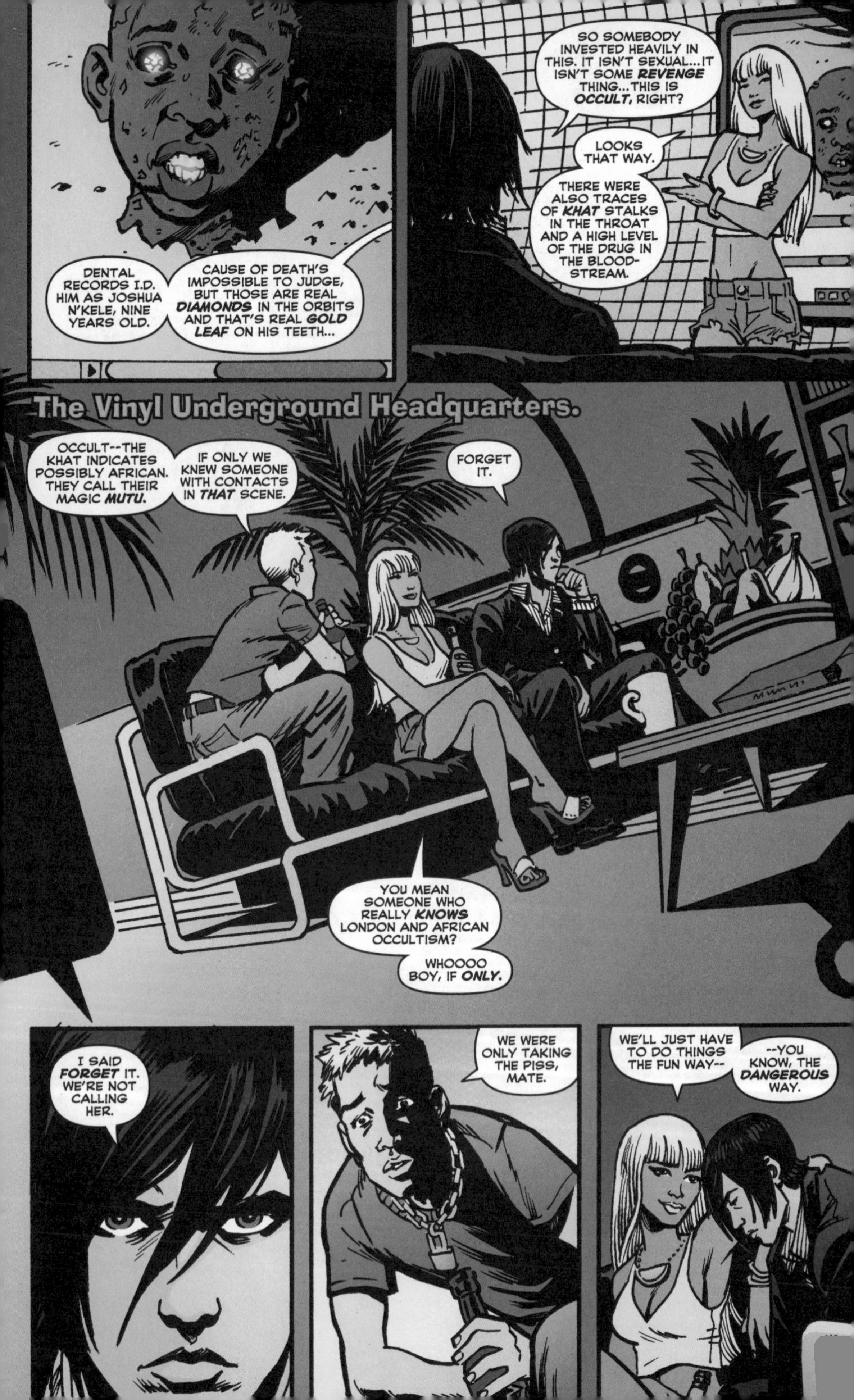
DENTAL RECORDS I.D. HIM AS JOSHUA N'KELE, NINE YEARS OLD.
CAUSE OF DEATH'S IMPOSSIBLE TO JUDGE, BUT THOSE ARE REAL DIAMONDS IN THE ORBITS AND THAT'S REAL GOLD LEAF ON HIS TEETH...
SO SOMEBODY INVESTED HEAVILY IN THIS. IT ISN'T SEXUAL...IT ISN'T SOME REVENGE THING...THIS IS OCCULT, RIGHT?
LOOKS THAT WAY.
THERE WERE ALSO TRACES OF KHAT STALKS IN THE THROAT AND A HIGH LEVEL OF THE DRUG IN THE BLOOD-STREAM.
The Vinyl Underground Headquarters.
OCCULT--THE KHAT INDICATES POSSIBLY AFRICAN. THEY CALL THEIR MAGIC MUTU.
IF ONLY WE KNEW SOMEONE WITH CONTACTS IN THAT SCENE.
FORGET IT.
YOU MEAN SOMEONE WHO REALLY KNOWS LONDON AND AFRICAN OCCULTISM?
WHOOOO BOY, IF ONLY.
I SAID FORGET IT. WE'RE NOT CALLING HER.
WE WERE ONLY TAKING THE PISS, MATE.
WE'LL JUST HAVE TO DO THINGS THE FUN WAY--
--YOU KNOW, THE DANGEROUS WAY.

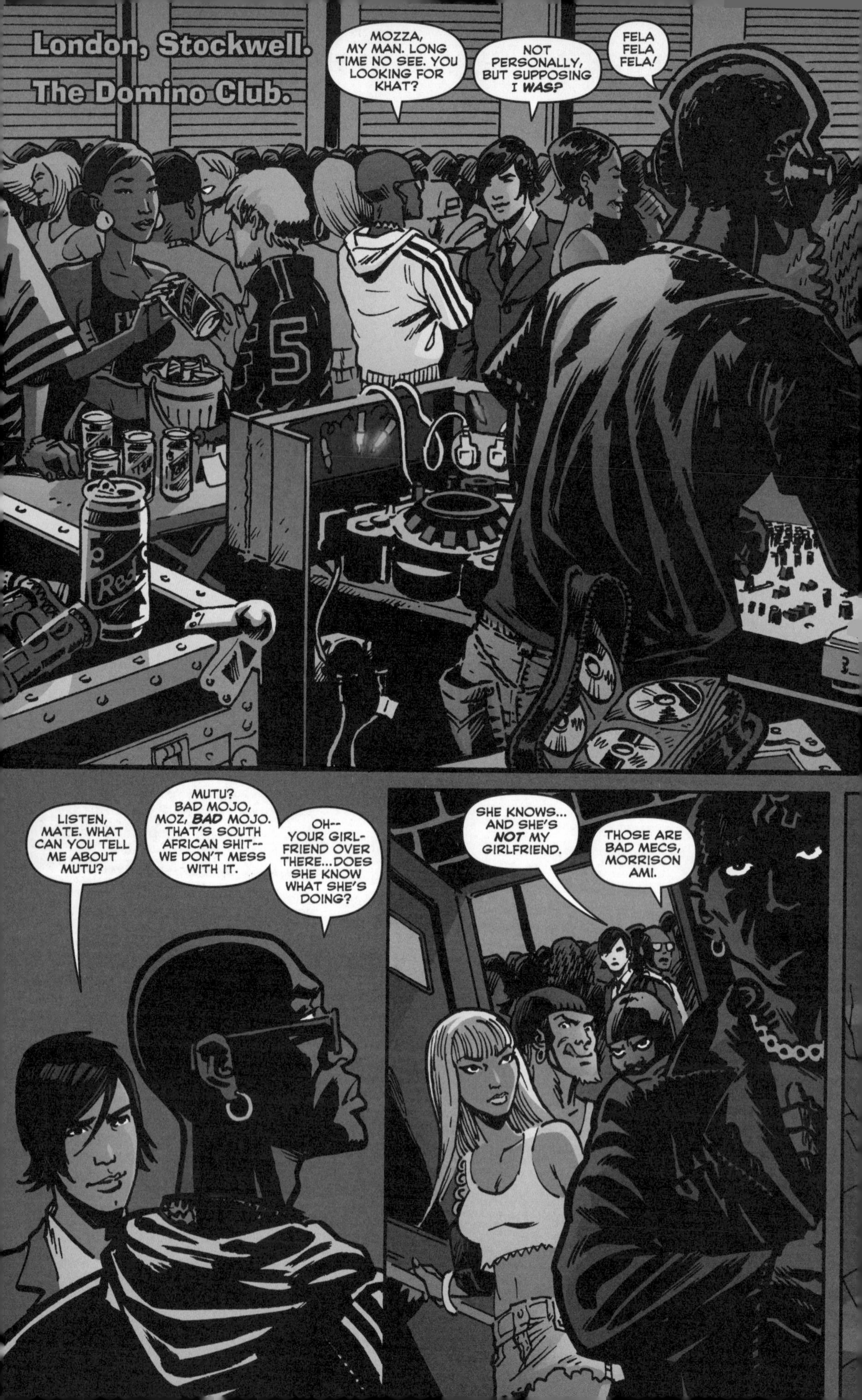
London, Stockwell.
The Domino Club.
MOZZA, MY MAN. LONG TIME NO SEE. YOU LOOKING FOR KHAT?
NOT PERSONALLY, BUT SUPPOSING I *WAS?*
FELA FELA FELA!
LISTEN, MATE. WHAT CAN YOU TELL ME ABOUT MUTU?
MUTU? BAD MOJO, MOZ, *BAD* MOJO. THAT'S SOUTH AFRICAN SHIT-- WE DON'T MESS WITH IT.
OH-- YOUR GIRL-FRIEND OVER THERE...DOES SHE KNOW WHAT SHE'S DOING?
SHE KNOWS... AND SHE'S *NOT* MY GIRLFRIEND.
THOSE ARE BAD MECS, MORRISON AMI.

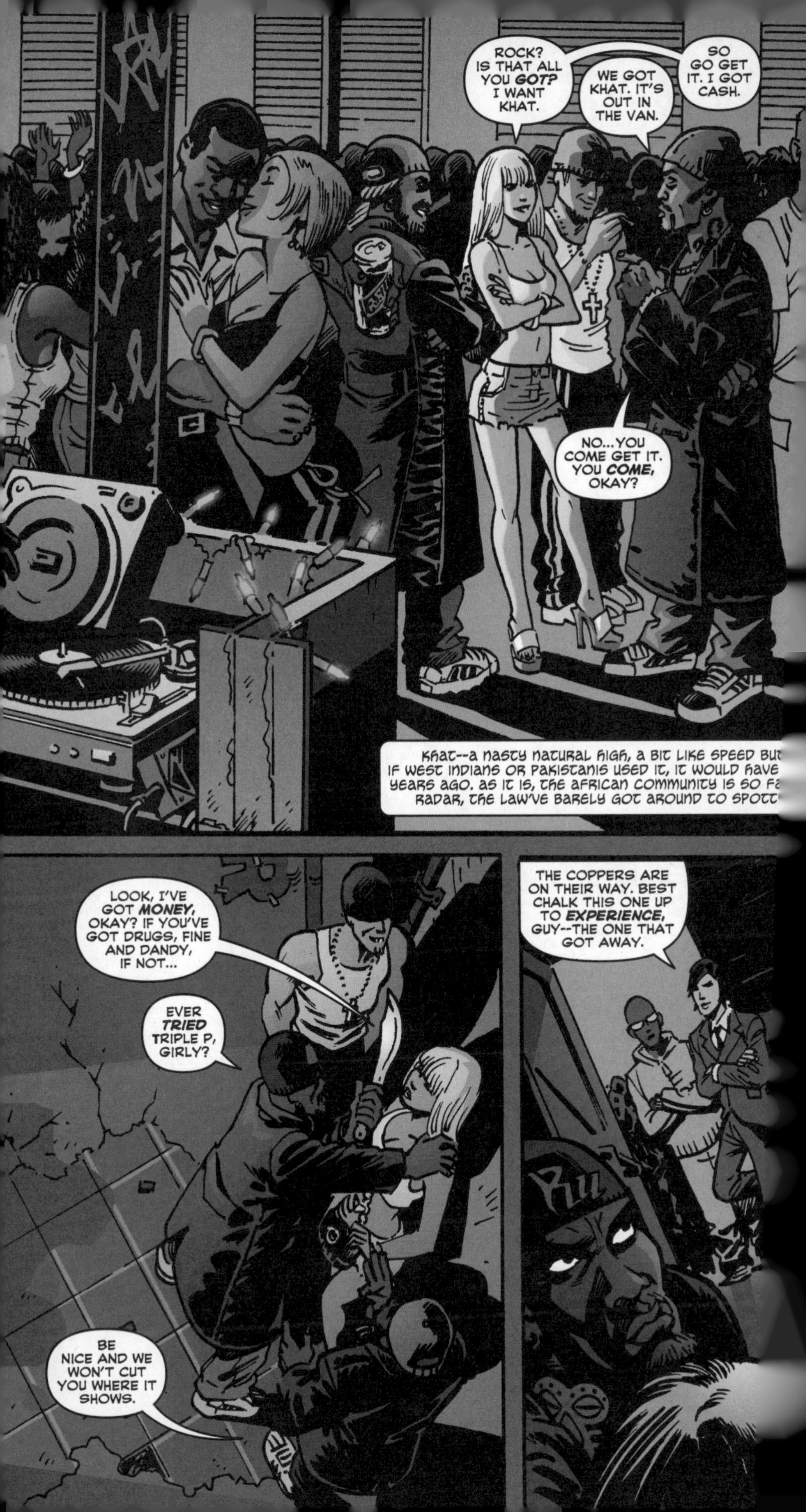

ROCK? IS THAT ALL YOU GOT? I WANT KHAT.
WE GOT KHAT. IT'S OUT IN THE VAN.
SO GO GET IT. I GOT CASH.
NO...YOU COME GET IT. YOU COME, OKAY?
KHAT--A NASTY NATURAL HIGH, A BIT LIKE SPEED BUT
IF WEST INDIANS OR PAKISTANIS USED IT, IT WOULD HAVE
YEARS AGO. AS IT IS, THE AFRICAN COMMUNITY IS SO
RADAR, THE LAW'VE BARELY GOT AROUND TO
LOOK, I'VE GOT MONEY, OKAY? IF YOU'VE GOT DRUGS, FINE AND DANDY, IF NOT...
EVER TRIED TRIPLE P, GIRLY?
BE NICE AND WE WON'T CUT YOU WHERE IT SHOWS.
THE COPPERS ARE ON THEIR WAY. BEST CHALK THIS ONE UP TO EXPERIENCE, GUY--THE ONE THAT GOT AWAY.

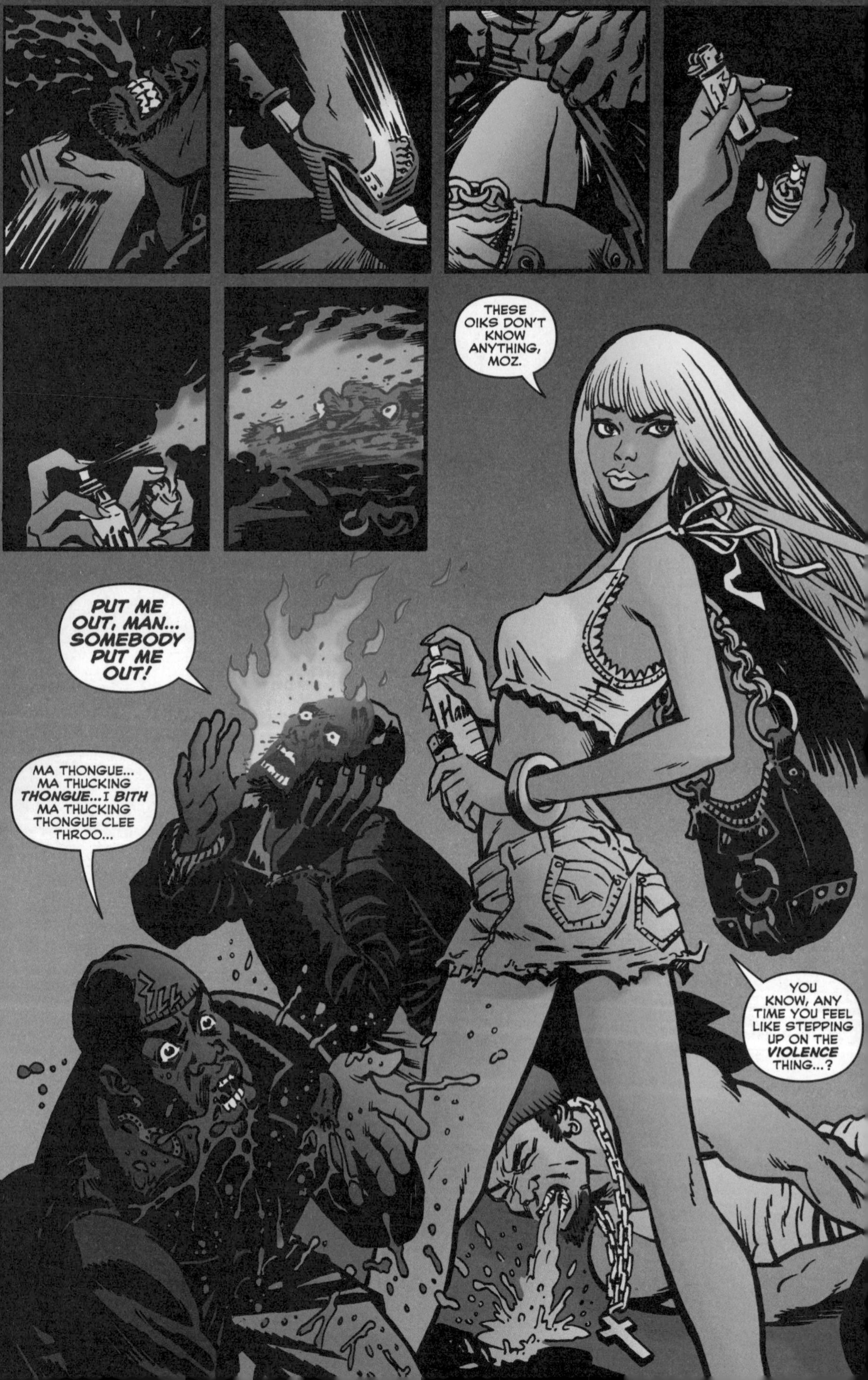
THESE OIKS DON'T KNOW ANYTHING, MOZ.
PUT ME OUT, MAN... SOMEBODY PUT ME OUT!
MA THONGUE... MA THUCKING THONGUE...I BITH MA THUCKING THONGUE CLEE THROO...
YOU KNOW, ANY TIME YOU FEEL LIKE STEPPING UP ON THE VIOLENCE THING...?

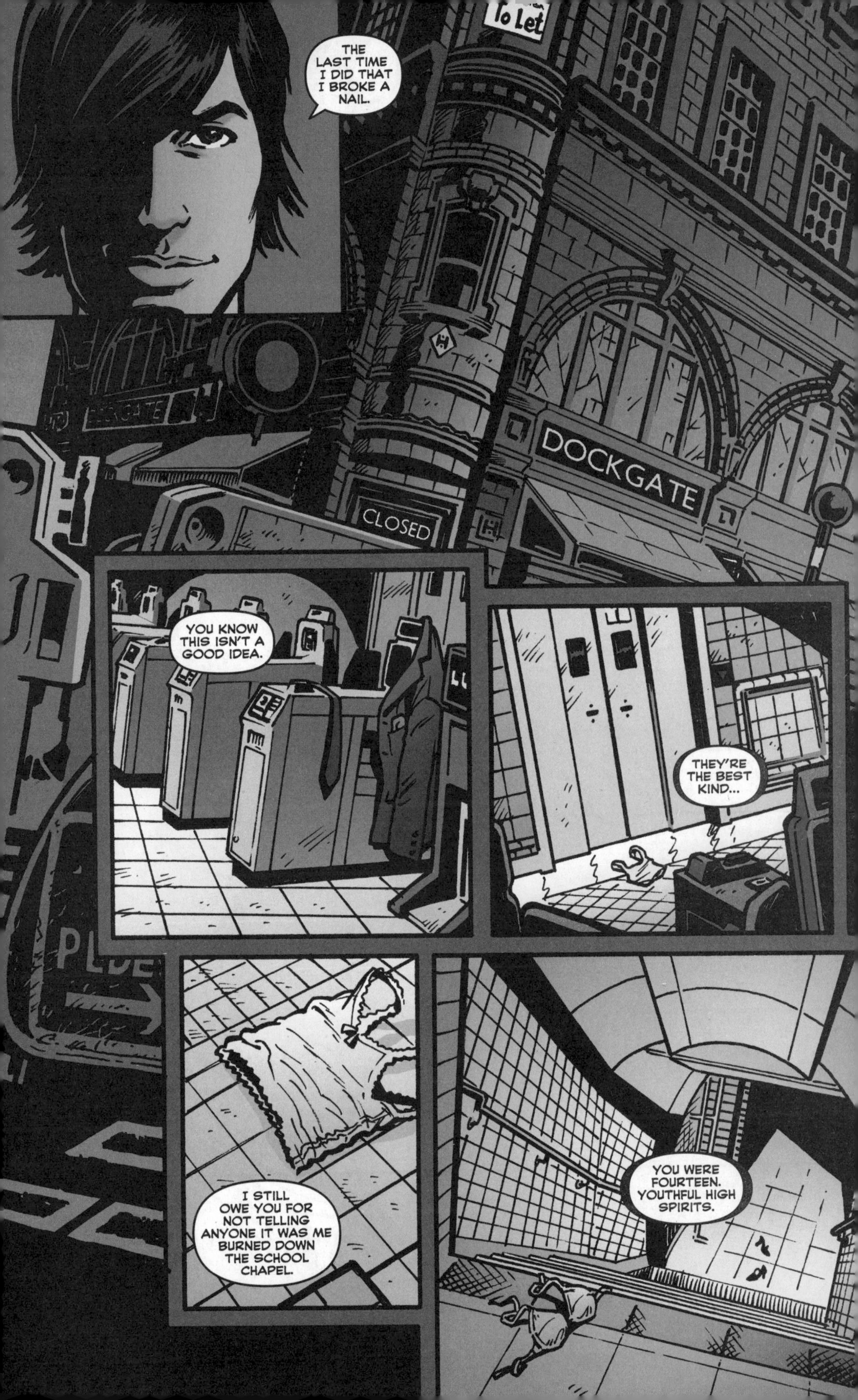
To Let
THE LAST TIME I DID THAT I BROKE A NAIL.
DOCKGATE
CLOSED
DOCKGATE
YOU KNOW THIS ISN'T A GOOD IDEA.
THEY'RE THE BEST KIND...
I STILL OWE YOU FOR NOT TELLING ANYONE IT WAS ME BURNED DOWN THE SCHOOL CHAPEL.
YOU WERE FOURTEEN. YOUTHFUL HIGH SPIRITS.

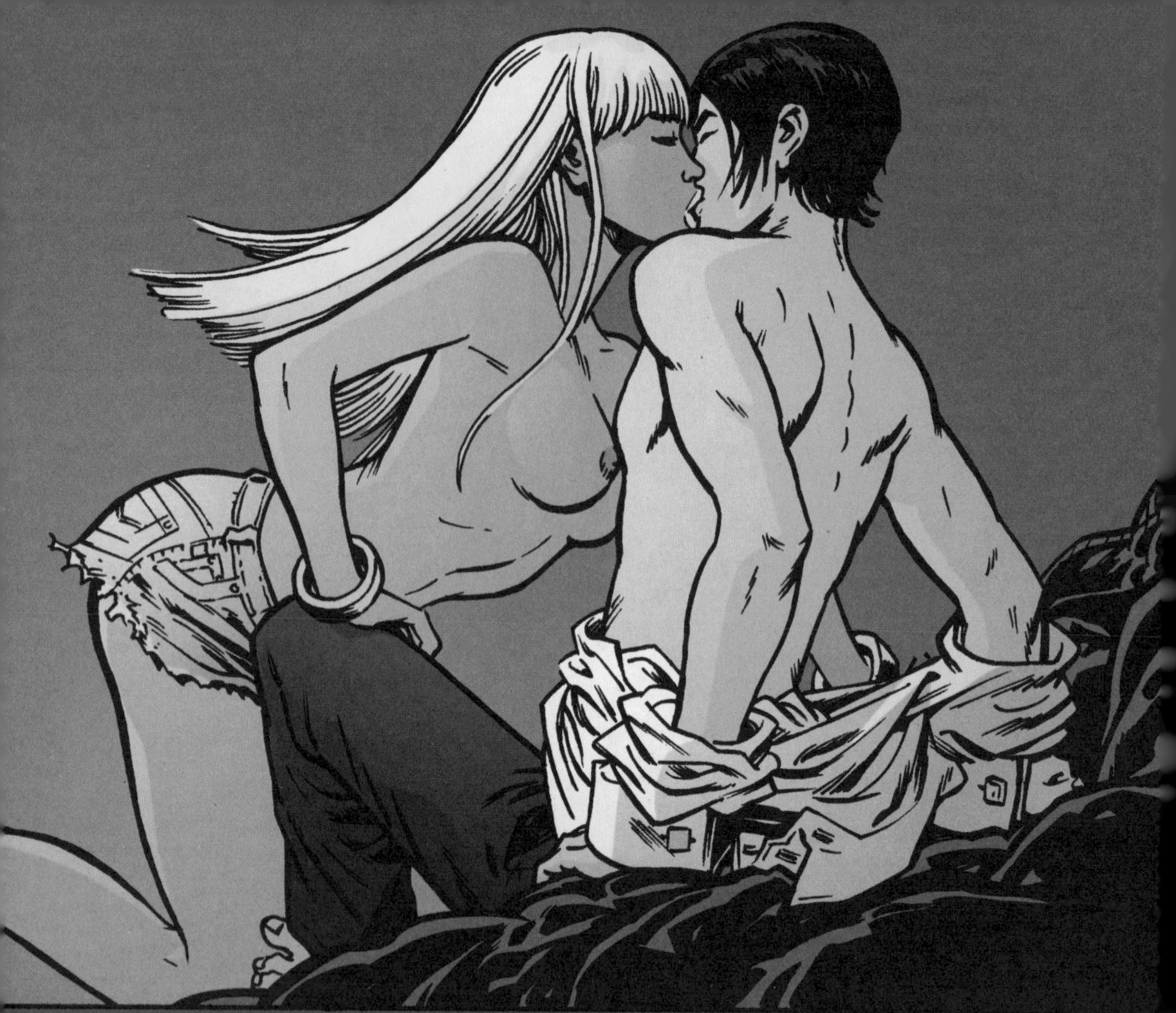

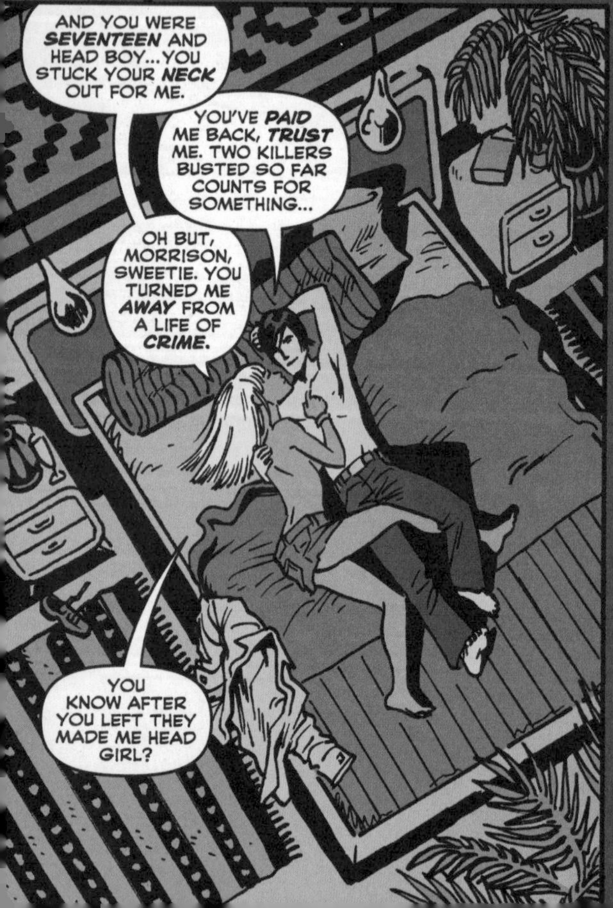
AND YOU WERE SEVENTEEN AND HEAD BOY...YOU STUCK YOUR NECK OUT FOR ME.
YOU'VE PAID ME BACK, TRUST ME. TWO KILLERS BUSTED SO FAR COUNTS FOR SOMETHING...
OH BUT, MORRISON, SWEETIE. YOU TURNED ME AWAY FROM A LIFE OF CRIME.
YOU KNOW AFTER YOU LEFT THEY MADE ME HEAD GIRL?

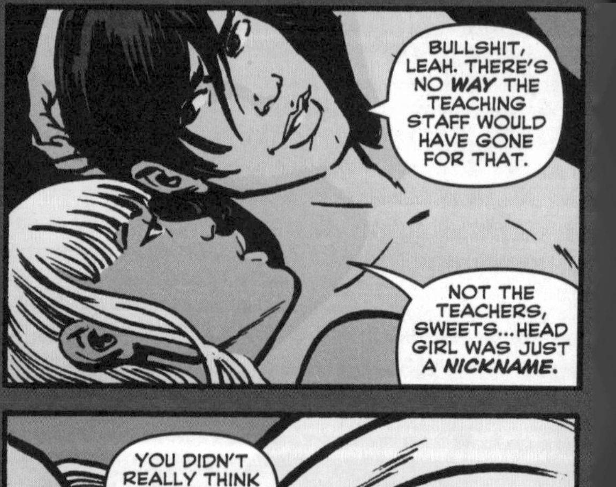
BULLSHIT, LEAH. THERE'S NO WAY THE TEACHING STAFF WOULD HAVE GONE FOR THAT.
NOT THE TEACHERS, SWEETS...HEAD GIRL WAS JUST A NICKNAME.

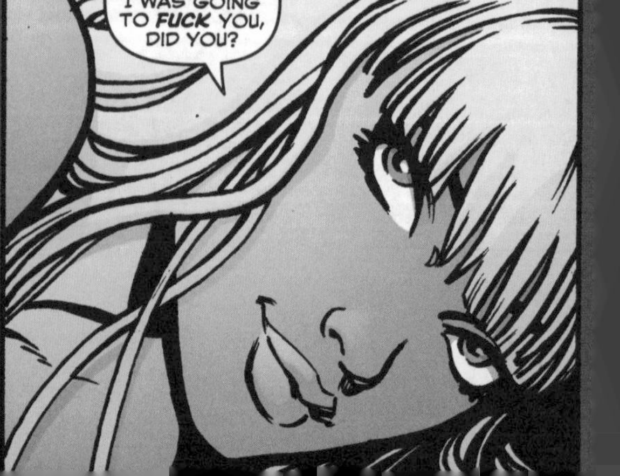
YOU DIDN'T REALLY THINK I WAS GOING TO FUCK YOU, DID YOU?

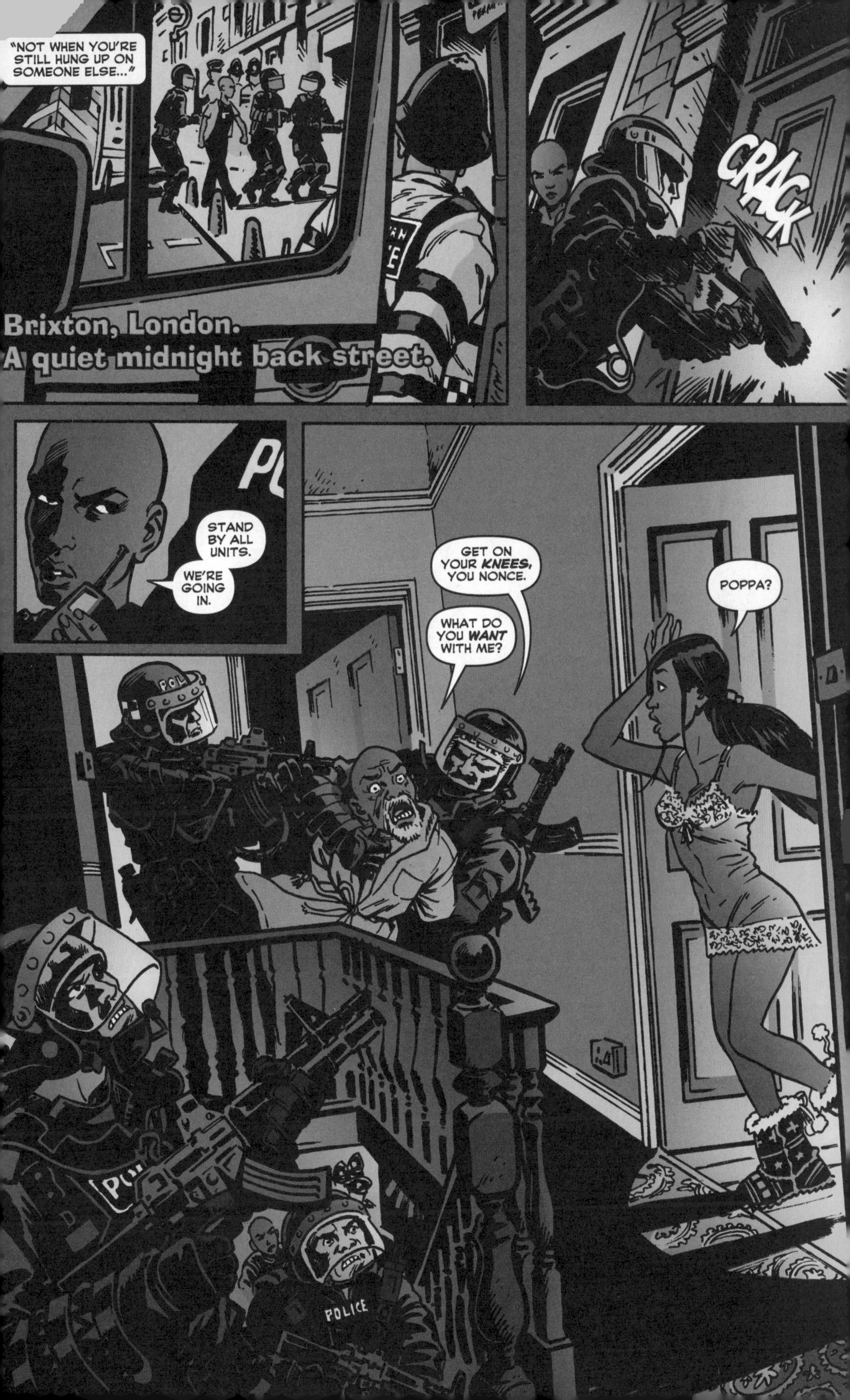
"NOT WHEN YOU'RE STILL HUNG UP ON SOMEONE ELSE..."
Brixton, London.
A quiet midnight back street.
CRACK
STAND BY ALL UNITS.
WE'RE GOING IN.
GET ON YOUR KNEES, YOU NONCE.
WHAT DO YOU WANT WITH ME?
POPPA?
POLICE

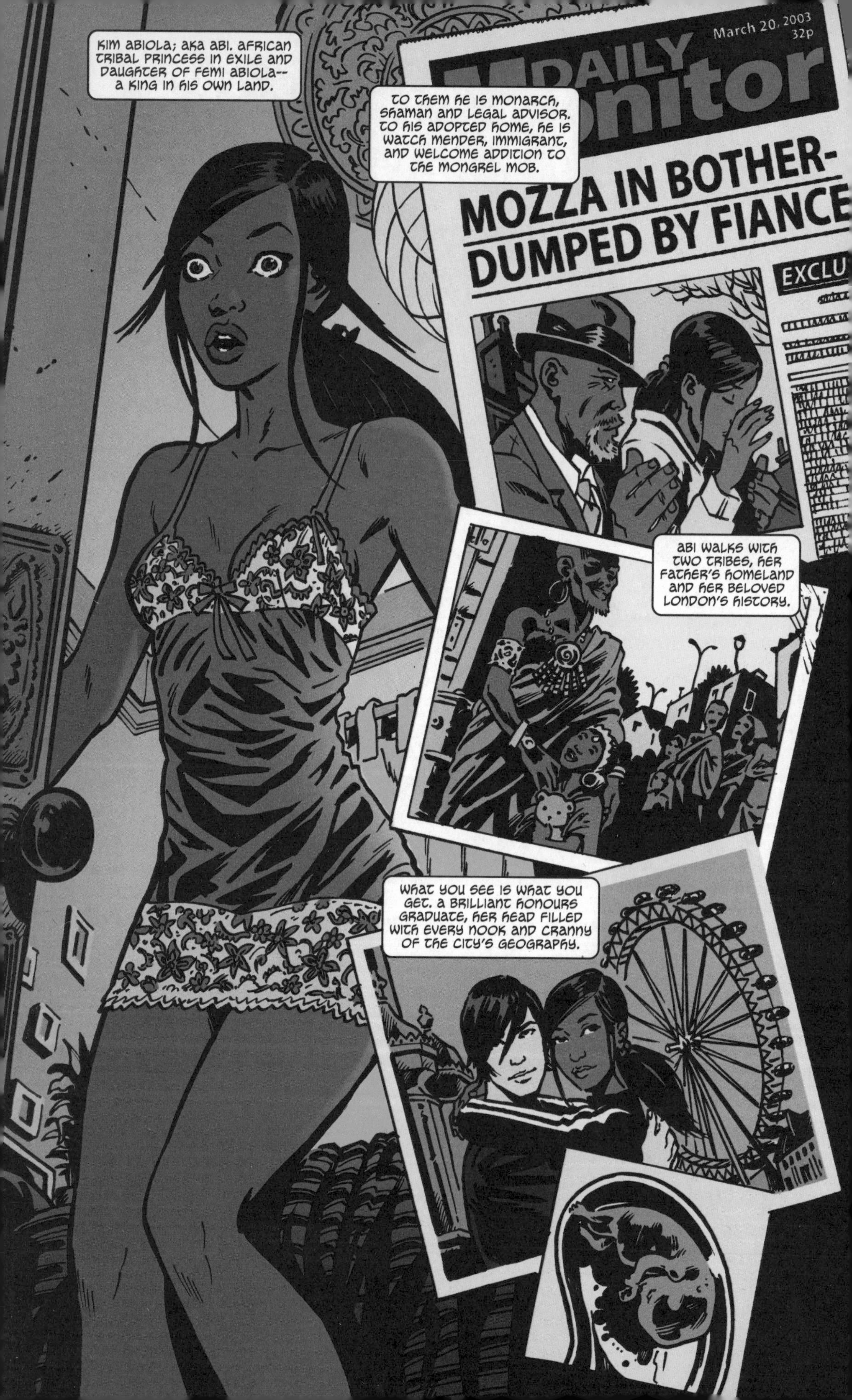
KIM ABIOLA; AKA ABI. AFRICAN TRIBAL PRINCESS IN EXILE AND DAUGHTER OF FEMI ABIOLA-- A KING IN HIS OWN LAND.
March 20, 2003
32p
DAILY
onitor
TO THEM HE IS MONARCH, SHAMAN AND LEGAL ADVISOR. TO HIS ADOPTED HOME, HE IS WATCH MENDER, IMMIGRANT, AND WELCOME ADDITION TO THE MONGREL MOB.
MOZZA IN BOTHER-
DUMPED BY FIANCE
EXCLU
ABI WALKS WITH TWO TRIBES, HER FATHER'S HOMELAND AND HER BELOVED LONDON'S HISTORY.
WHAT YOU SEE IS WHAT YOU GET. A BRILLIANT HONOURS GRADUATE, HER HEAD FILLED WITH EVERY NOOK AND CRANNY OF THE CITY'S GEOGRAPHY.

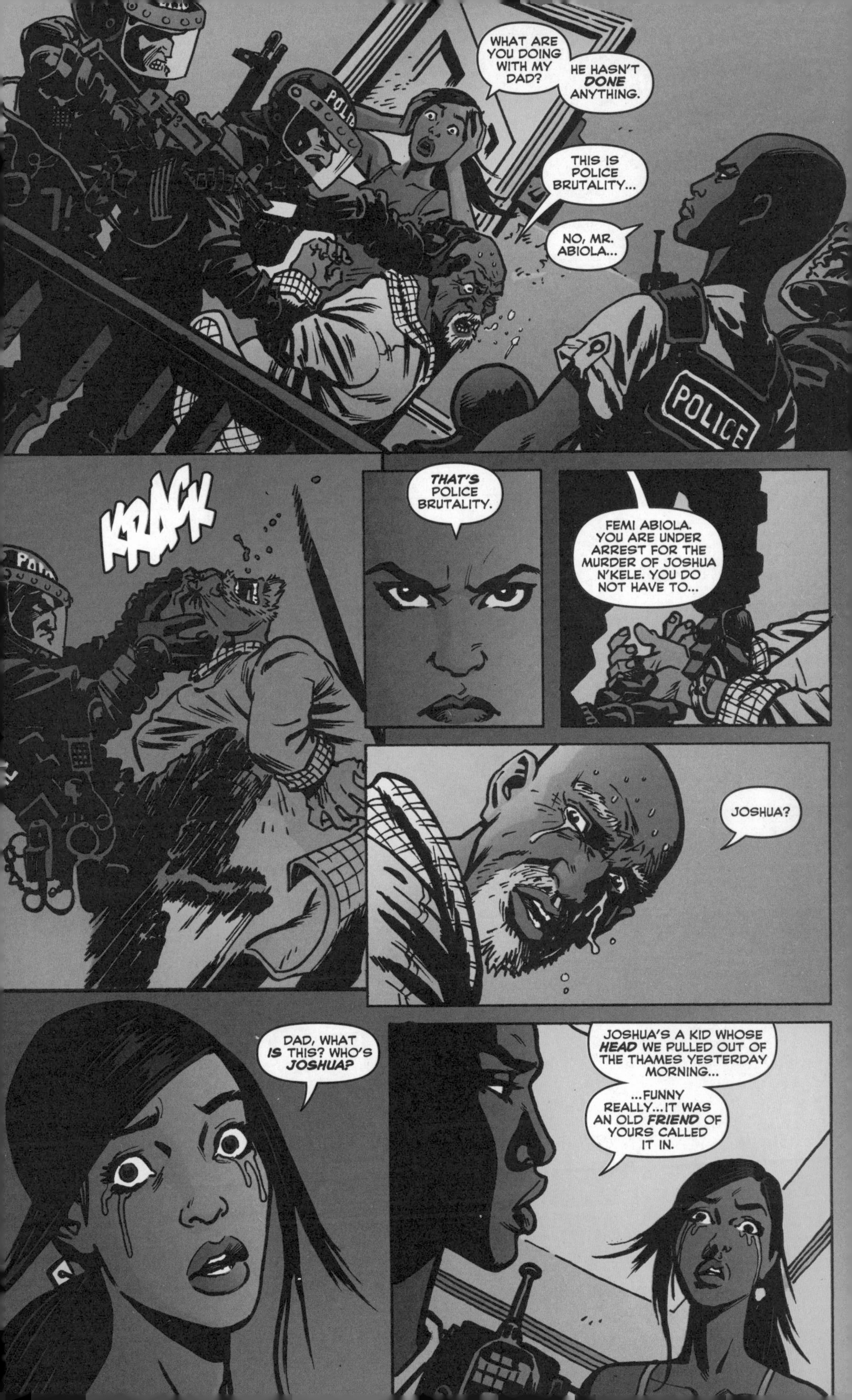
WHAT ARE YOU DOING WITH MY DAD?
HE HASN'T DONE ANYTHING.
THIS IS POLICE BRUTALITY...
NO, MR. ABIOLA...
POLICE
KRACK
THAT'S POLICE BRUTALITY.
FEMI ABIOLA. YOU ARE UNDER ARREST FOR THE MURDER OF JOSHUA N'KELE. YOU DO NOT HAVE TO...
JOSHUA?
DAD, WHAT IS THIS? WHO'S JOSHUA?
JOSHUA'S A KID WHOSE HEAD WE PULLED OUT OF THE THAMES YESTERDAY MORNING...
...FUNNY REALLY...IT WAS AN OLD FRIEND OF YOURS CALLED IT IN.

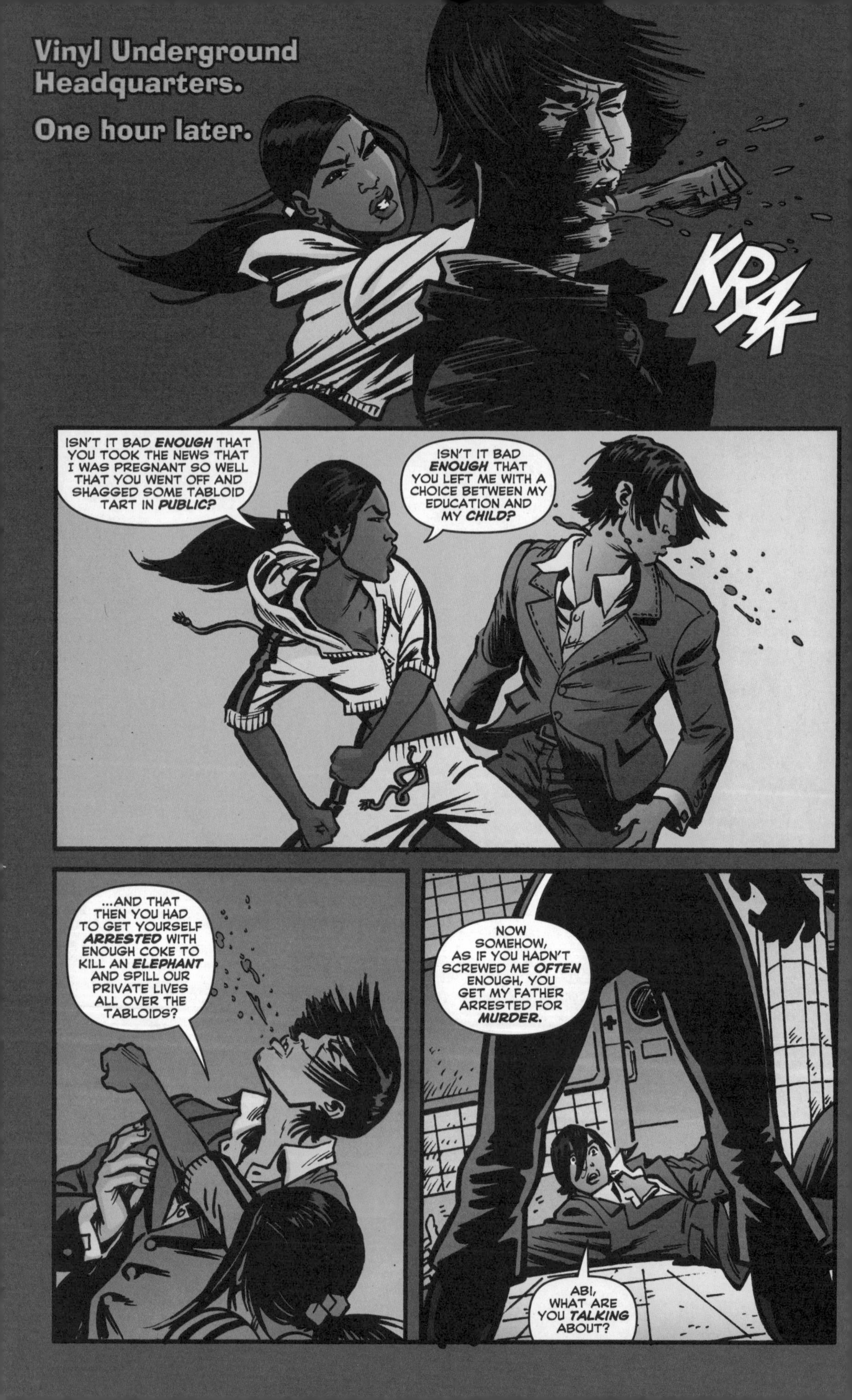
Vinyl Underground Headquarters.
One hour later.
KRAK
ISN'T IT BAD ENOUGH THAT YOU TOOK THE NEWS THAT I WAS PREGNANT SO WELL THAT YOU WENT OFF AND SHAGGED SOME TABLOID TART IN PUBLIC?
ISN'T IT BAD ENOUGH THAT YOU LEFT ME WITH A CHOICE BETWEEN MY EDUCATION AND MY CHILD?
...AND THAT THEN YOU HAD TO GET YOURSELF ARRESTED WITH ENOUGH COKE TO KILL AN ELEPHANT AND SPILL OUR PRIVATE LIVES ALL OVER THE TABLOIDS?
NOW SOMEHOW, AS IF YOU HADN'T SCREWED ME OFTEN ENOUGH, YOU GET MY FATHER ARRESTED FOR MURDER.
ABI, WHAT ARE YOU TALKING ABOUT?

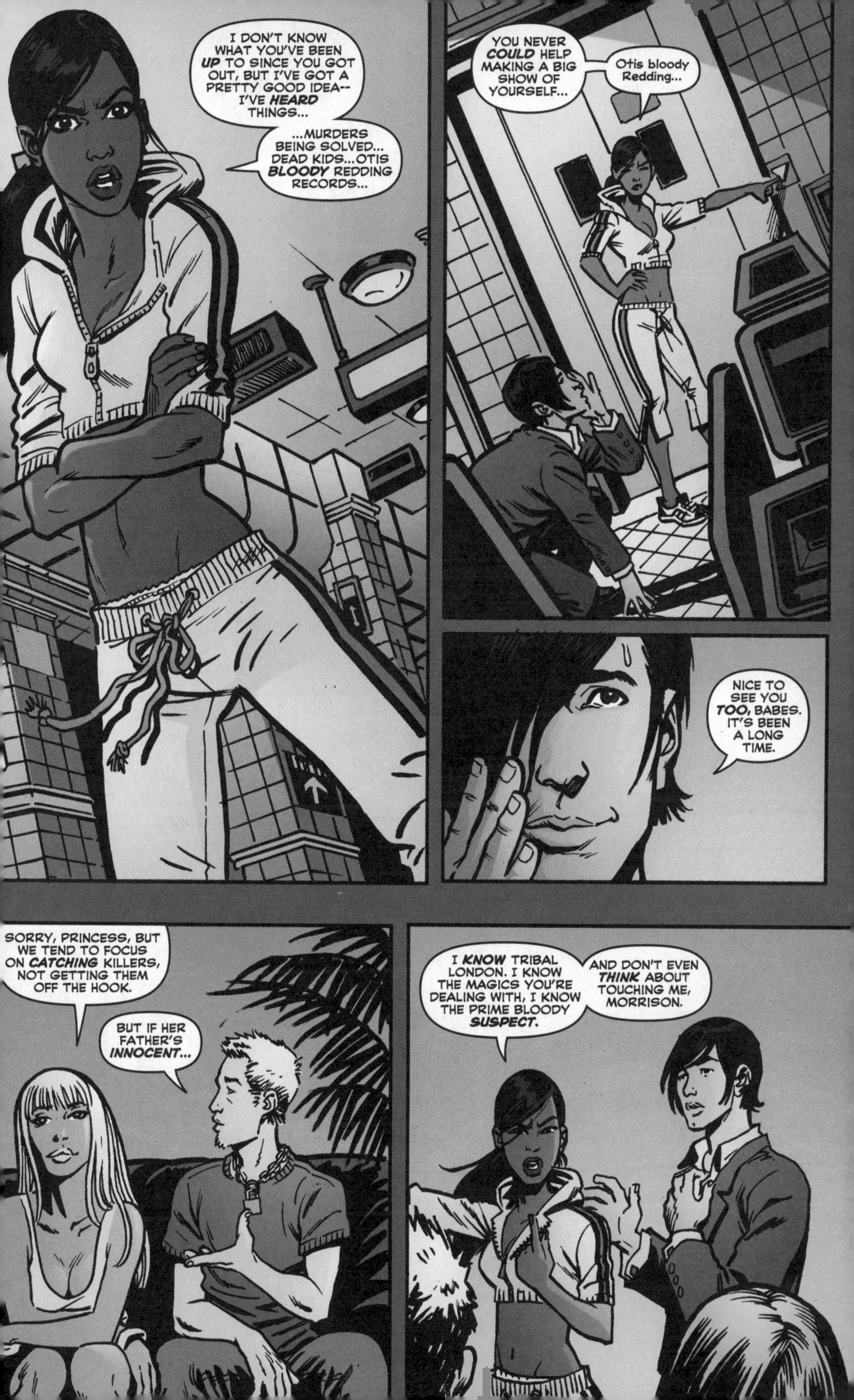
I DON'T KNOW WHAT YOU'VE BEEN UP TO SINCE YOU GOT OUT, BUT I'VE GOT A PRETTY GOOD IDEA-- I'VE HEARD THINGS...
...MURDERS BEING SOLVED... DEAD KIDS...OTIS BLOODY REDDING RECORDS...
YOU NEVER COULD HELP MAKING A BIG SHOW OF YOURSELF...
Otis bloody Redding...
NICE TO SEE YOU TOO, BABES. IT'S BEEN A LONG TIME.
SORRY, PRINCESS, BUT WE TEND TO FOCUS ON CATCHING KILLERS, NOT GETTING THEM OFF THE HOOK.
BUT IF HER FATHER'S INNOCENT...
I KNOW TRIBAL LONDON. I KNOW THE MAGICS YOU'RE DEALING WITH, I KNOW THE PRIME BLOODY SUSPECT.
AND DON'T EVEN THINK ABOUT TOUCHING ME, MORRISON.

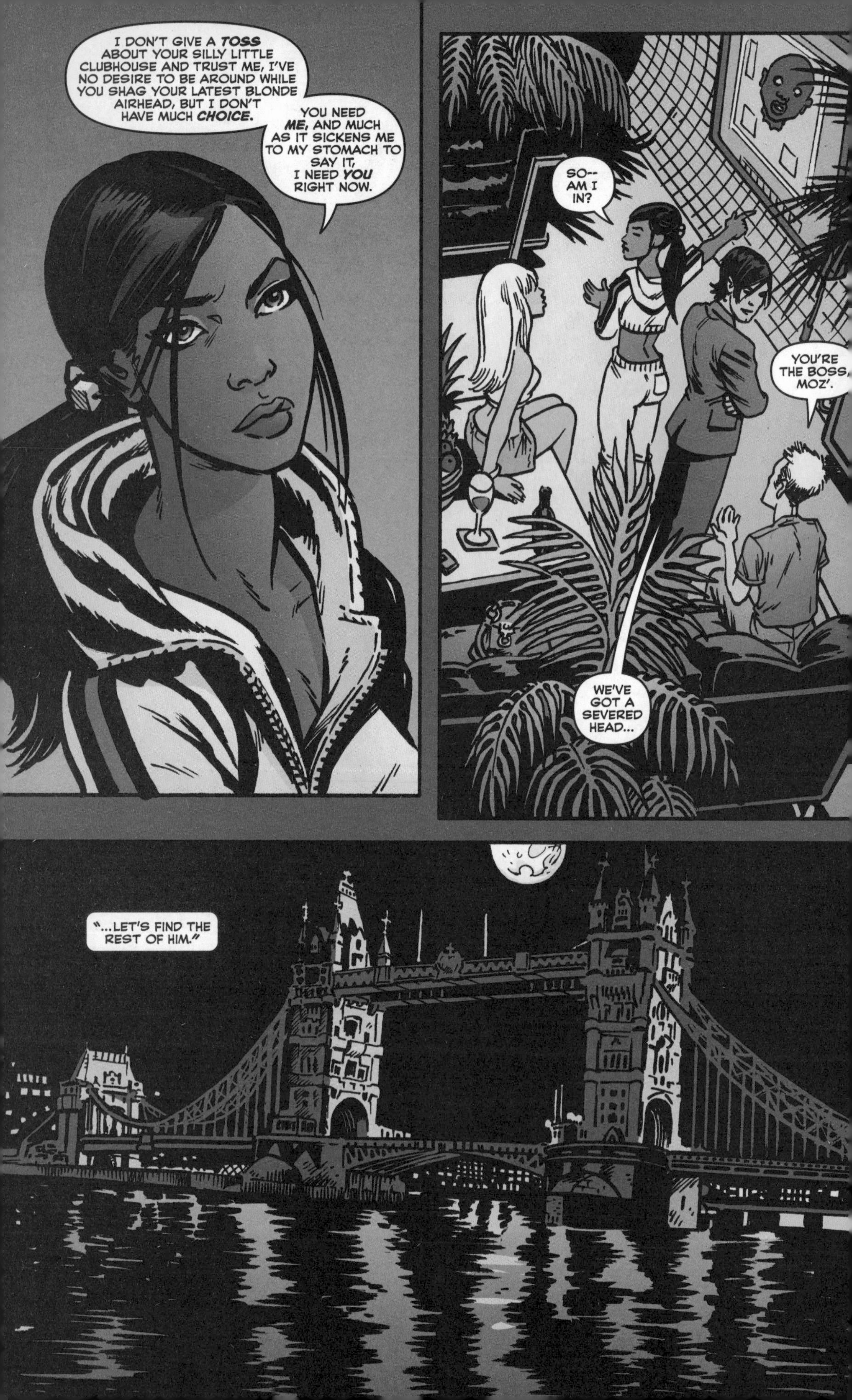
I DON'T GIVE A TOSS ABOUT YOUR SILLY LITTLE CLUBHOUSE AND TRUST ME, I'VE NO DESIRE TO BE AROUND WHILE YOU SHAG YOUR LATEST BLONDE AIRHEAD, BUT I DON'T HAVE MUCH CHOICE.
YOU NEED ME, AND MUCH AS IT SICKENS ME TO MY STOMACH TO SAY IT, I NEED YOU RIGHT NOW.
SO-- AM I IN?
YOU'RE THE BOSS, MOZ'.
WE'VE GOT A SEVERED HEAD...
"...LET'S FIND THE REST OF HIM."

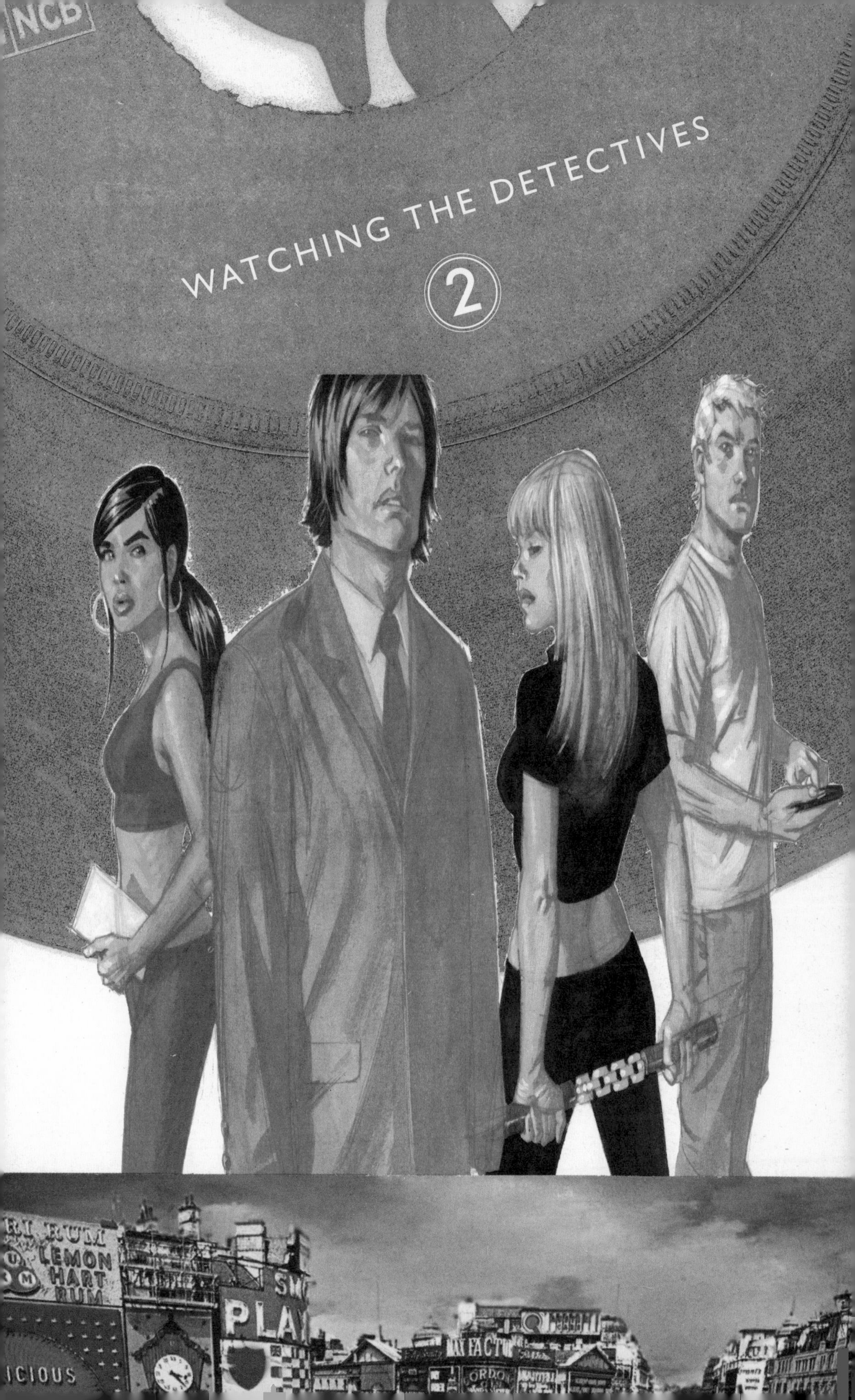
NCB
WATCHING THE DETECTIVES
2
LEMON
HART
RUM
PLA
ICIOUS

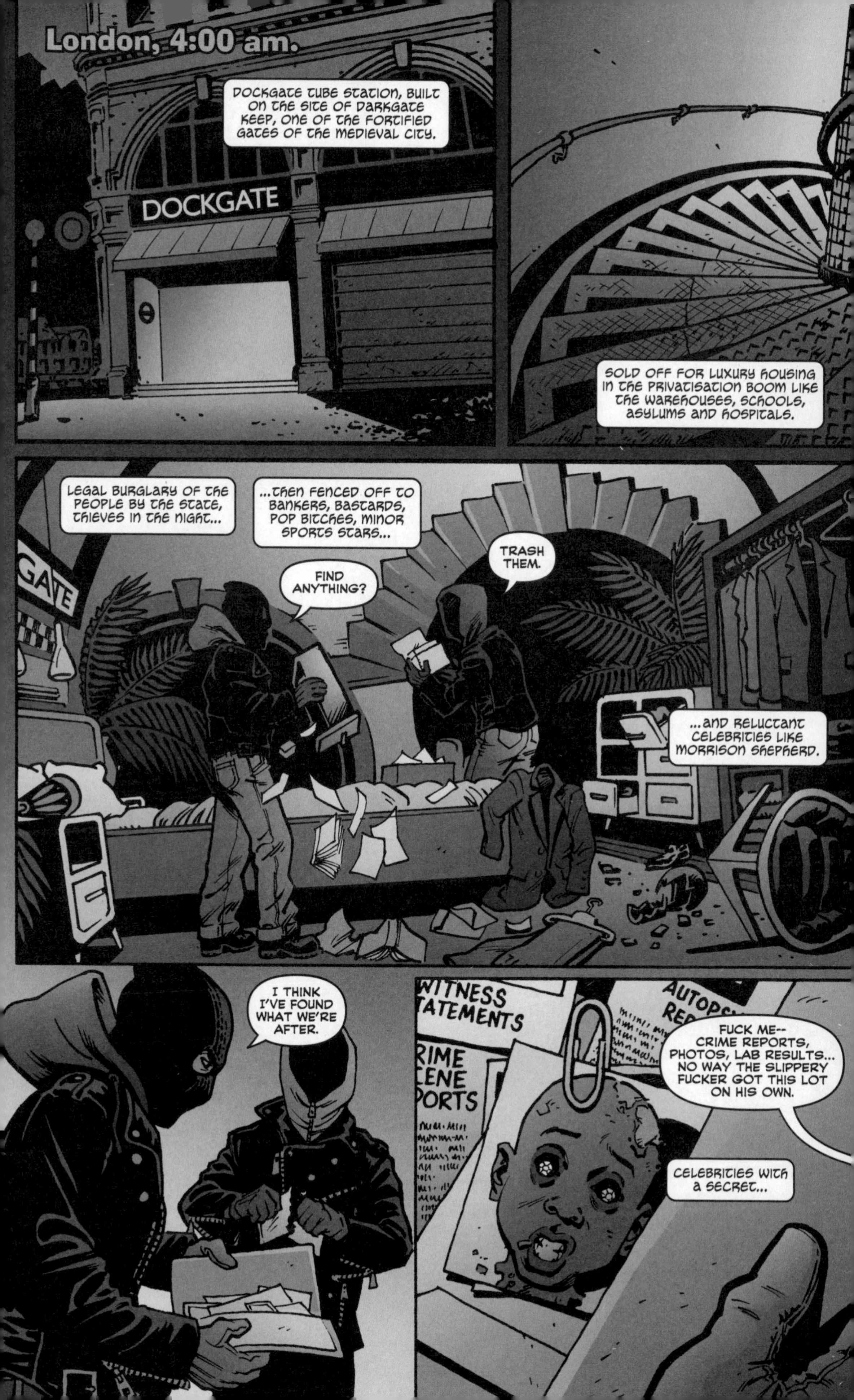
London, 4:00 am.
DOCKGATE TUBE STATION, BUILT ON THE SITE OF DARKGATE KEEP, ONE OF THE FORTIFIED GATES OF THE MEDIEVAL CITY.
DOCKGATE
SOLD OFF FOR LUXURY HOUSING IN THE PRIVATISATION BOOM LIKE THE WAREHOUSES, SCHOOLS, ASYLUMS AND HOSPITALS.
LEGAL BURGLARY OF THE PEOPLE BY THE STATE, THIEVES IN THE NIGHT...
...THEN FENCED OFF TO BANKERS, BASTARDS, POP BITCHES, MINOR SPORTS STARS...
FIND ANYTHING?
TRASH THEM.
...AND RELUCTANT CELEBRITIES LIKE MORRISON SHEPHERD.
I THINK I'VE FOUND WHAT WE'RE AFTER.
FUCK ME-- CRIME REPORTS, PHOTOS, LAB RESULTS... NO WAY THE SLIPPERY FUCKER GOT THIS LOT ON HIS OWN.
CELEBRITIES WITH A SECRET...

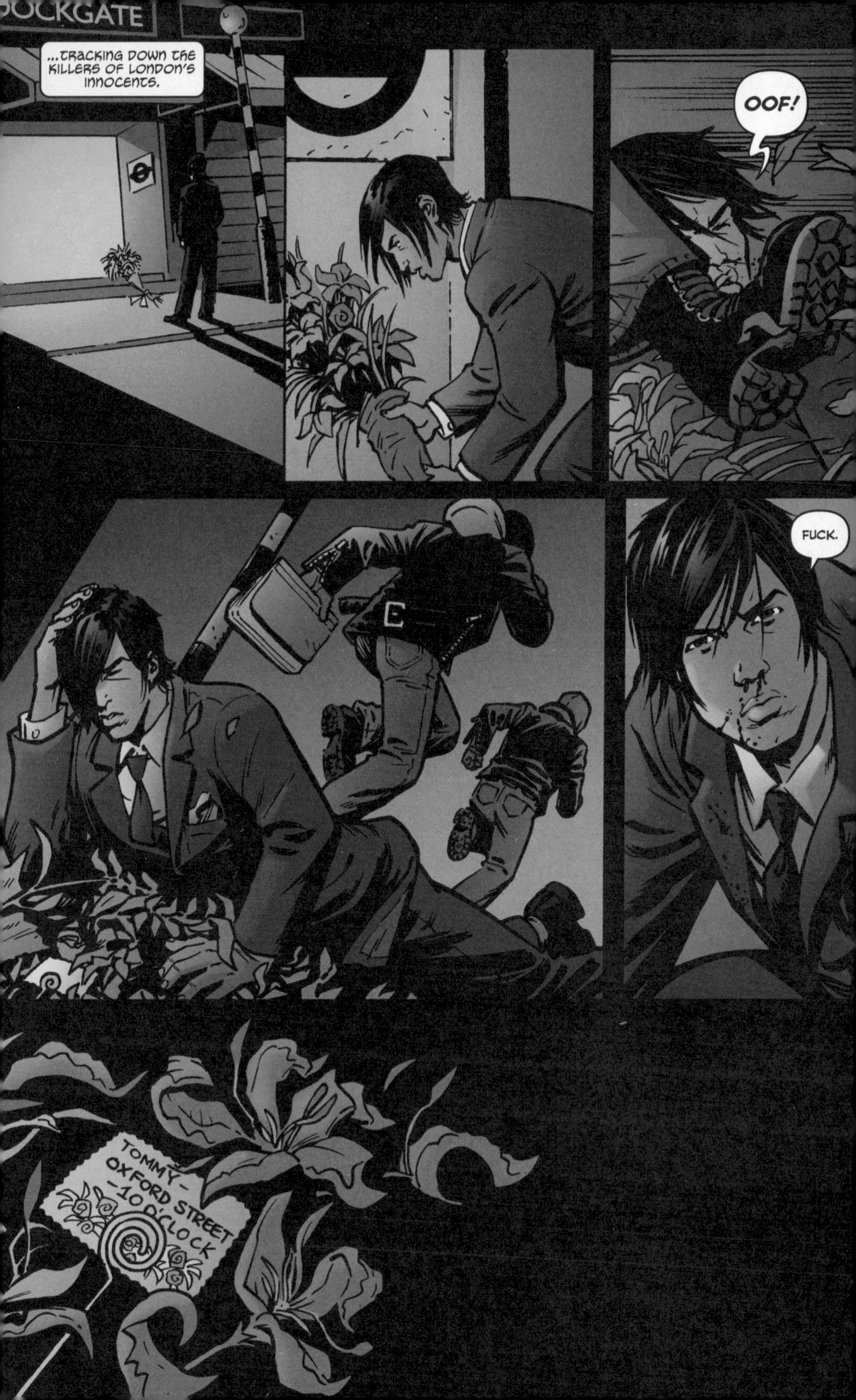
DOCKGATE
...TRACKING DOWN THE KILLERS OF LONDON'S INNOCENTS.
OOF!
FUCK.
TOMMY
OXFORD STREET
10 O'CLOCK

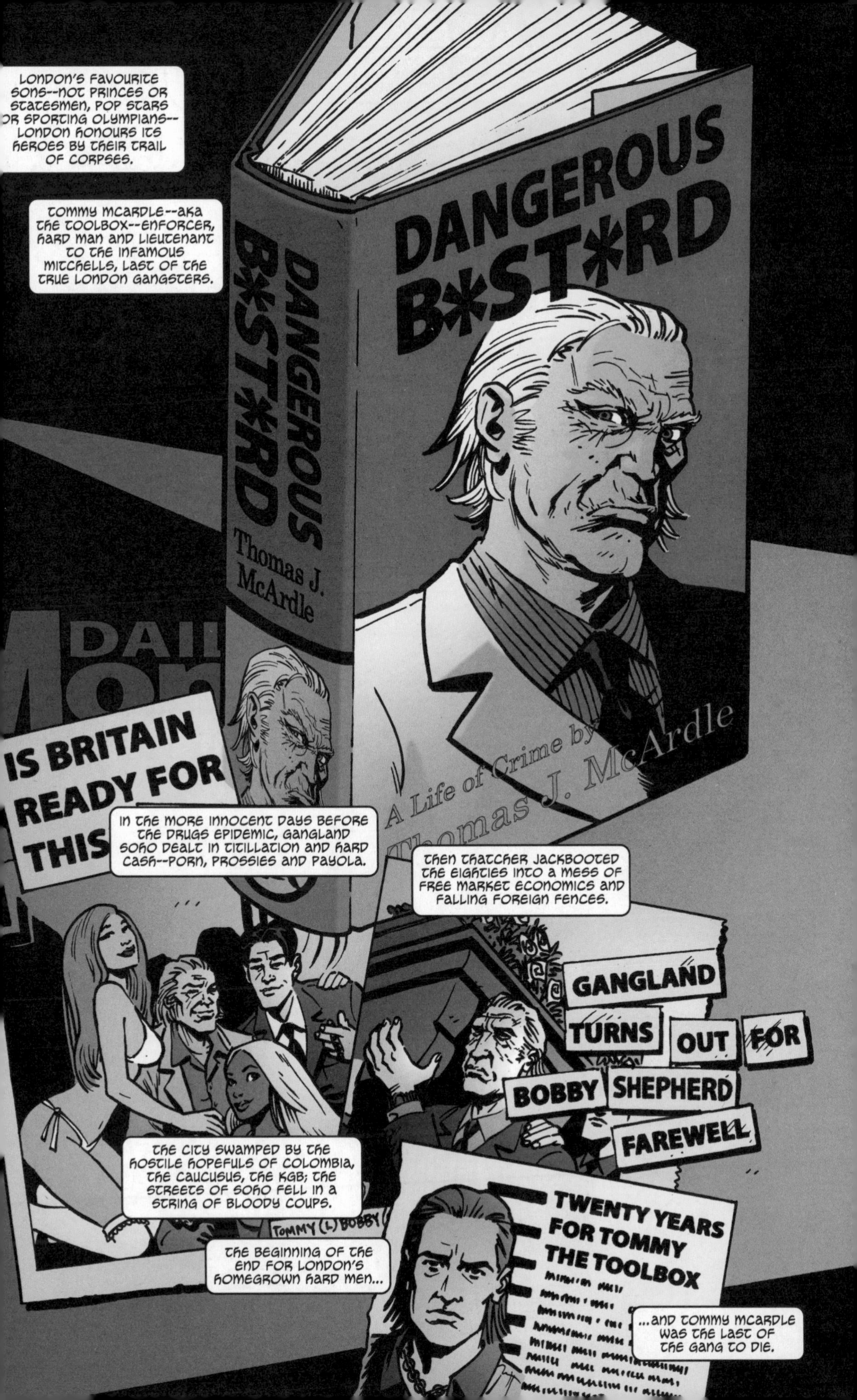
LONDON'S FAVOURITE SONS--NOT PRINCES OR STATESMEN, POP STARS OR SPORTING OLYMPIANS--LONDON HONOURS ITS HEROES BY THEIR TRAIL OF CORPSES.
TOMMY MCARDLE--AKA THE TOOLBOX--ENFORCER, HARD MAN AND LIEUTENANT TO THE INFAMOUS MITCHELLS, LAST OF THE TRUE LONDON GANGSTERS.
DANGEROUS B*ST*RD
DANGEROUS B*ST*RD
Thomas J. McArdle
A Life of Crime by Thomas J. McArdle
DAIL
IS BRITAIN READY FOR THIS
IN THE MORE INNOCENT DAYS BEFORE THE DRUGS EPIDEMIC, GANGLAND SOHO DEALT IN TITILLATION AND HARD CASH--PORN, PROSSIES AND PAYOLA.
THEN THATCHER JACKBOOTED THE EIGHTIES INTO A MESS OF FREE MARKET ECONOMICS AND FALLING FOREIGN FENCES.
GANGLAND TURNS OUT FOR BOBBY SHEPHERD FAREWELL
THE CITY SWAMPED BY THE HOSTILE HOPEFULS OF COLOMBIA, THE CAUCUSUS, THE KGB; THE STREETS OF SOHO FELL IN A STRING OF BLOODY COUPS.
TOMMY (L) BOBBY
THE BEGINNING OF THE END FOR LONDON'S HOMEGROWN HARD MEN...
TWENTY YEARS FOR TOMMY THE TOOLBOX
...AND TOMMY MCARDLE WAS THE LAST OF THE GANG TO DIE.

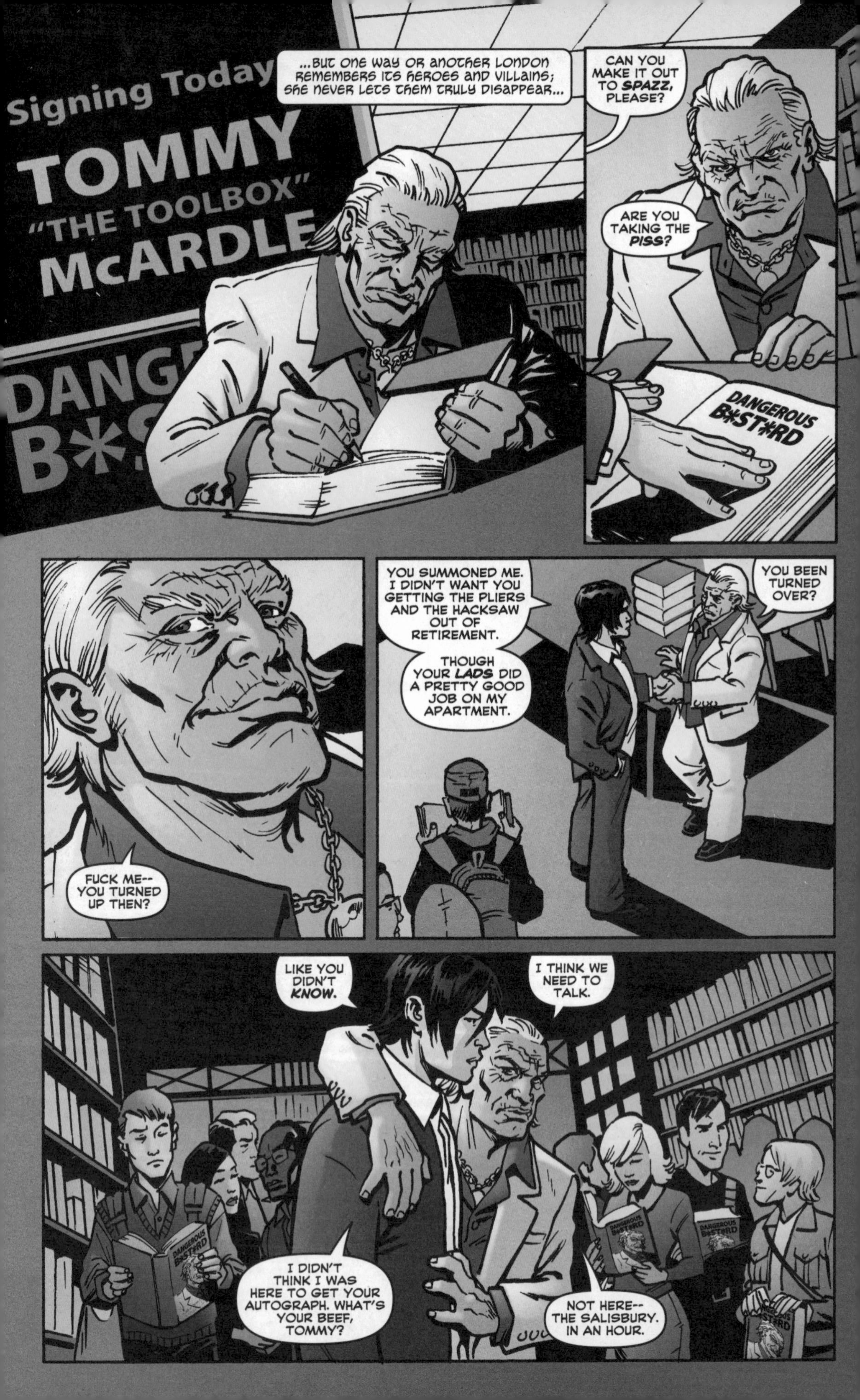
Signing Today
TOMMY
"THE TOOLBOX"
McARDLE
DANG
B*S
...BUT ONE WAY OR ANOTHER LONDON REMEMBERS ITS HEROES AND VILLAINS; SHE NEVER LETS THEM TRULY DISAPPEAR...
CAN YOU MAKE IT OUT TO SPAZZ, PLEASE?
ARE YOU TAKING THE PISS?
DANGEROUS B*ST*RD
FUCK ME-- YOU TURNED UP THEN?
YOU SUMMONED ME. I DIDN'T WANT YOU GETTING THE PLIERS AND THE HACKSAW OUT OF RETIREMENT.
THOUGH YOUR LADS DID A PRETTY GOOD JOB ON MY APARTMENT.
YOU BEEN TURNED OVER?
LIKE YOU DIDN'T KNOW.
I THINK WE NEED TO TALK.
I DIDN'T THINK I WAS HERE TO GET YOUR AUTOGRAPH. WHAT'S YOUR BEEF, TOMMY?
NOT HERE-- THE SALISBURY. IN AN HOUR.

JUICYLOU/ Whisper: All right, Perv? I assume Moz isn't around?
CALLUMPERV/ Whisper: He was following up on the break- in – then he said he was going up Green Lanes to chase up some khat dealer…
JUICYLOU/Whisper: You think he knows who did it?
CALLUMPERV: Like he'd tell me.
JUICYLOU: We might get further with this detective shit if he shared a little more.
CALLUMPERV/ Whisper: Like you do? Sharing his bed?
JUICYLOU/ Whisper: Just a one-off. You know how fire and fighting get me horny.
CALLUMPERV/ Whisper: Just as long as you don't share too much. If Moz finds out about this little business…

JUICYLOU/ Whisper: He won't find out from me.
WELLHUNGSTUD: Hi baby, you horny?
JUICYLOU: Hi, wellhung. I'm always horny.
JUICYLOU/Whisper: Great, this guy's an asshole… so who do you think wanted all our paperwork?
CALLUMPERV/Whisper: Search me. Maybe Abi's dad isn't as guilty as you thought.
JUICYLOU/Whisper: They found the kid's blood all over the workshop!
CALLUMPERV/Whisper: So who turned us over?
WELLHUNGSTUD: Show me your tits, babes
JUICYLOU: You got to pay to see tits, wellhung, sorry.

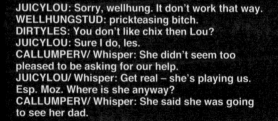

DIRTYLES: Hi, baby. I'm horny, you horny?
JUICYLOU: Hi, Les. You nice and hard for juicy lou?
JUICYLOU/ Whisper: How about short, dark and stupid?
CALLUMPERV/ Whisper: Abi? She's not stupid. She's just worried about her dad.
JUICYLOU/ Whisper: So she comes running to her ex to sort it out?
CALLUMPERV/ Whisper: lol you sound jealous.
WELLHUNGSTUD: Tits first, then I'll pay.
DIRTYLES: I'm a woman actually. A dirty les. You like chix, Lou?

JUICYLOU: Sorry, wellhung. It don't work that way.
WELLHUNGSTUD: prickteasing bitch.
DIRTYLES: You don't like chix then Lou?
JUICYLOU: Sure I do, les.
CALLUMPERV/ Whisper: She didn't seem too pleased to be asking for our help.
JUICYLOU/ Whisper: Get real – she's playing us. Esp. Moz. Where is she anyway?
CALLUMPERV/ Whisper: She said she was going to see her dad.

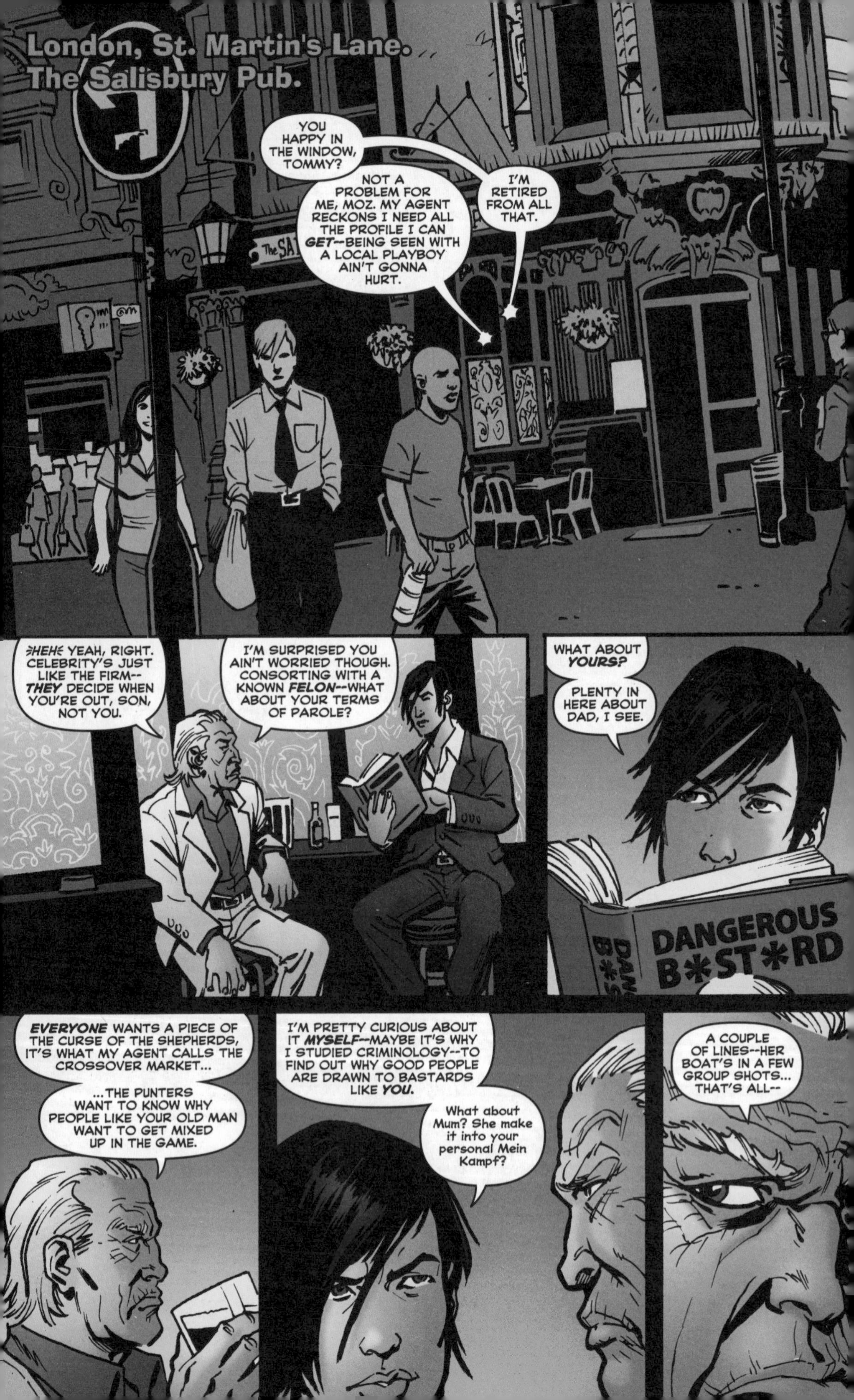
London, St. Martin's Lane.
The Salisbury Pub.
YOU HAPPY IN THE WINDOW, TOMMY?
I'M RETIRED FROM ALL THAT.
NOT A PROBLEM FOR ME, MOZ. MY AGENT RECKONS I NEED ALL THE PROFILE I CAN GET--BEING SEEN WITH A LOCAL PLAYBOY AIN'T GONNA HURT.
The SA
HEH YEAH, RIGHT. CELEBRITY'S JUST LIKE THE FIRM--THEY DECIDE WHEN YOU'RE OUT, SON, NOT YOU.
I'M SURPRISED YOU AIN'T WORRIED THOUGH. CONSORTING WITH A KNOWN FELON--WHAT ABOUT YOUR TERMS OF PAROLE?
WHAT ABOUT YOURS?
PLENTY IN HERE ABOUT DAD, I SEE.
DANGEROUS B*ST*RD
EVERYONE WANTS A PIECE OF THE CURSE OF THE SHEPHERDS, IT'S WHAT MY AGENT CALLS THE CROSSOVER MARKET...
...THE PUNTERS WANT TO KNOW WHY PEOPLE LIKE YOUR OLD MAN WANT TO GET MIXED UP IN THE GAME.
I'M PRETTY CURIOUS ABOUT IT MYSELF--MAYBE IT'S WHY I STUDIED CRIMINOLOGY--TO FIND OUT WHY GOOD PEOPLE ARE DRAWN TO BASTARDS LIKE YOU.
What about Mum? She make it into your personal Mein Kampf?
A COUPLE OF LINES--HER BOAT'S IN A FEW GROUP SHOTS... THAT'S ALL--

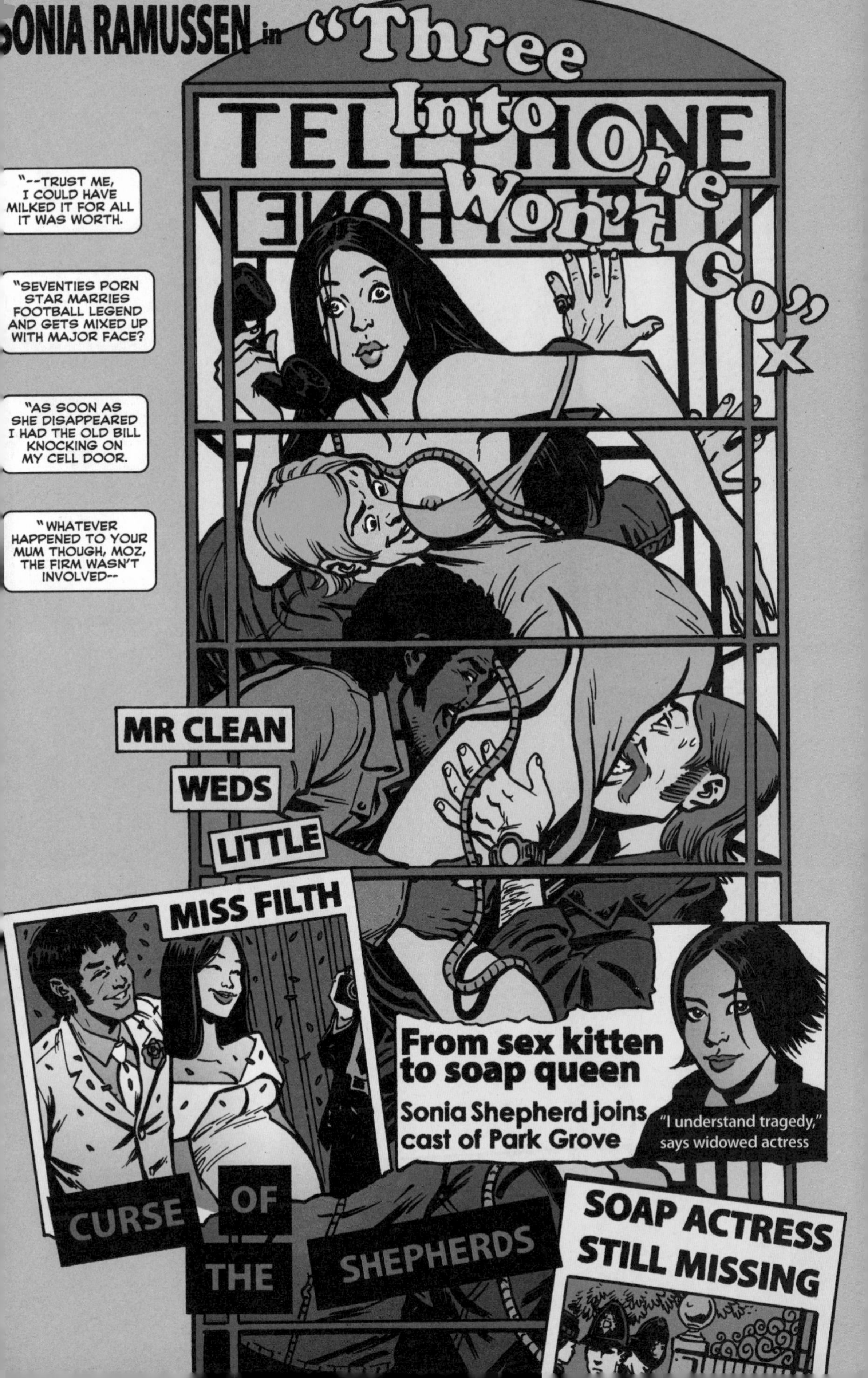
SONIA RAMUSSEN in "Three Into One Won't Go" x
"--TRUST ME, I COULD HAVE MILKED IT FOR ALL IT WAS WORTH.
"SEVENTIES PORN STAR MARRIES FOOTBALL LEGEND AND GETS MIXED UP WITH MAJOR FACE?
"AS SOON AS SHE DISAPPEARED I HAD THE OLD BILL KNOCKING ON MY CELL DOOR.
"WHATEVER HAPPENED TO YOUR MUM THOUGH, MOZ, THE FIRM WASN'T INVOLVED--
MR CLEAN
WEDS
LITTLE
MISS FILTH
From sex kitten to soap queen
Sonia Shepherd joins cast of Park Grove
"I understand tragedy," says widowed actress
CURSE OF THE SHEPHERDS
SOAP ACTRESS STILL MISSING

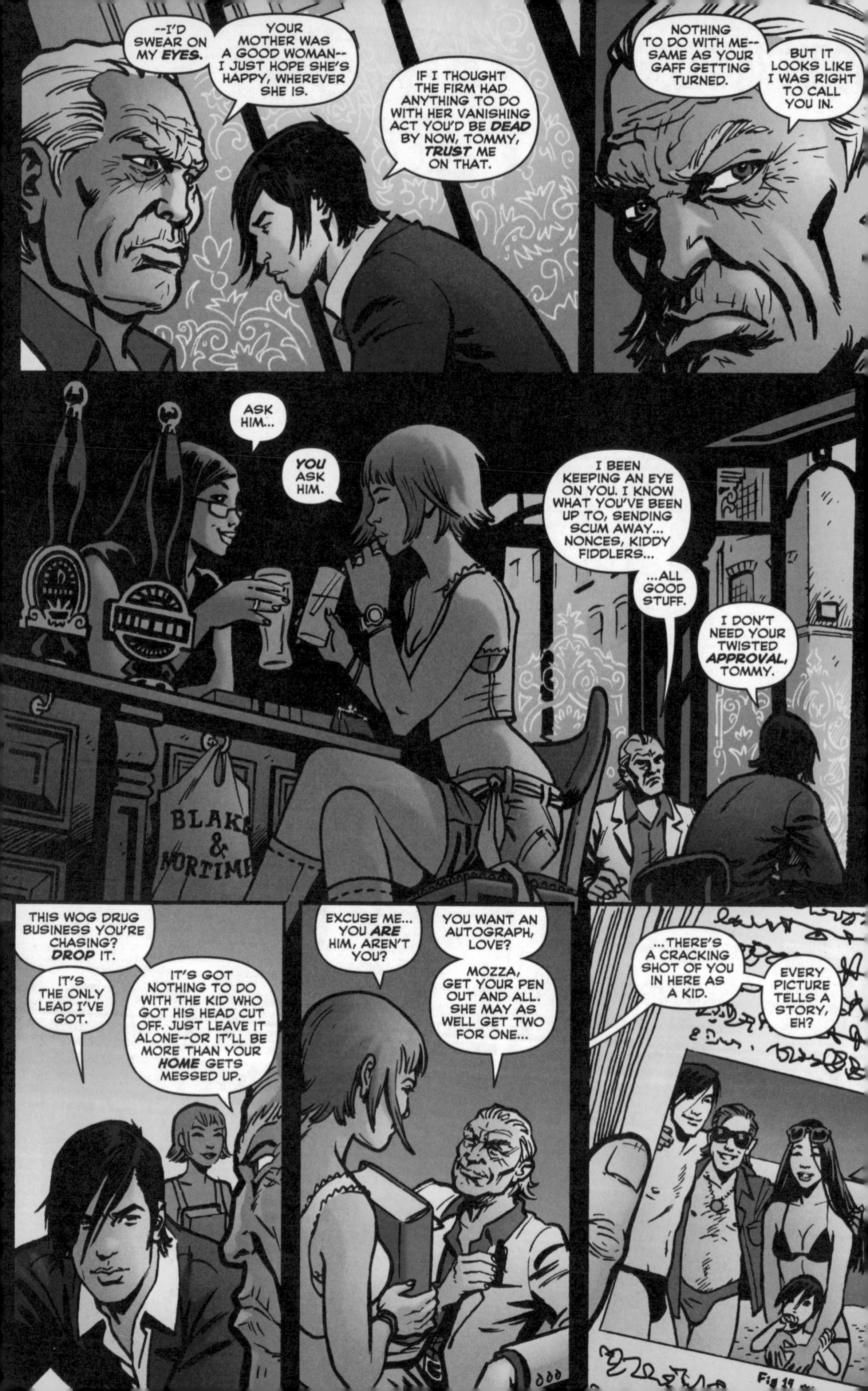
--I'D SWEAR ON MY EYES.
YOUR MOTHER WAS A GOOD WOMAN--I JUST HOPE SHE'S HAPPY, WHEREVER SHE IS.
IF I THOUGHT THE FIRM HAD ANYTHING TO DO WITH HER VANISHING ACT YOU'D BE DEAD BY NOW, TOMMY, TRUST ME ON THAT.
NOTHING TO DO WITH ME--SAME AS YOUR GAFF GETTING TURNED.
BUT IT LOOKS LIKE I WAS RIGHT TO CALL YOU IN.
ASK HIM...
YOU ASK HIM.
I BEEN KEEPING AN EYE ON YOU. I KNOW WHAT YOU'VE BEEN UP TO, SENDING SCUM AWAY... NONCES, KIDDY FIDDLERS...
...ALL GOOD STUFF.
I DON'T NEED YOUR TWISTED APPROVAL, TOMMY.
BLAKE & MORTIME
THIS WOG DRUG BUSINESS YOU'RE CHASING? DROP IT.
IT'S THE ONLY LEAD I'VE GOT.
IT'S GOT NOTHING TO DO WITH THE KID WHO GOT HIS HEAD CUT OFF. JUST LEAVE IT ALONE--OR IT'LL BE MORE THAN YOUR HOME GETS MESSED UP.
EXCUSE ME... YOU ARE HIM, AREN'T YOU?
YOU WANT AN AUTOGRAPH, LOVE?
MOZZA, GET YOUR PEN OUT AND ALL. SHE MAY AS WELL GET TWO FOR ONE...
...THERE'S A CRACKING SHOT OF YOU IN HERE AS A KID.
EVERY PICTURE TELLS A STORY, EH?

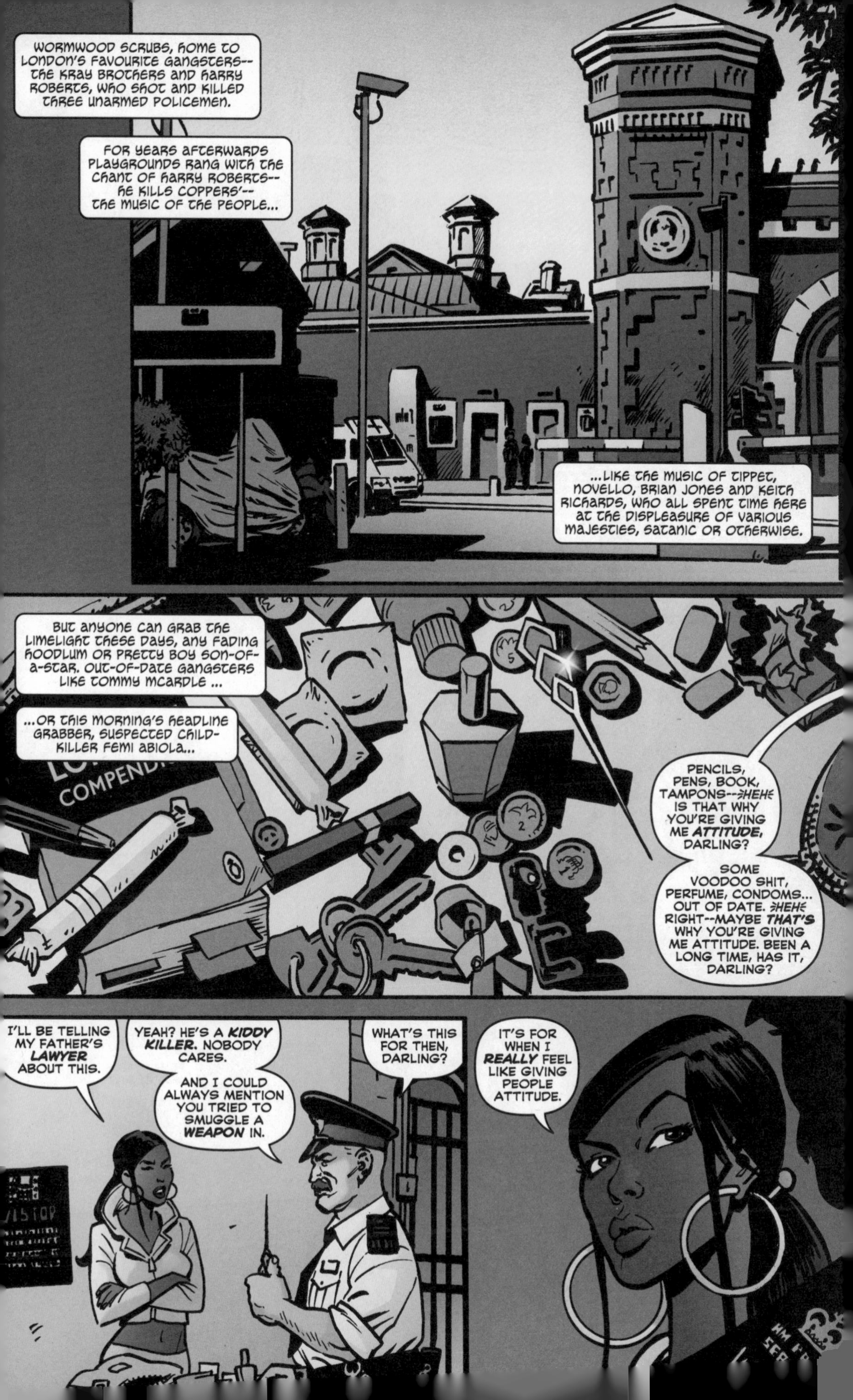
WORMWOOD SCRUBS, HOME TO LONDON'S FAVOURITE GANGSTERS--THE KRAY BROTHERS AND HARRY ROBERTS, WHO SHOT AND KILLED THREE UNARMED POLICEMEN.
FOR YEARS AFTERWARDS PLAYGROUNDS RANG WITH THE CHANT OF HARRY ROBERTS--HE KILLS COPPERS'--THE MUSIC OF THE PEOPLE...
...LIKE THE MUSIC OF TIPPET, NOVELLO, BRIAN JONES AND KEITH RICHARDS, WHO ALL SPENT TIME HERE AT THE DISPLEASURE OF VARIOUS MAJESTIES, SATANIC OR OTHERWISE.
BUT ANYONE CAN GRAB THE LIMELIGHT THESE DAYS, ANY FADING HOODLUM OR PRETTY BOY SON-OF-A-STAR. OUT-OF-DATE GANGSTERS LIKE TOMMY MCARDLE ...
...OR THIS MORNING'S HEADLINE GRABBER, SUSPECTED CHILD-KILLER FEMI ABIOLA...
COMPENDI
PENCILS, PENS, BOOK, TAMPONS--HEHE IS THAT WHY YOU'RE GIVING ME ATTITUDE, DARLING?
SOME VOODOO SHIT, PERFUME, CONDOMS... OUT OF DATE. HEHE RIGHT--MAYBE THAT'S WHY YOU'RE GIVING ME ATTITUDE. BEEN A LONG TIME, HAS IT, DARLING?
I'LL BE TELLING MY FATHER'S LAWYER ABOUT THIS.
YEAH? HE'S A KIDDY KILLER. NOBODY CARES.
AND I COULD ALWAYS MENTION YOU TRIED TO SMUGGLE A WEAPON IN.
WHAT'S THIS FOR THEN, DARLING?
IT'S FOR WHEN I REALLY FEEL LIKE GIVING PEOPLE ATTITUDE.

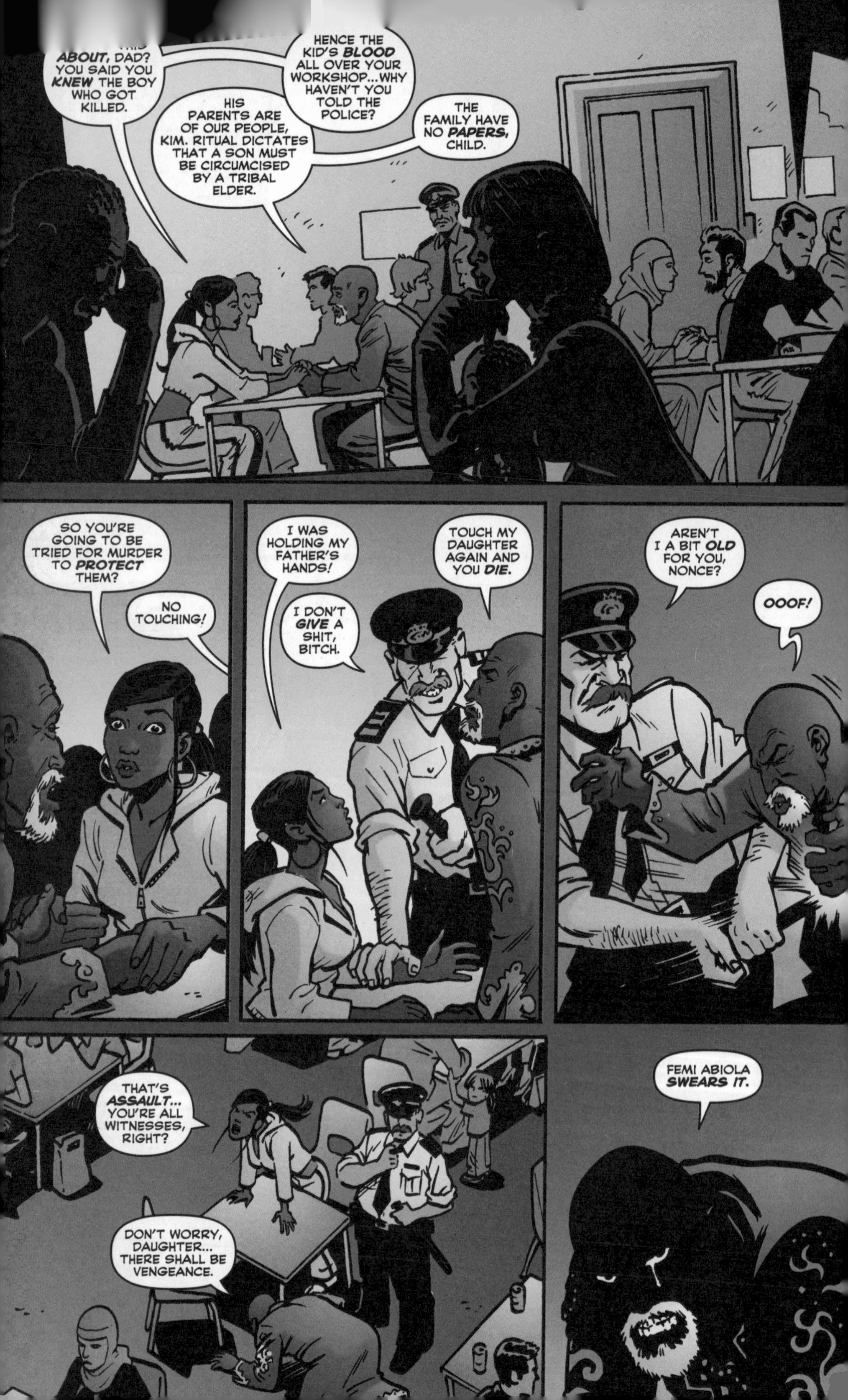
ABOUT, DAD? YOU SAID YOU KNEW THE BOY WHO GOT KILLED.
HIS PARENTS ARE OF OUR PEOPLE, KIM. RITUAL DICTATES THAT A SON MUST BE CIRCUMCISED BY A TRIBAL ELDER.
HENCE THE KID'S BLOOD ALL OVER YOUR WORKSHOP...WHY HAVEN'T YOU TOLD THE POLICE?
THE FAMILY HAVE NO PAPERS, CHILD.
SO YOU'RE GOING TO BE TRIED FOR MURDER TO PROTECT THEM?
NO TOUCHING!
I WAS HOLDING MY FATHER'S HANDS!
I DON'T GIVE A SHIT, BITCH.
TOUCH MY DAUGHTER AGAIN AND YOU DIE.
AREN'T I A BIT OLD FOR YOU, NONCE?
OOOF!
THAT'S ASSAULT... YOU'RE ALL WITNESSES, RIGHT?
DON'T WORRY, DAUGHTER... THERE SHALL BE VENGEANCE.
FEMI ABIOLA SWEARS IT.

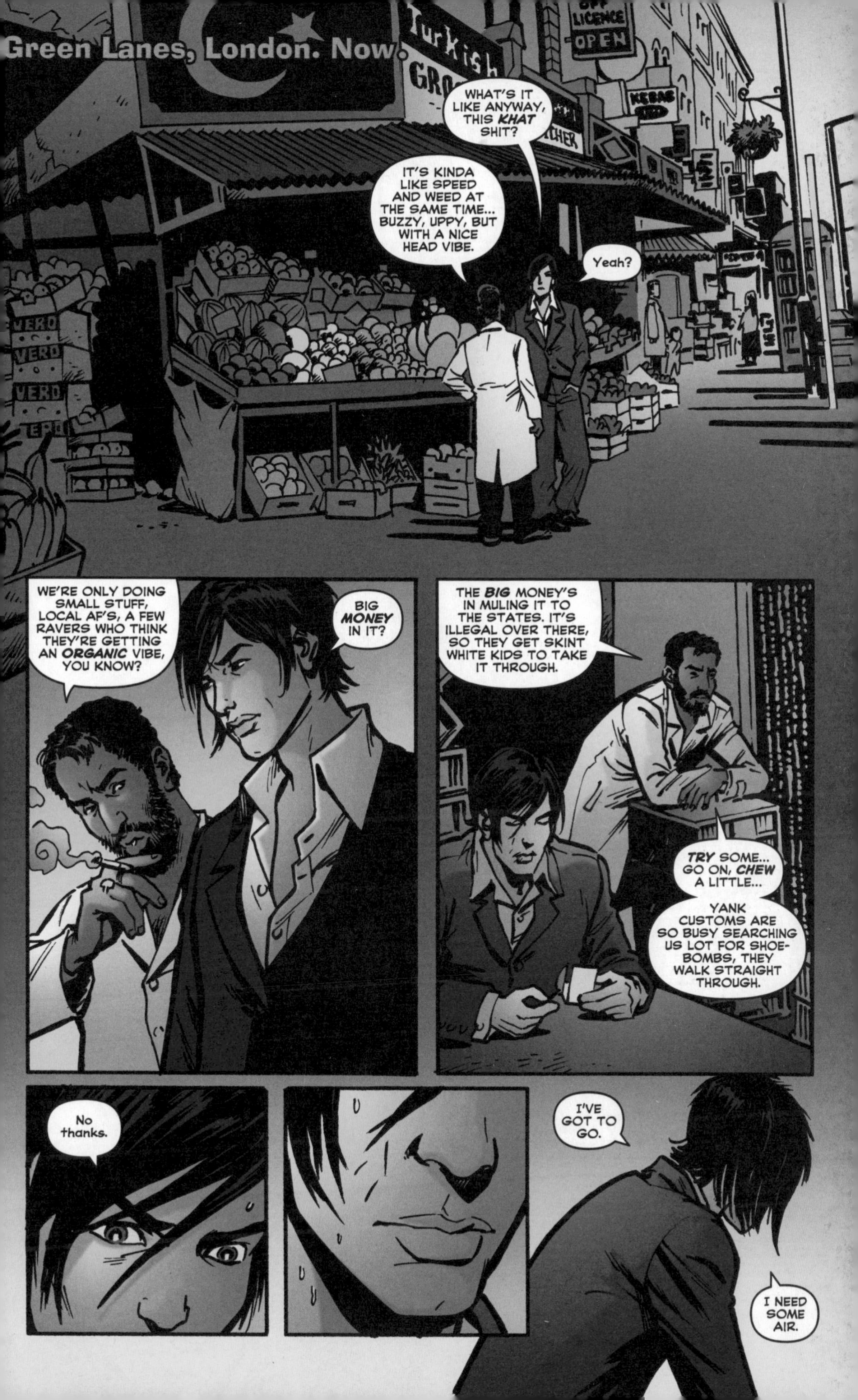
Green Lanes, London. Now.
Turkish
OFF LICENCE
OPEN
KEBABS
WHAT'S IT LIKE ANYWAY, THIS KHAT SHIT?
IT'S KINDA LIKE SPEED AND WEED AT THE SAME TIME... BUZZY, UPPY, BUT WITH A NICE HEAD VIBE.
Yeah?
WE'RE ONLY DOING SMALL STUFF, LOCAL AF'S, A FEW RAVERS WHO THINK THEY'RE GETTING AN ORGANIC VIBE, YOU KNOW?
BIG MONEY IN IT?
THE BIG MONEY'S IN MULING IT TO THE STATES. IT'S ILLEGAL OVER THERE, SO THEY GET SKINT WHITE KIDS TO TAKE IT THROUGH.
TRY SOME... GO ON, CHEW A LITTLE...
YANK CUSTOMS ARE SO BUSY SEARCHING US LOT FOR SHOE-BOMBS, THEY WALK STRAIGHT THROUGH.
No thanks.
I'VE GOT TO GO.
I NEED SOME AIR.

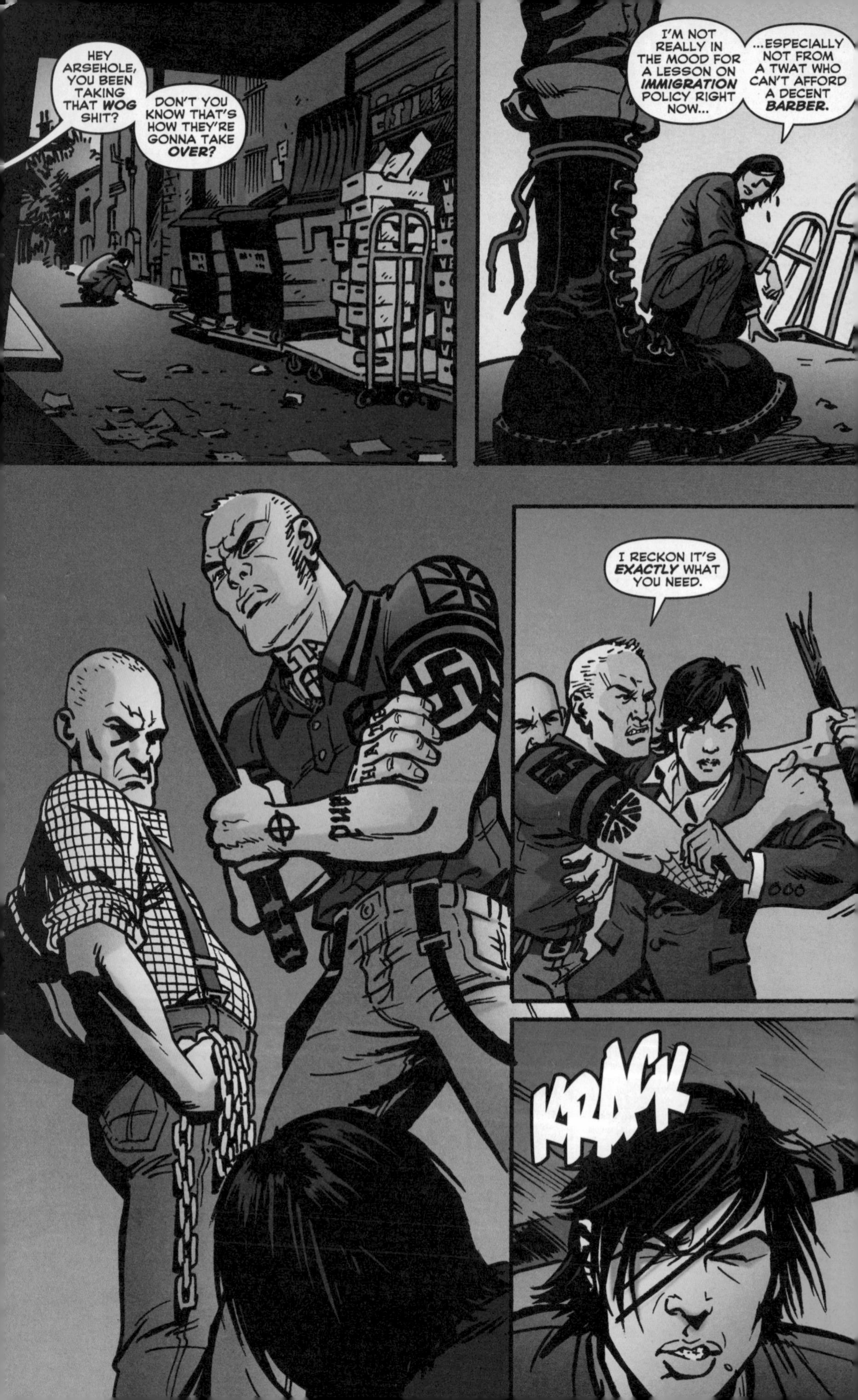
HEY ARSEHOLE, YOU BEEN TAKING THAT WOG SHIT?
DON'T YOU KNOW THAT'S HOW THEY'RE GONNA TAKE OVER?
I'M NOT REALLY IN THE MOOD FOR A LESSON ON IMMIGRATION POLICY RIGHT NOW...
...ESPECIALLY NOT FROM A TWAT WHO CAN'T AFFORD A DECENT BARBER.
I RECKON IT'S EXACTLY WHAT YOU NEED.
KRACK

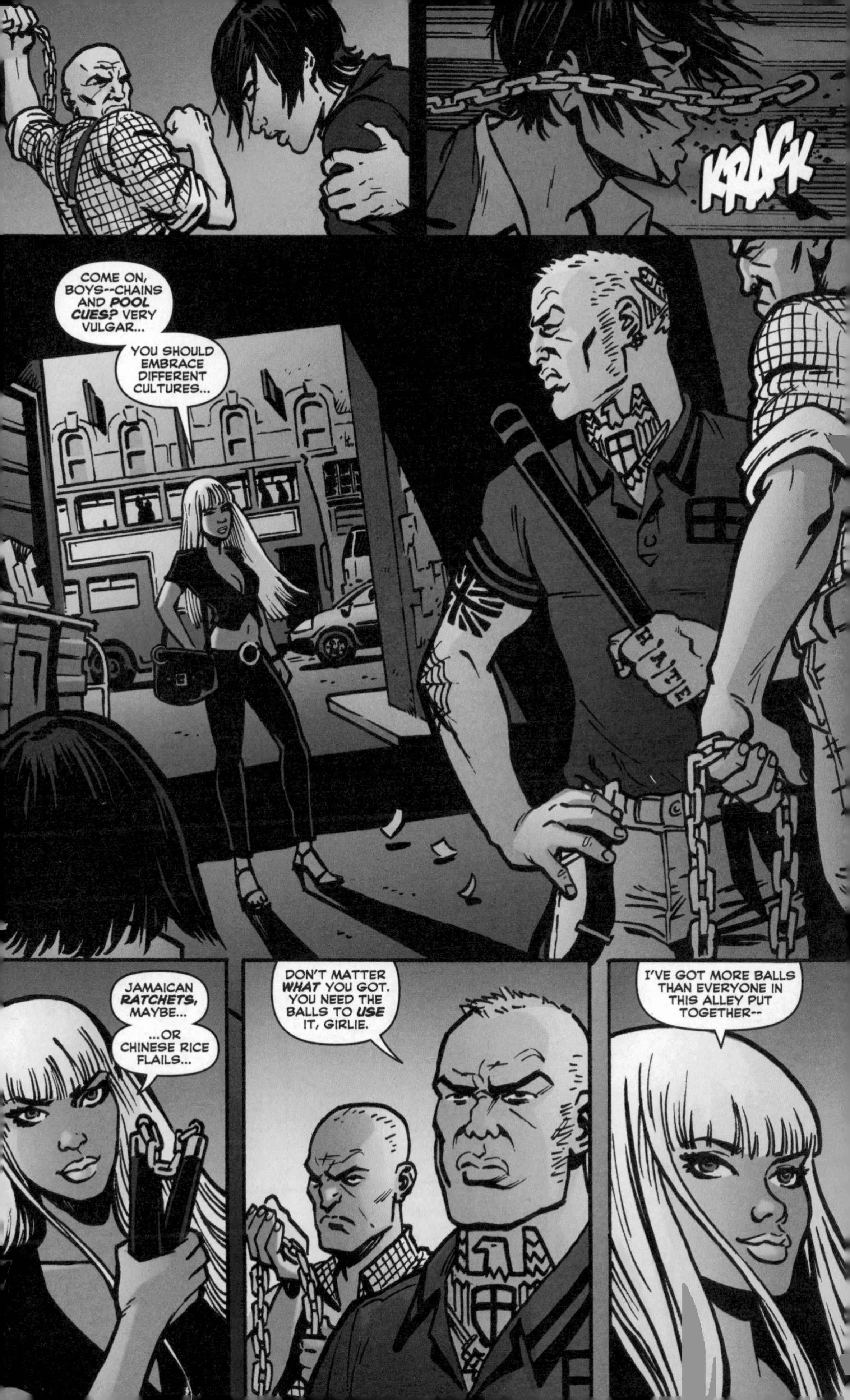
KRACK
COME ON, BOYS--CHAINS AND POOL CUES? VERY VULGAR...
YOU SHOULD EMBRACE DIFFERENT CULTURES...
HATE
JAMAICAN RATCHETS, MAYBE...
...OR CHINESE RICE FLAILS...
DON'T MATTER WHAT YOU GOT. YOU NEED THE BALLS TO USE IT, GIRLIE.
I'VE GOT MORE BALLS THAN EVERYONE IN THIS ALLEY PUT TOGETHER--

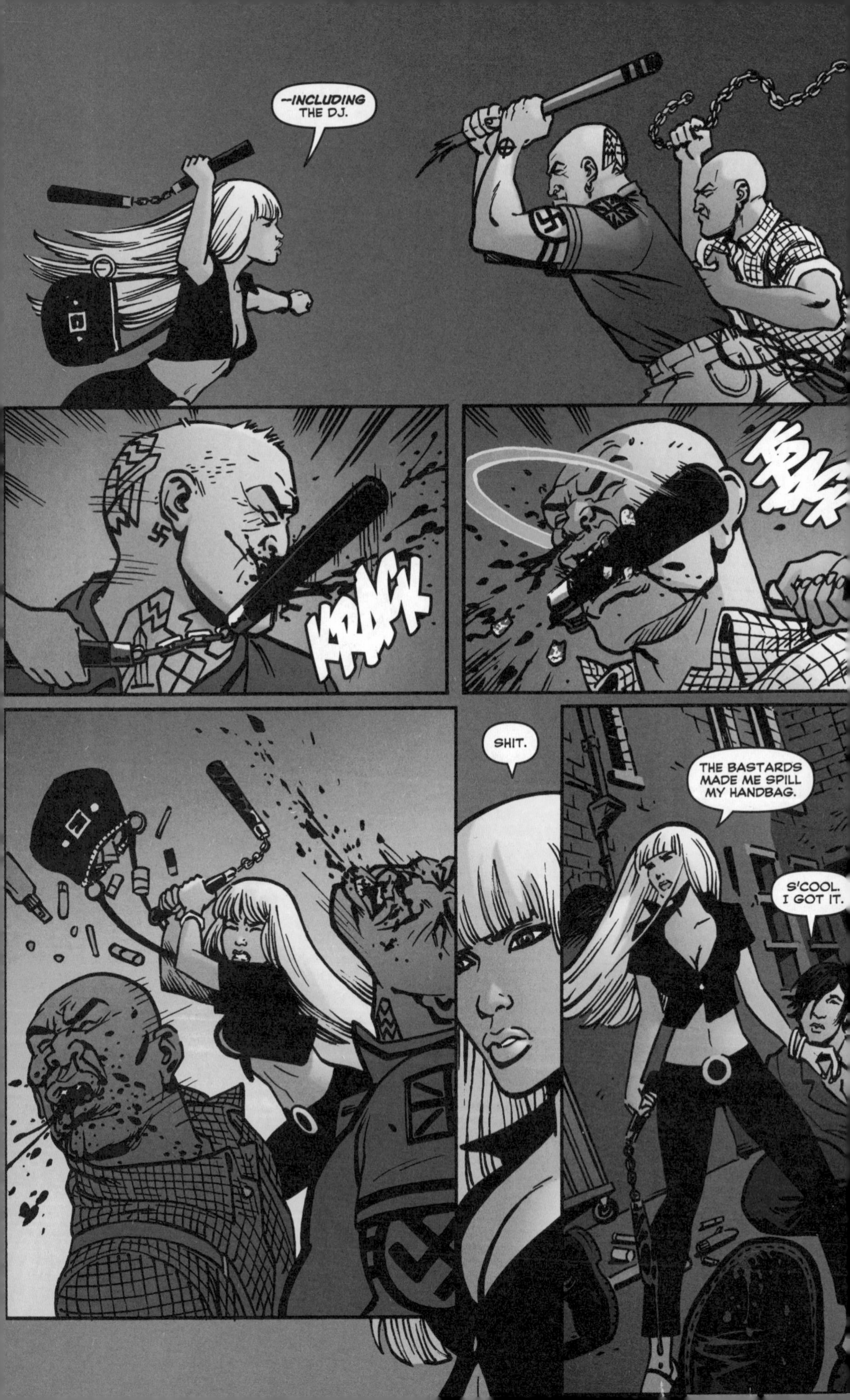
—INCLUDING THE DJ.
KRACK
KRACK
SHIT.
THE BASTARDS MADE ME SPILL MY HANDBAG.
S'COOL. I GOT IT.

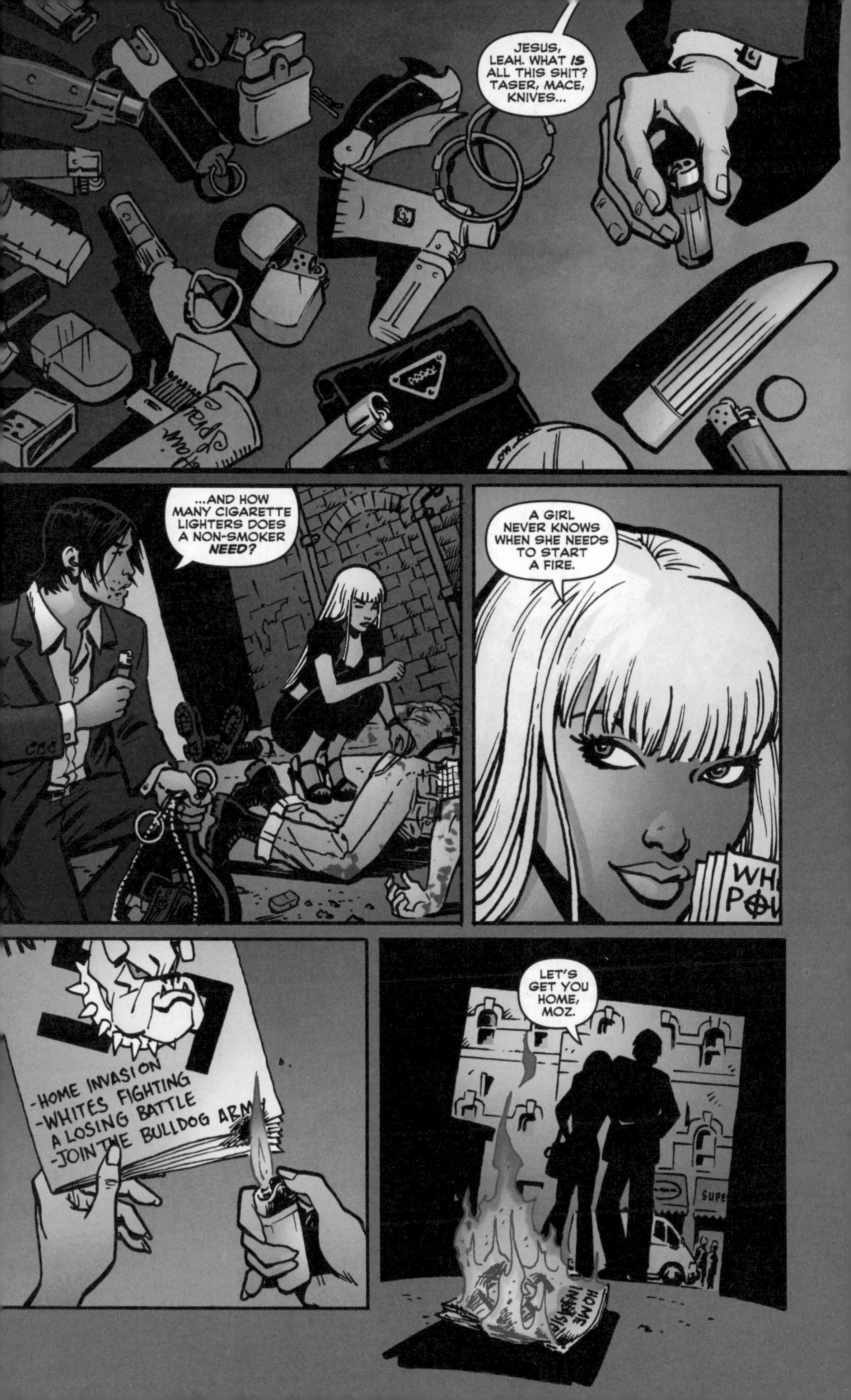
JESUS, LEAH. WHAT IS ALL THIS SHIT? TASER, MACE, KNIVES...
...AND HOW MANY CIGARETTE LIGHTERS DOES A NON-SMOKER NEED?
A GIRL NEVER KNOWS WHEN SHE NEEDS TO START A FIRE.
-HOME INVASION
-WHITES FIGHTING
A LOSING BATTLE
-JOIN THE BULLDOG ARMY
LET'S GET YOU HOME, MOZ.

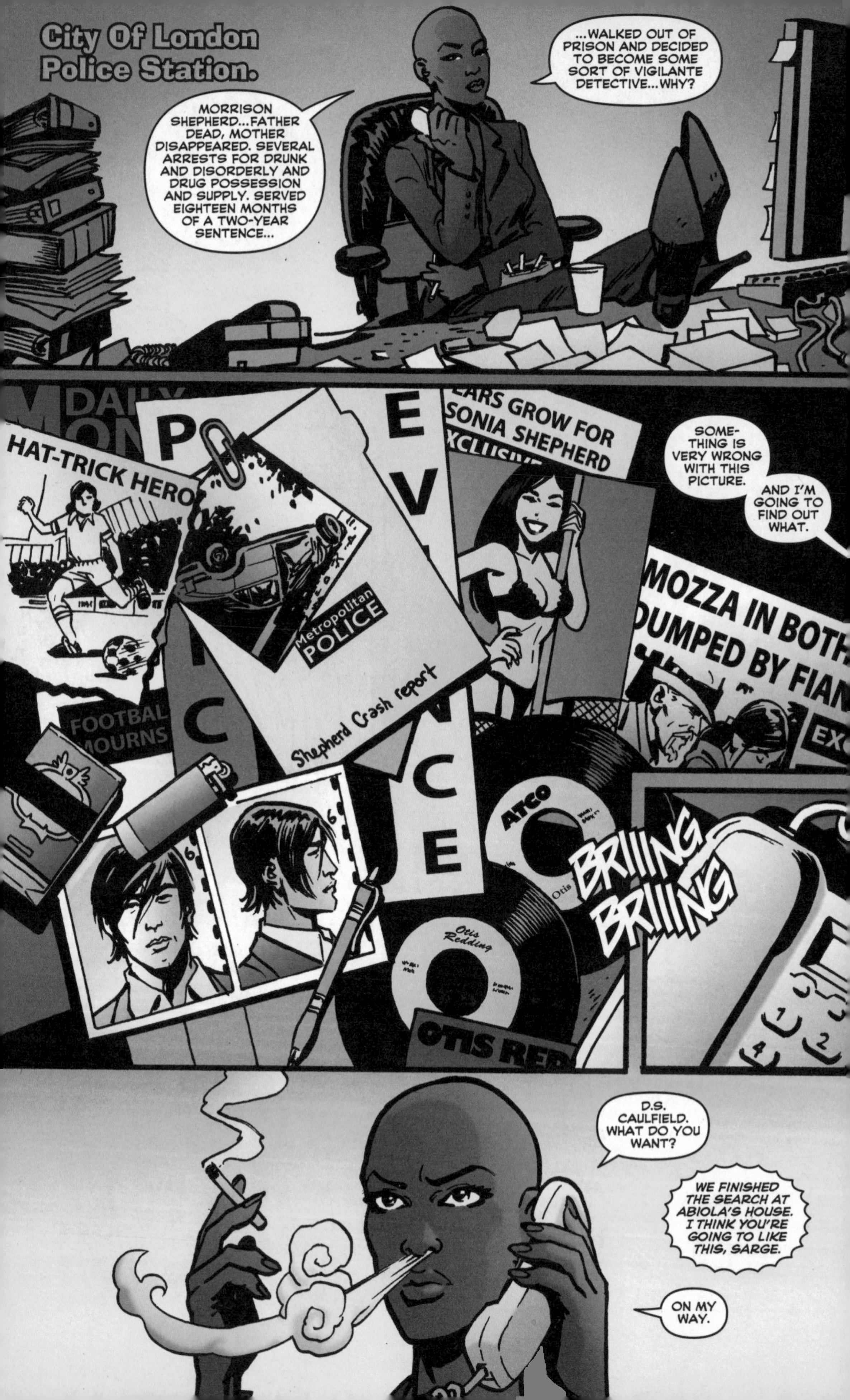
City Of London Police Station.
MORRISON SHEPHERD...FATHER DEAD, MOTHER DISAPPEARED. SEVERAL ARRESTS FOR DRUNK AND DISORDERLY AND DRUG POSSESSION AND SUPPLY. SERVED EIGHTEEN MONTHS OF A TWO-YEAR SENTENCE...
...WALKED OUT OF PRISON AND DECIDED TO BECOME SOME SORT OF VIGILANTE DETECTIVE...WHY?
HAT-TRICK HERO
SONIA SHEPHERD
Metropolitan POLICE
Shepherd Crash report
SOME-THING IS VERY WRONG WITH THIS PICTURE.
AND I'M GOING TO FIND OUT WHAT.
ATCO
Otis Redding
BRIIING BRIIING
D.S. CAULFIELD. WHAT DO YOU WANT?
WE FINISHED THE SEARCH AT ABIOLA'S HOUSE. I THINK YOU'RE GOING TO LIKE THIS, SARGE.
ON MY WAY.

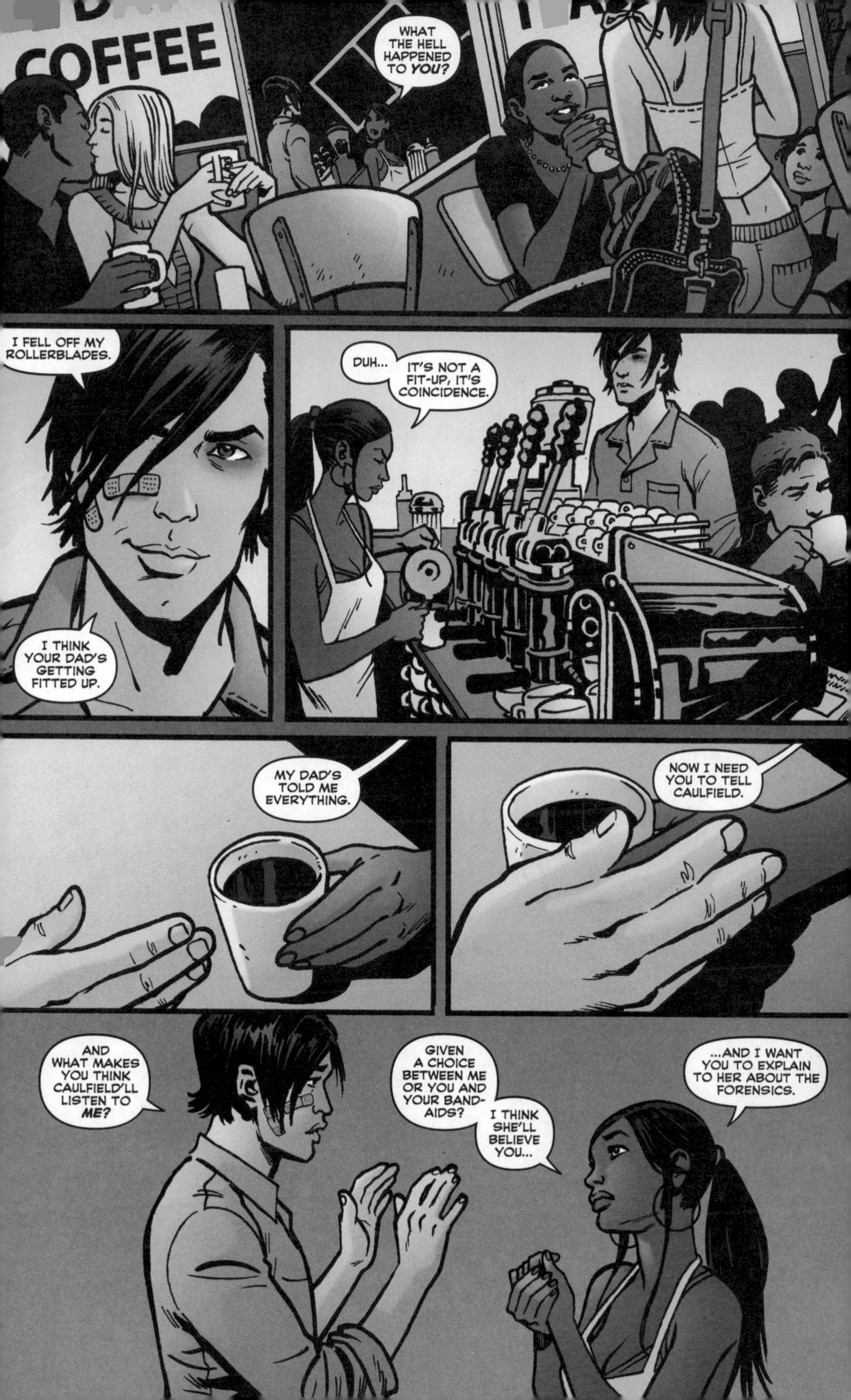
COFFEE
WHAT THE HELL HAPPENED TO *YOU*?
I FELL OFF MY ROLLERBLADES.
I THINK YOUR DAD'S GETTING FITTED UP.
DUH...
IT'S NOT A FIT-UP, IT'S COINCIDENCE.
MY DAD'S TOLD ME EVERYTHING.
NOW I NEED YOU TO TELL CAULFIELD.
AND WHAT MAKES YOU THINK CAULFIELD'LL LISTEN TO *ME?*
GIVEN A CHOICE BETWEEN ME OR YOU AND YOUR BAND-AIDS?
I THINK SHE'LL BELIEVE YOU...
...AND I WANT YOU TO EXPLAIN TO HER ABOUT THE FORENSICS.

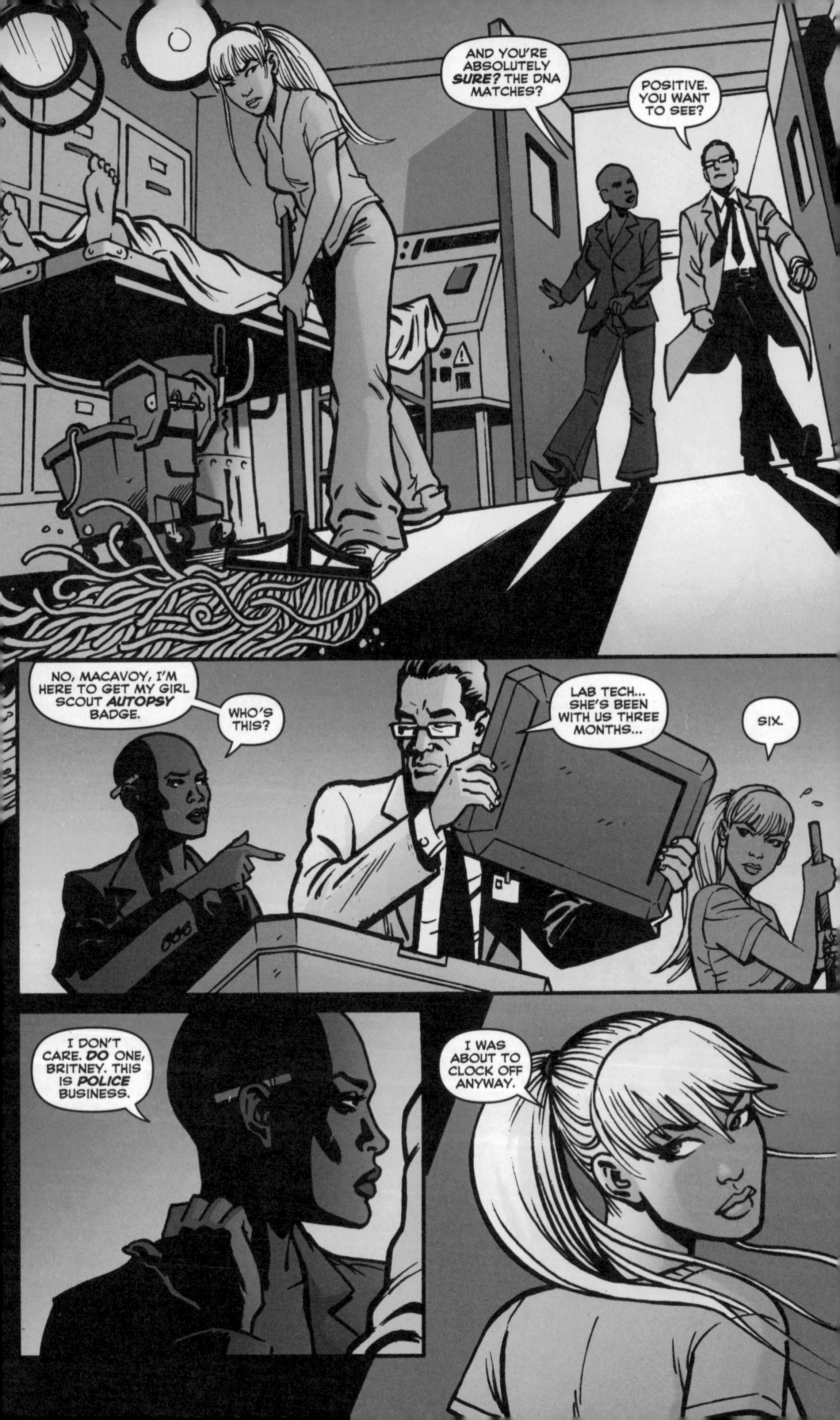
AND YOU'RE ABSOLUTELY SURE? THE DNA MATCHES?
POSITIVE. YOU WANT TO SEE?
NO, MACAVOY, I'M HERE TO GET MY GIRL SCOUT AUTOPSY BADGE.
WHO'S THIS?
LAB TECH... SHE'S BEEN WITH US THREE MONTHS...
SIX.
I DON'T CARE. DO ONE, BRITNEY. THIS IS POLICE BUSINESS.
I WAS ABOUT TO CLOCK OFF ANYWAY.

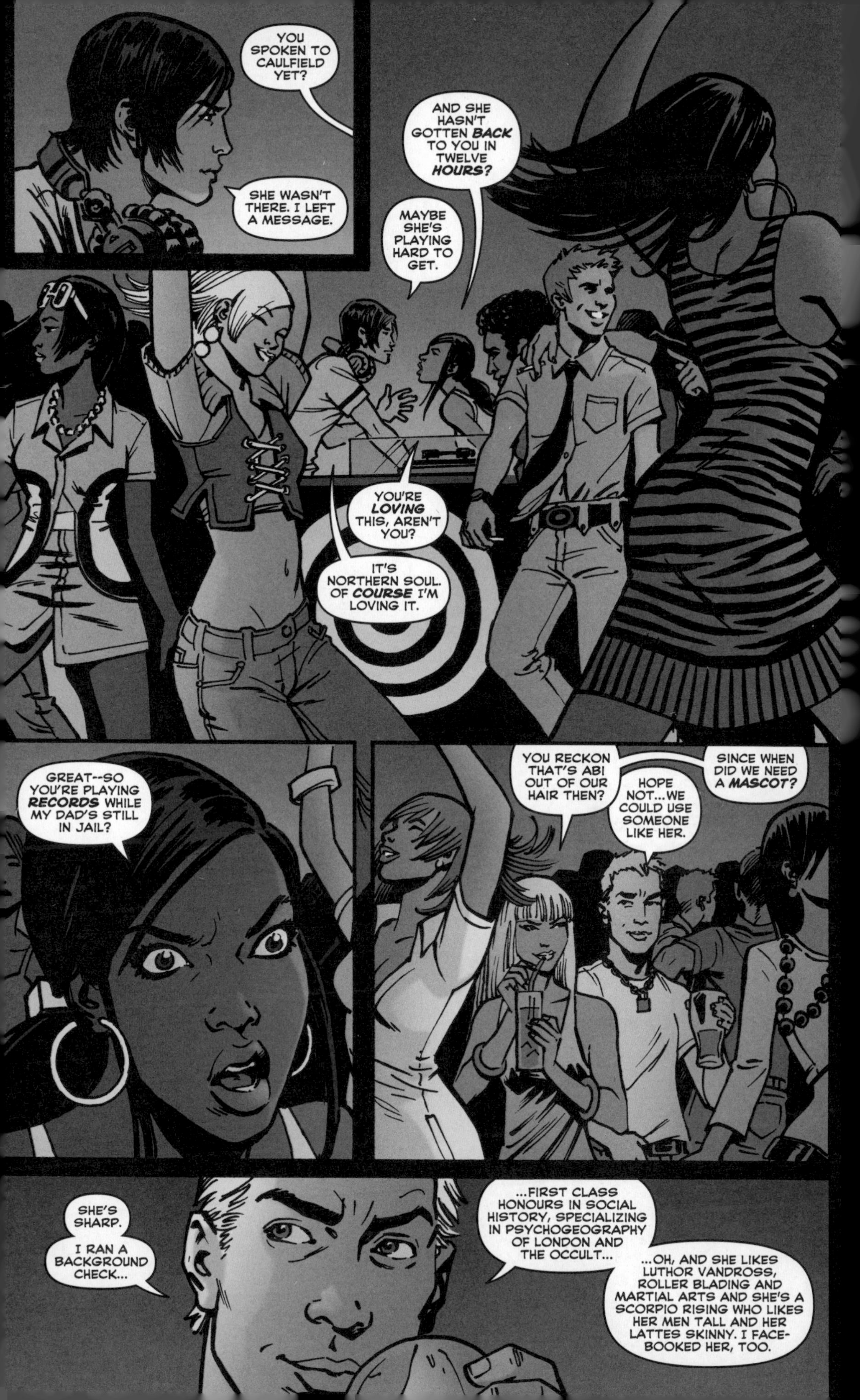
YOU SPOKEN TO CAULFIELD YET?
SHE WASN'T THERE. I LEFT A MESSAGE.
AND SHE HASN'T GOTTEN BACK TO YOU IN TWELVE HOURS?
MAYBE SHE'S PLAYING HARD TO GET.
YOU'RE LOVING THIS, AREN'T YOU?
IT'S NORTHERN SOUL. OF COURSE I'M LOVING IT.
GREAT--SO YOU'RE PLAYING RECORDS WHILE MY DAD'S STILL IN JAIL?
YOU RECKON THAT'S ABI OUT OF OUR HAIR THEN?
SINCE WHEN DID WE NEED A MASCOT?
HOPE NOT...WE COULD USE SOMEONE LIKE HER.
SHE'S SHARP.
I RAN A BACKGROUND CHECK...
...FIRST CLASS HONOURS IN SOCIAL HISTORY, SPECIALIZING IN PSYCHOGEOGRAPHY OF LONDON AND THE OCCULT...
...OH, AND SHE LIKES LUTHOR VANDROSS, ROLLER BLADING AND MARTIAL ARTS AND SHE'S A SCORPIO RISING WHO LIKES HER MEN TALL AND HER LATTES SKINNY. I FACE-BOOKED HER, TOO.

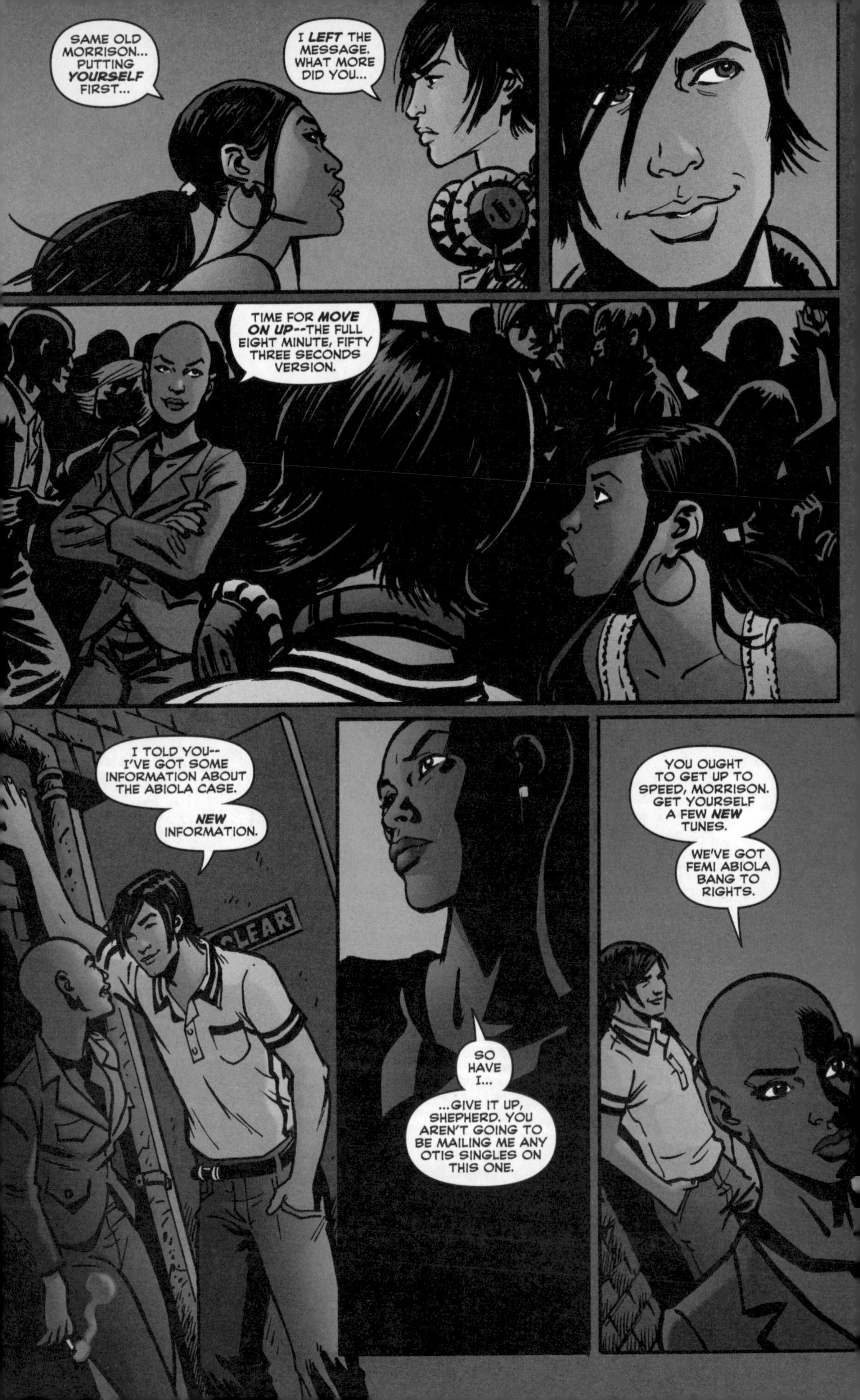
SAME OLD MORRISON... PUTTING YOURSELF FIRST...
I LEFT THE MESSAGE. WHAT MORE DID YOU...
TIME FOR MOVE ON UP--THE FULL EIGHT MINUTE, FIFTY THREE SECONDS VERSION.
I TOLD YOU-- I'VE GOT SOME INFORMATION ABOUT THE ABIOLA CASE.
NEW INFORMATION.
CLEAR
SO HAVE I...
...GIVE IT UP, SHEPHERD. YOU AREN'T GOING TO BE MAILING ME ANY OTIS SINGLES ON THIS ONE.
YOU OUGHT TO GET UP TO SPEED, MORRISON. GET YOURSELF A FEW NEW TUNES.
WE'VE GOT FEMI ABIOLA BANG TO RIGHTS.

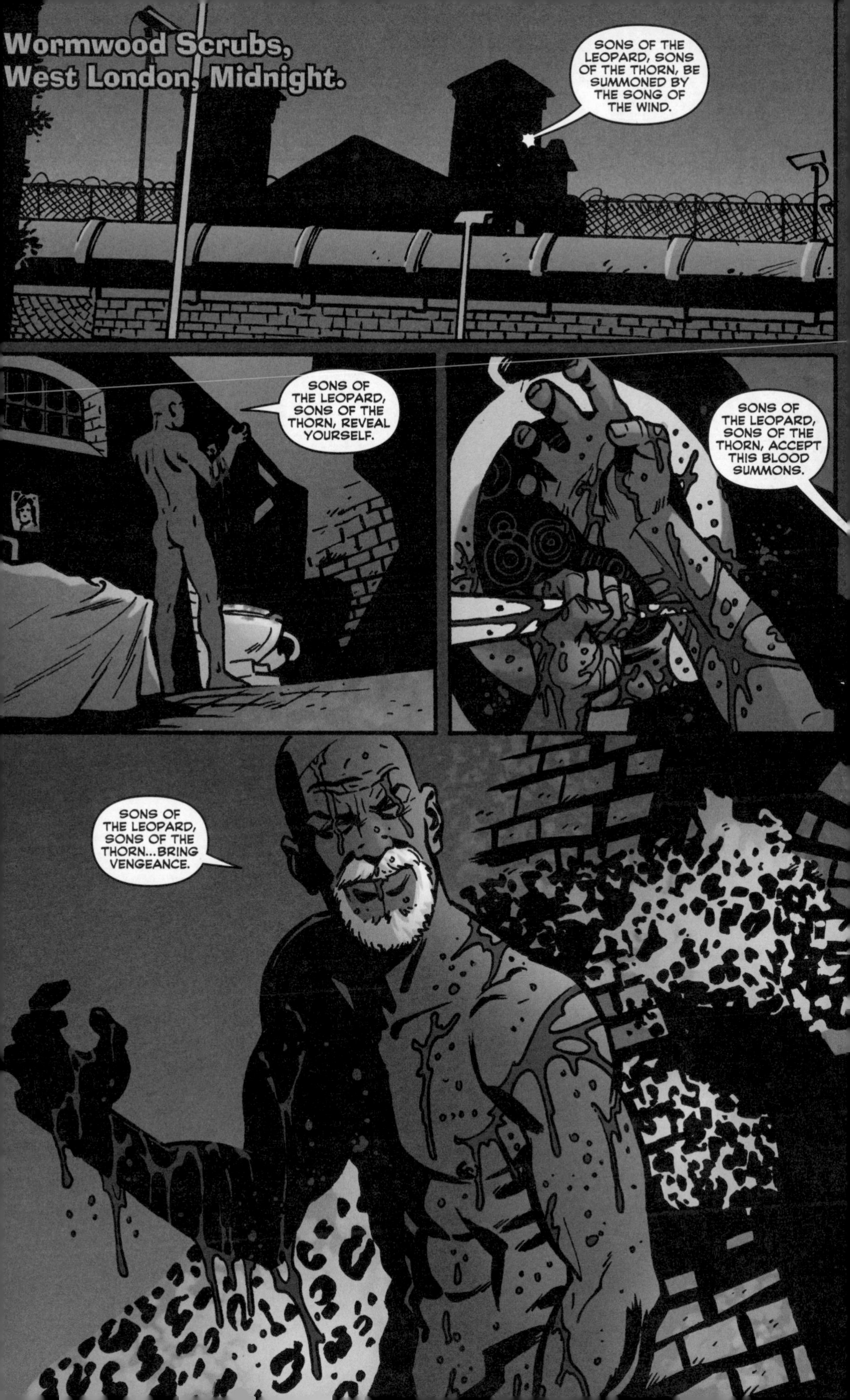
Wormwood Scrubs, West London, Midnight.
SONS OF THE LEOPARD, SONS OF THE THORN, BE SUMMONED BY THE SONG OF THE WIND.
SONS OF THE LEOPARD, SONS OF THE THORN, REVEAL YOURSELF.
SONS OF THE LEOPARD, SONS OF THE THORN, ACCEPT THIS BLOOD SUMMONS.
SONS OF THE LEOPARD, SONS OF THE THORN...BRING VENGEANCE.

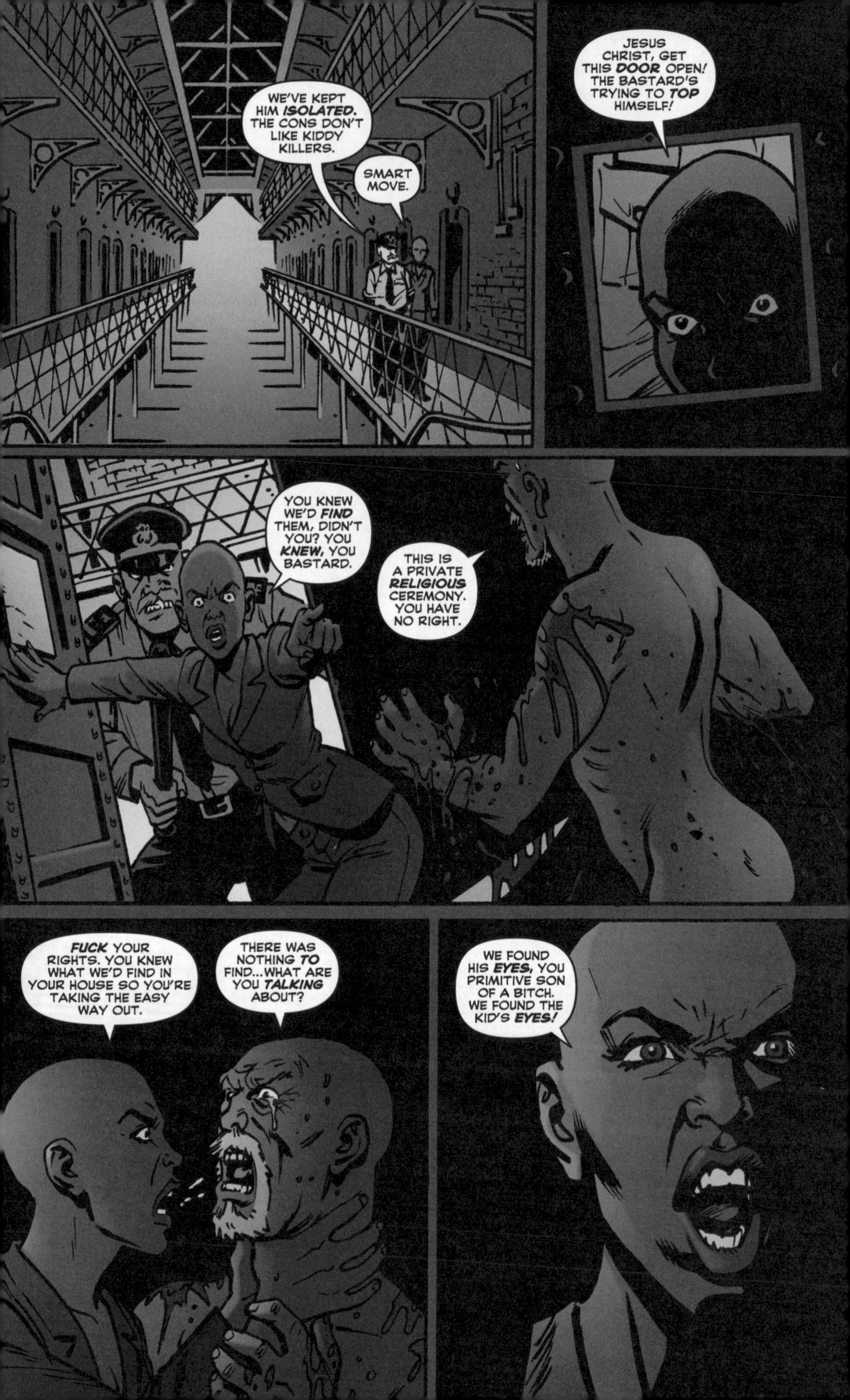
WE'VE KEPT HIM ISOLATED. THE CONS DON'T LIKE KIDDY KILLERS.
SMART MOVE.
JESUS CHRIST, GET THIS DOOR OPEN! THE BASTARD'S TRYING TO TOP HIMSELF!
YOU KNEW WE'D FIND THEM, DIDN'T YOU? YOU KNEW, YOU BASTARD.
THIS IS A PRIVATE RELIGIOUS CEREMONY. YOU HAVE NO RIGHT.
FUCK YOUR RIGHTS. YOU KNEW WHAT WE'D FIND IN YOUR HOUSE SO YOU'RE TAKING THE EASY WAY OUT.
THERE WAS NOTHING TO FIND...WHAT ARE YOU TALKING ABOUT?
WE FOUND HIS EYES, YOU PRIMITIVE SON OF A BITCH. WE FOUND THE KID'S EYES!

NIGHT SHIFT

3

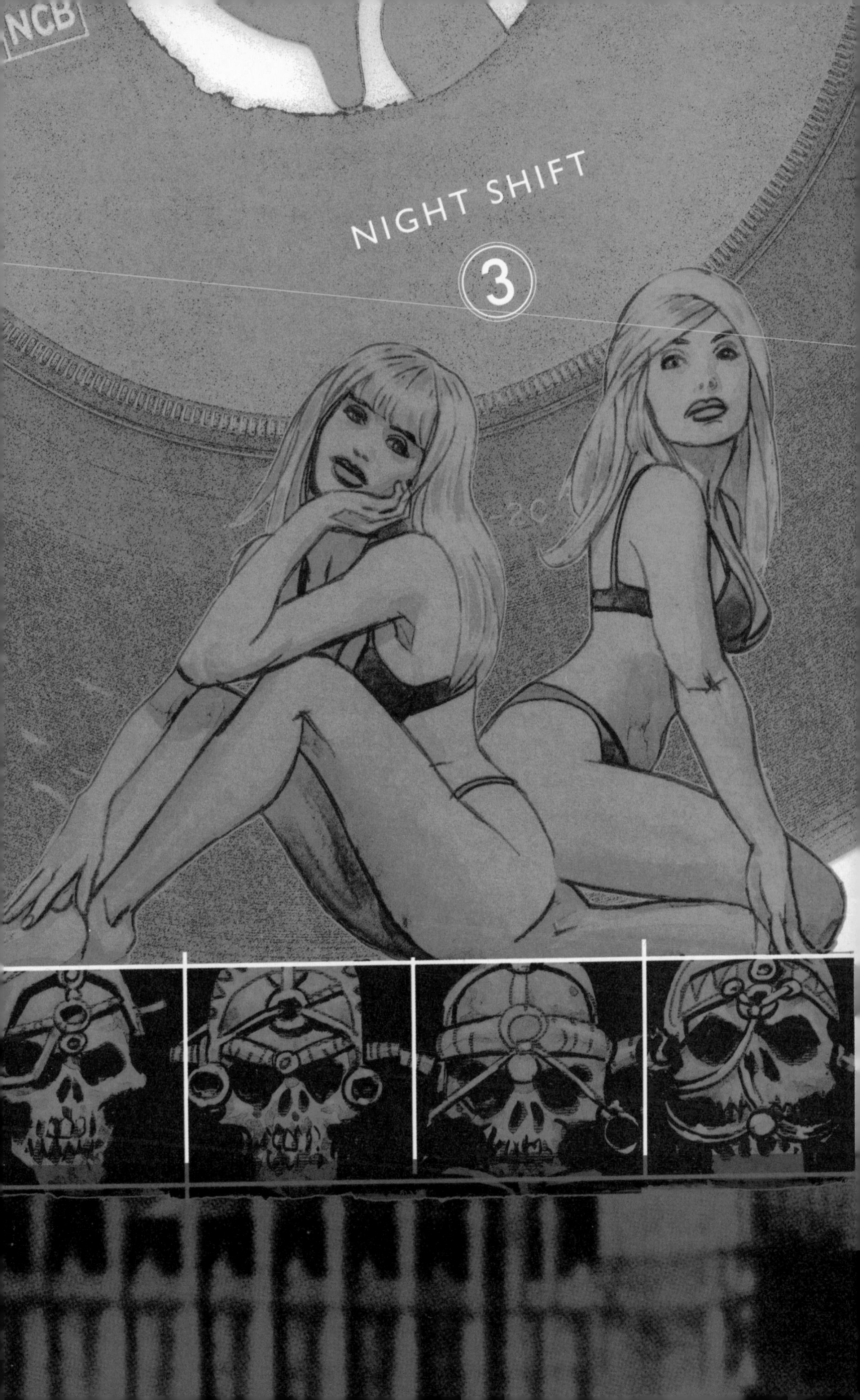
NCB

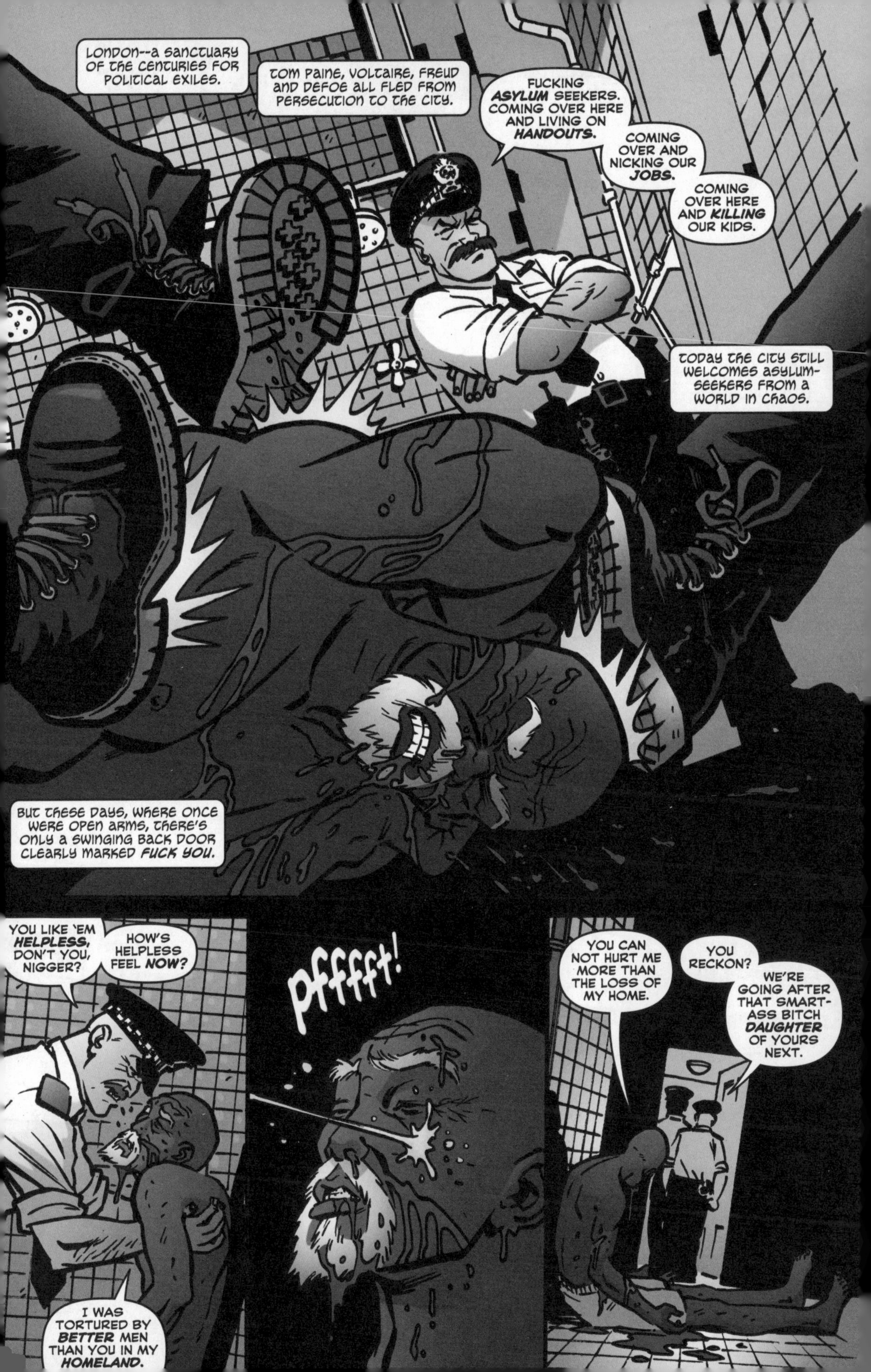

LONDON--A SANCTUARY OF THE CENTURIES FOR POLITICAL EXILES.
TOM PAINE, VOLTAIRE, FREUD AND DEFOE ALL FLED FROM PERSECUTION TO THE CITY.
FUCKING ASYLUM SEEKERS. COMING OVER HERE AND LIVING ON HANDOUTS.
COMING OVER AND NICKING OUR JOBS.
COMING OVER HERE AND KILLING OUR KIDS.
TODAY THE CITY STILL WELCOMES ASYLUM-SEEKERS FROM A WORLD IN CHAOS.
BUT THESE DAYS, WHERE ONCE WERE OPEN ARMS, THERE'S ONLY A SWINGING BACK DOOR CLEARLY MARKED FUCK YOU.
YOU LIKE 'EM HELPLESS, DON'T YOU, NIGGER?
HOW'S HELPLESS FEEL NOW?
I WAS TORTURED BY BETTER MEN THAN YOU IN MY HOMELAND.
PFFFFT!
YOU CAN NOT HURT ME MORE THAN THE LOSS OF MY HOME.
YOU RECKON?
WE'RE GOING AFTER THAT SMART-ASS BITCH DAUGHTER OF YOURS NEXT.

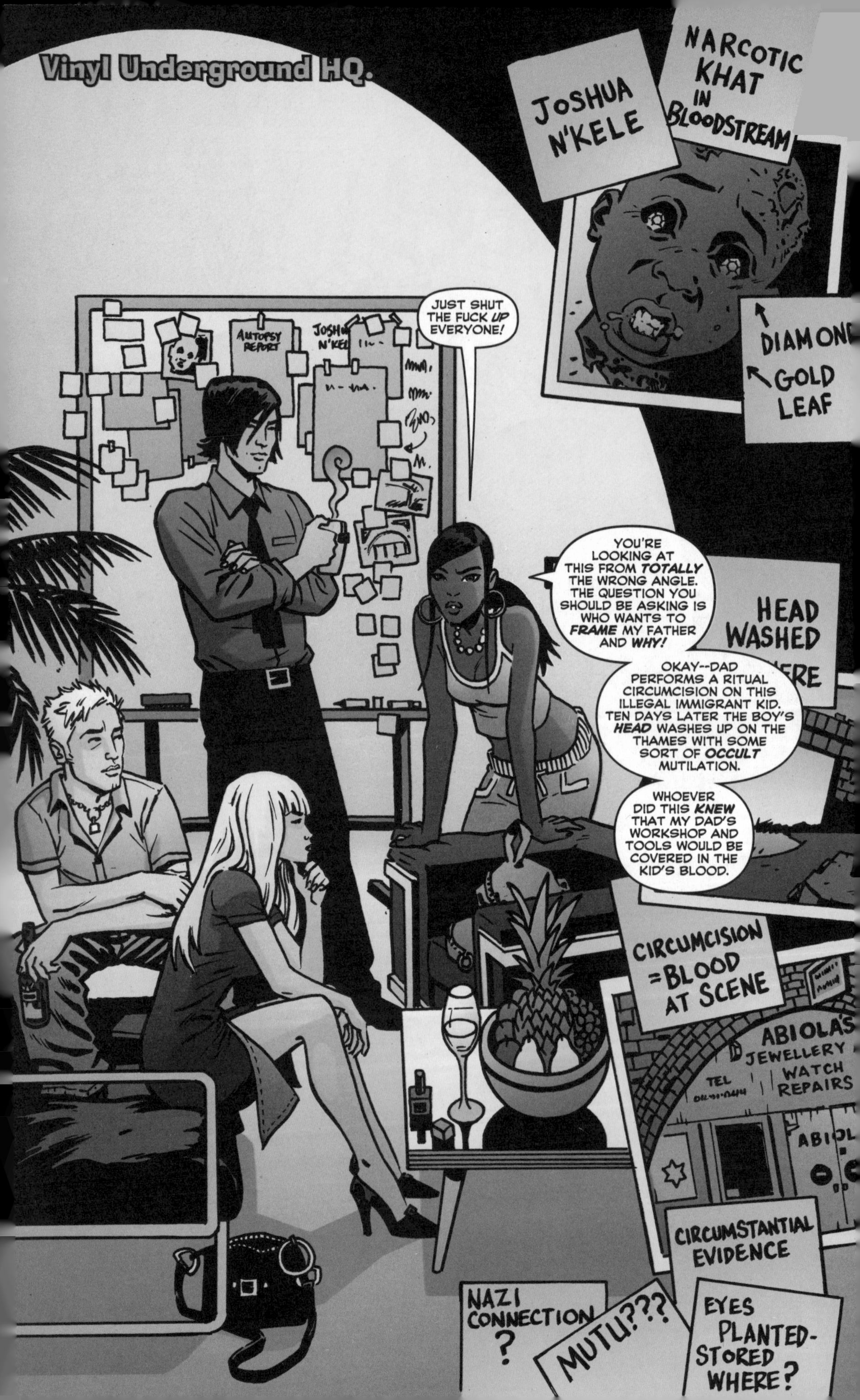
Vinyl Underground HQ.
JOSHUA N'KELE
NARCOTIC KHAT IN BLOODSTREAM
DIAMOND
GOLD LEAF
AUTOPSY REPORT
JUST SHUT THE FUCK *UP* EVERYONE!
YOU'RE LOOKING AT THIS FROM *TOTALLY* THE WRONG ANGLE. THE QUESTION YOU SHOULD BE ASKING IS WHO WANTS TO *FRAME* MY FATHER AND *WHY!*
HEAD WASHED
OKAY--DAD PERFORMS A RITUAL CIRCUMCISION ON THIS ILLEGAL IMMIGRANT KID. TEN DAYS LATER THE BOY'S *HEAD* WASHES UP ON THE THAMES WITH SOME SORT OF *OCCULT* MUTILATION.
WHOEVER DID THIS *KNEW* THAT MY DAD'S WORKSHOP AND TOOLS WOULD BE COVERED IN THE KID'S BLOOD.
CIRCUMCISION =BLOOD AT SCENE
ABIOLA'S JEWELLERY WATCH REPAIRS
TEL
CIRCUMSTANTIAL EVIDENCE
NAZI CONNECTION ?
MUTU???
EYES PLANTED- STORED WHERE?

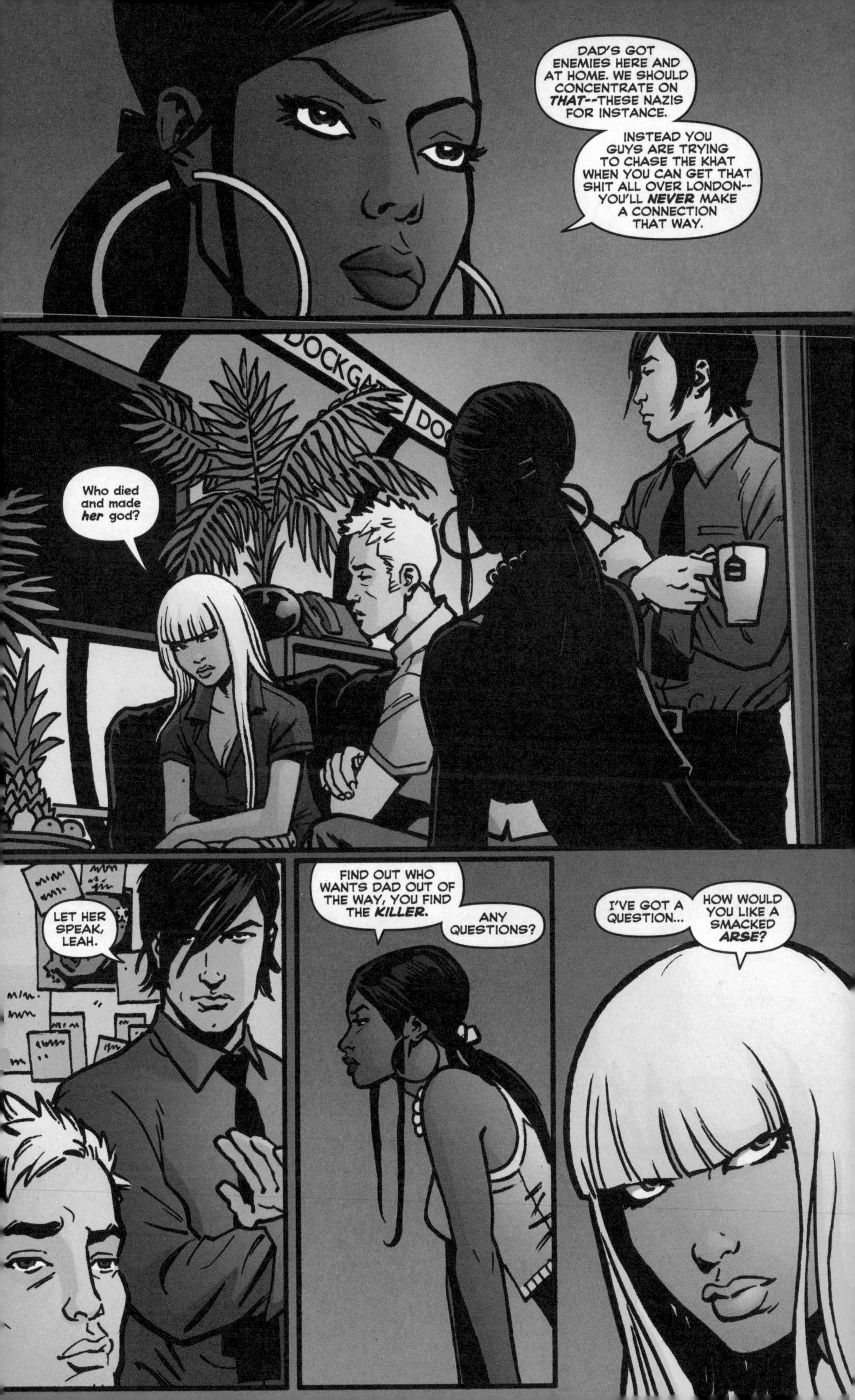
DAD'S GOT ENEMIES HERE AND AT HOME. WE SHOULD CONCENTRATE ON *THAT*--THESE NAZIS FOR INSTANCE.
INSTEAD YOU GUYS ARE TRYING TO CHASE THE KHAT WHEN YOU CAN GET THAT SHIT ALL OVER LONDON--YOU'LL *NEVER* MAKE A CONNECTION THAT WAY.
DOCKGA
DOC
Who died and made *her* god?
LET HER SPEAK, LEAH.
FIND OUT WHO WANTS DAD OUT OF THE WAY, YOU FIND THE *KILLER*.
ANY QUESTIONS?
I'VE GOT A QUESTION...
HOW WOULD YOU LIKE A SMACKED *ARSE*?

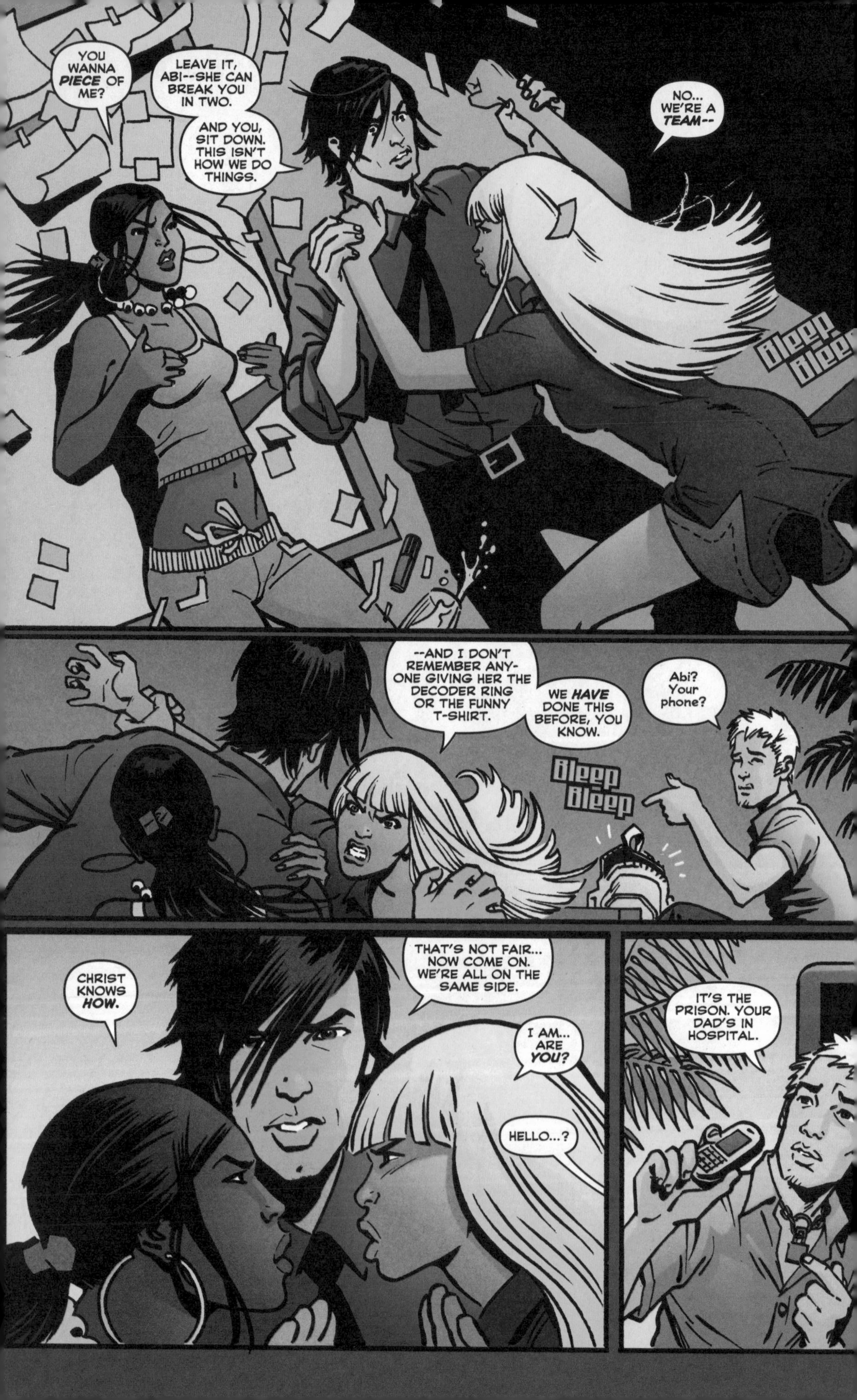
YOU WANNA PIECE OF ME?
LEAVE IT, ABI--SHE CAN BREAK YOU IN TWO.
AND YOU, SIT DOWN. THIS ISN'T HOW WE DO THINGS.
NO... WE'RE A TEAM--
Bleep Bleep
--AND I DON'T REMEMBER ANY-ONE GIVING HER THE DECODER RING OR THE FUNNY T-SHIRT.
WE HAVE DONE THIS BEFORE, YOU KNOW.
Abi? Your phone?
Bleep Bleep
CHRIST KNOWS HOW.
THAT'S NOT FAIR... NOW COME ON. WE'RE ALL ON THE SAME SIDE.
I AM... ARE YOU?
HELLO...?
IT'S THE PRISON. YOUR DAD'S IN HOSPITAL.

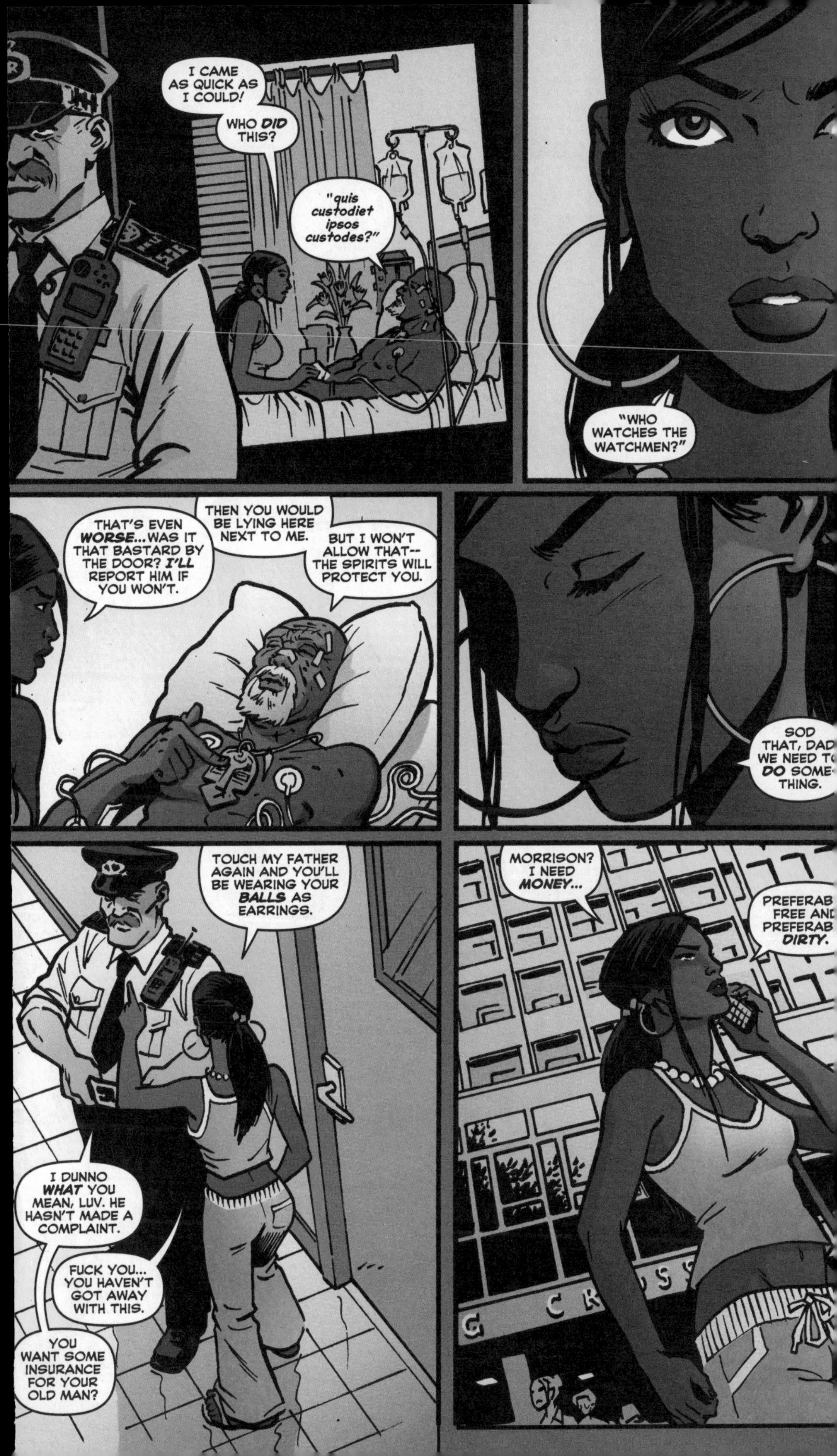
I CAME AS QUICK AS I COULD!
WHO DID THIS?
"quis custodiet ipsos custodes?"
"WHO WATCHES THE WATCHMEN?"
THAT'S EVEN WORSE...WAS IT THAT BASTARD BY THE DOOR? I'LL REPORT HIM IF YOU WON'T.
THEN YOU WOULD BE LYING HERE NEXT TO ME.
BUT I WON'T ALLOW THAT-- THE SPIRITS WILL PROTECT YOU.
SOD THAT, DAD WE NEED TO DO SOME-THING.
TOUCH MY FATHER AGAIN AND YOU'LL BE WEARING YOUR BALLS AS EARRINGS.
I DUNNO WHAT YOU MEAN, LUV. HE HASN'T MADE A COMPLAINT.
FUCK YOU... YOU HAVEN'T GOT AWAY WITH THIS.
YOU WANT SOME INSURANCE FOR YOUR OLD MAN?
MORRISON? I NEED MONEY...
PREFERAB FREE AND PREFERAB DIRTY.

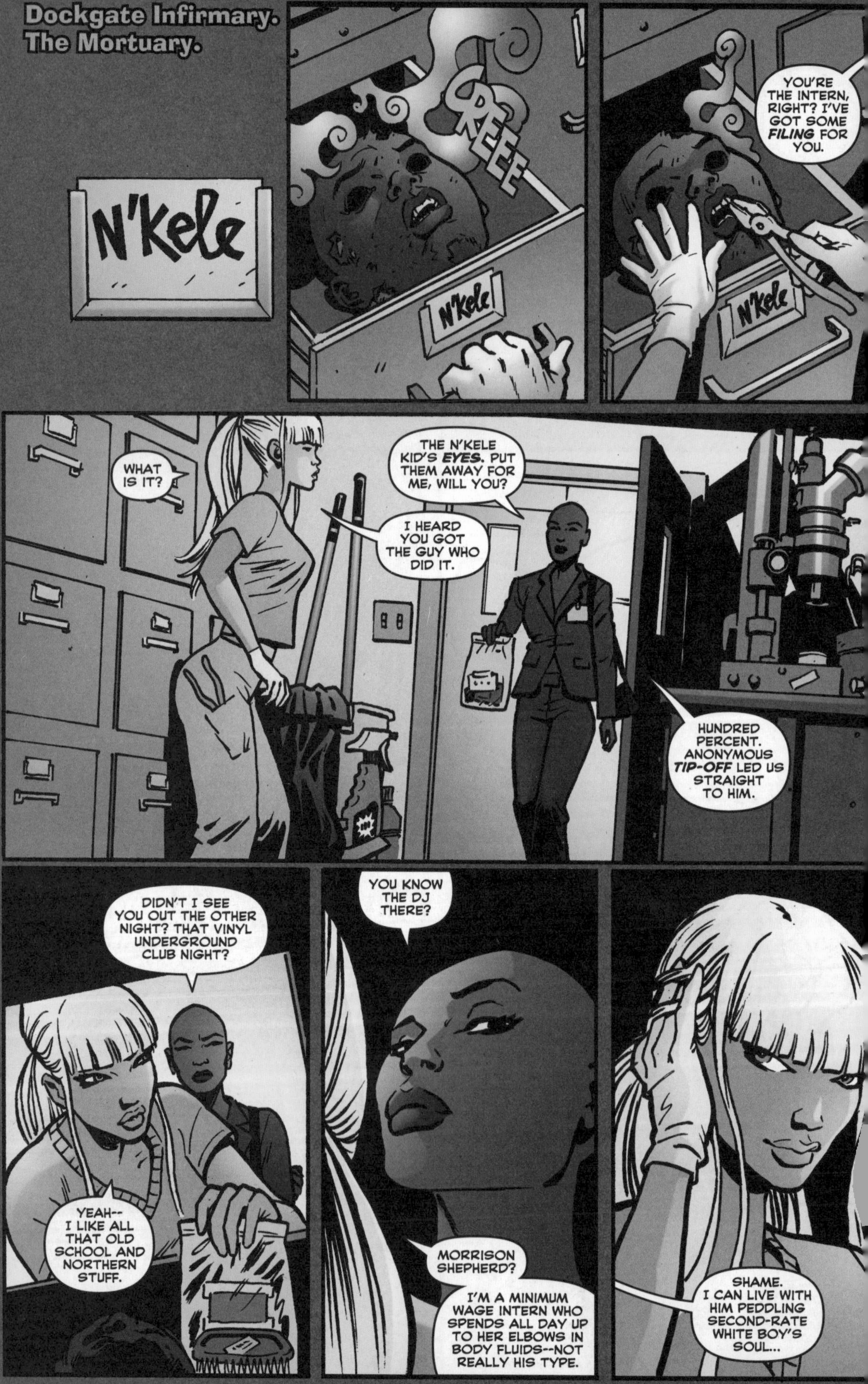
Dockgate Infirmary.
The Mortuary.
N'Kele
CREEE
N'Kele
YOU'RE THE INTERN, RIGHT? I'VE GOT SOME FILING FOR YOU.
N'Kele
WHAT IS IT?
THE N'KELE KID'S EYES. PUT THEM AWAY FOR ME, WILL YOU?
I HEARD YOU GOT THE GUY WHO DID IT.
HUNDRED PERCENT. ANONYMOUS TIP-OFF LED US STRAIGHT TO HIM.
DIDN'T I SEE YOU OUT THE OTHER NIGHT? THAT VINYL UNDERGROUND CLUB NIGHT?
YEAH-- I LIKE ALL THAT OLD SCHOOL AND NORTHERN STUFF.
YOU KNOW THE DJ THERE?
MORRISON SHEPHERD?
I'M A MINIMUM WAGE INTERN WHO SPENDS ALL DAY UP TO HER ELBOWS IN BODY FLUIDS--NOT REALLY HIS TYPE.
SHAME. I CAN LIVE WITH HIM PEDDLING SECOND-RATE WHITE BOY'S SOUL...

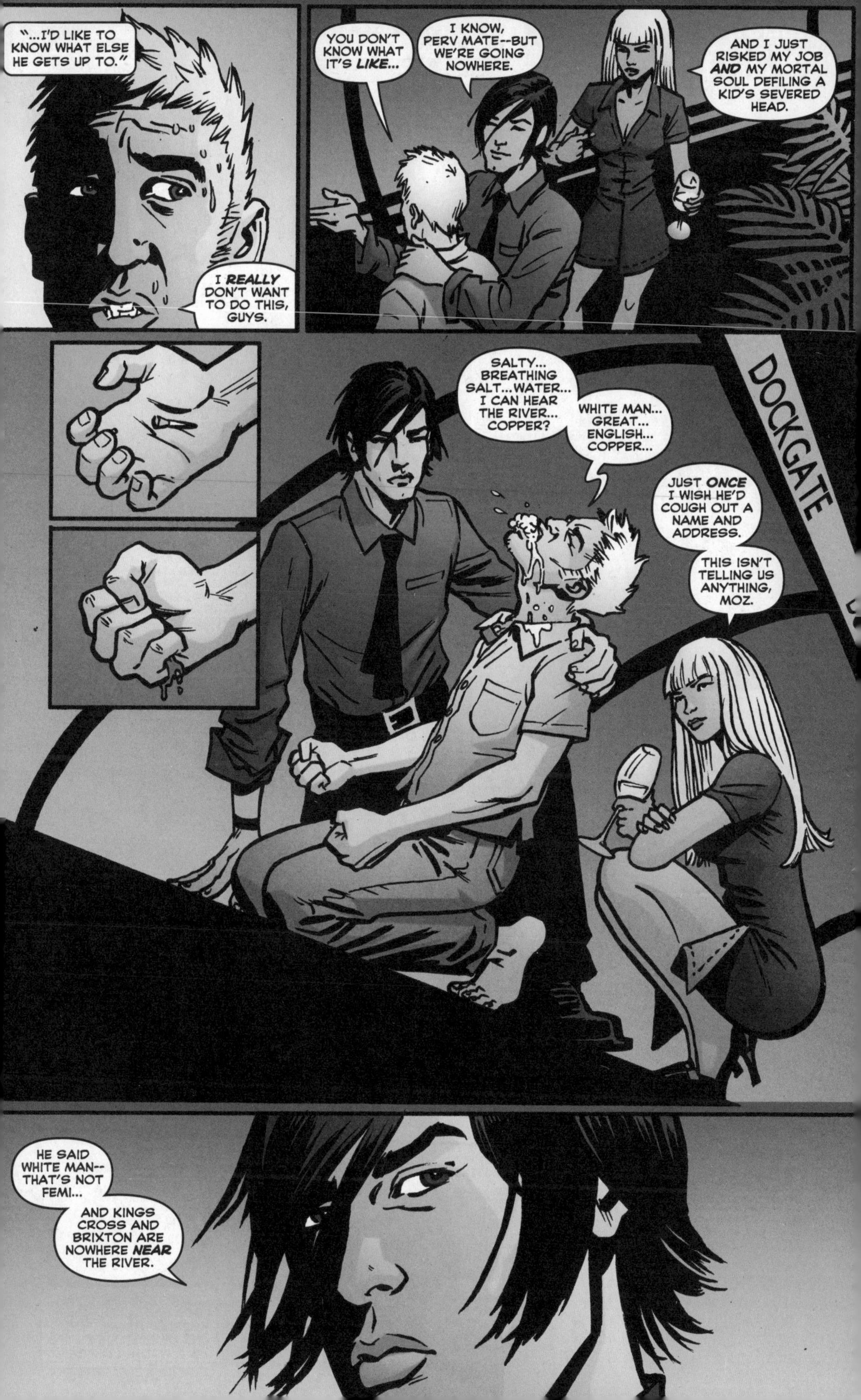
"...I'D LIKE TO KNOW WHAT ELSE HE GETS UP TO."
I **REALLY** DON'T WANT TO DO THIS, GUYS.
YOU DON'T KNOW WHAT IT'S **LIKE**...
I KNOW, PERV MATE--BUT WE'RE GOING NOWHERE.
AND I JUST RISKED MY JOB **AND** MY MORTAL SOUL DEFILING A KID'S SEVERED HEAD.
SALTY... BREATHING SALT...WATER... I CAN HEAR THE RIVER... COPPER?
WHITE MAN... GREAT... ENGLISH... COPPER...
DOCKGATE
JUST **ONCE** I WISH HE'D COUGH OUT A NAME AND ADDRESS.
THIS ISN'T TELLING US ANYTHING, MOZ.
HE SAID WHITE MAN-- THAT'S NOT FEMI...
AND KINGS CROSS AND BRIXTON ARE NOWHERE **NEAR** THE RIVER.

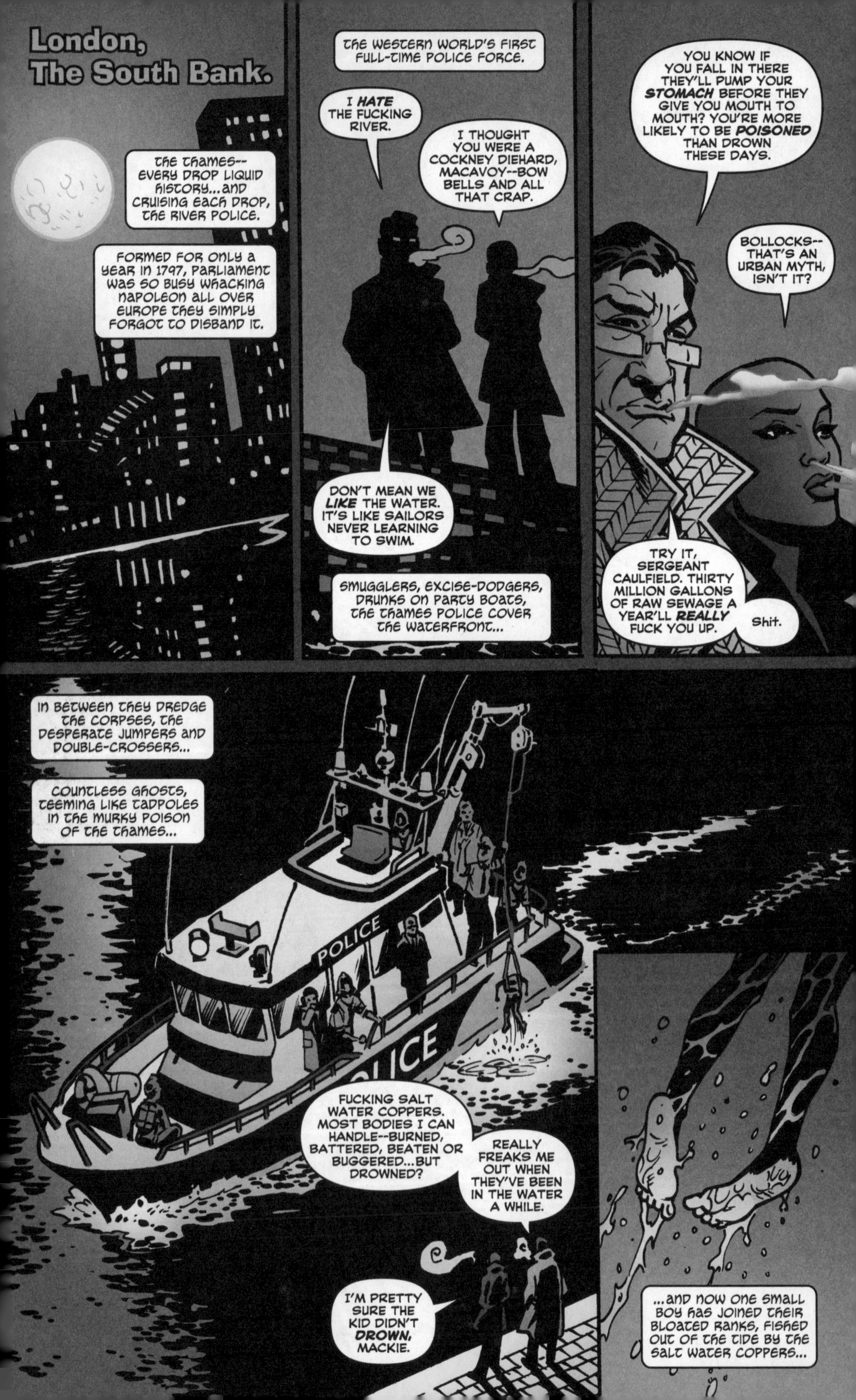
London,
The South Bank.
THE THAMES-- EVERY DROP LIQUID HISTORY...AND CRUISING EACH DROP, THE RIVER POLICE.
FORMED FOR ONLY A YEAR IN 1797, PARLIAMENT WAS SO BUSY WHACKING NAPOLEON ALL OVER EUROPE THEY SIMPLY FORGOT TO DISBAND IT.
THE WESTERN WORLD'S FIRST FULL-TIME POLICE FORCE.
I HATE THE FUCKING RIVER.
I THOUGHT YOU WERE A COCKNEY DIEHARD, MACAVOY--BOW BELLS AND ALL THAT CRAP.
DON'T MEAN WE LIKE THE WATER. IT'S LIKE SAILORS NEVER LEARNING TO SWIM.
SMUGGLERS, EXCISE-DODGERS, DRUNKS ON PARTY BOATS, THE THAMES POLICE COVER THE WATERFRONT...
YOU KNOW IF YOU FALL IN THERE THEY'LL PUMP YOUR STOMACH BEFORE THEY GIVE YOU MOUTH TO MOUTH? YOU'RE MORE LIKELY TO BE POISONED THAN DROWN THESE DAYS.
BOLLOCKS-- THAT'S AN URBAN MYTH, ISN'T IT?
TRY IT, SERGEANT CAULFIELD. THIRTY MILLION GALLONS OF RAW SEWAGE A YEAR'LL REALLY FUCK YOU UP.
Shit.
IN BETWEEN THEY DREDGE THE CORPSES, THE DESPERATE JUMPERS AND DOUBLE-CROSSERS...
COUNTLESS GHOSTS, TEEMING LIKE TADPOLES IN THE MURKY POISON OF THE THAMES...
POLICE
POLICE
FUCKING SALT WATER COPPERS. MOST BODIES I CAN HANDLE--BURNED, BATTERED, BEATEN OR BUGGERED...BUT DROWNED?
REALLY FREAKS ME OUT WHEN THEY'VE BEEN IN THE WATER A WHILE.
I'M PRETTY SURE THE KID DIDN'T DROWN, MACKIE.
...AND NOW ONE SMALL BOY HAS JOINED THEIR BLOATED RANKS, FISHED OUT OF THE TIDE BY THE SALT WATER COPPERS...

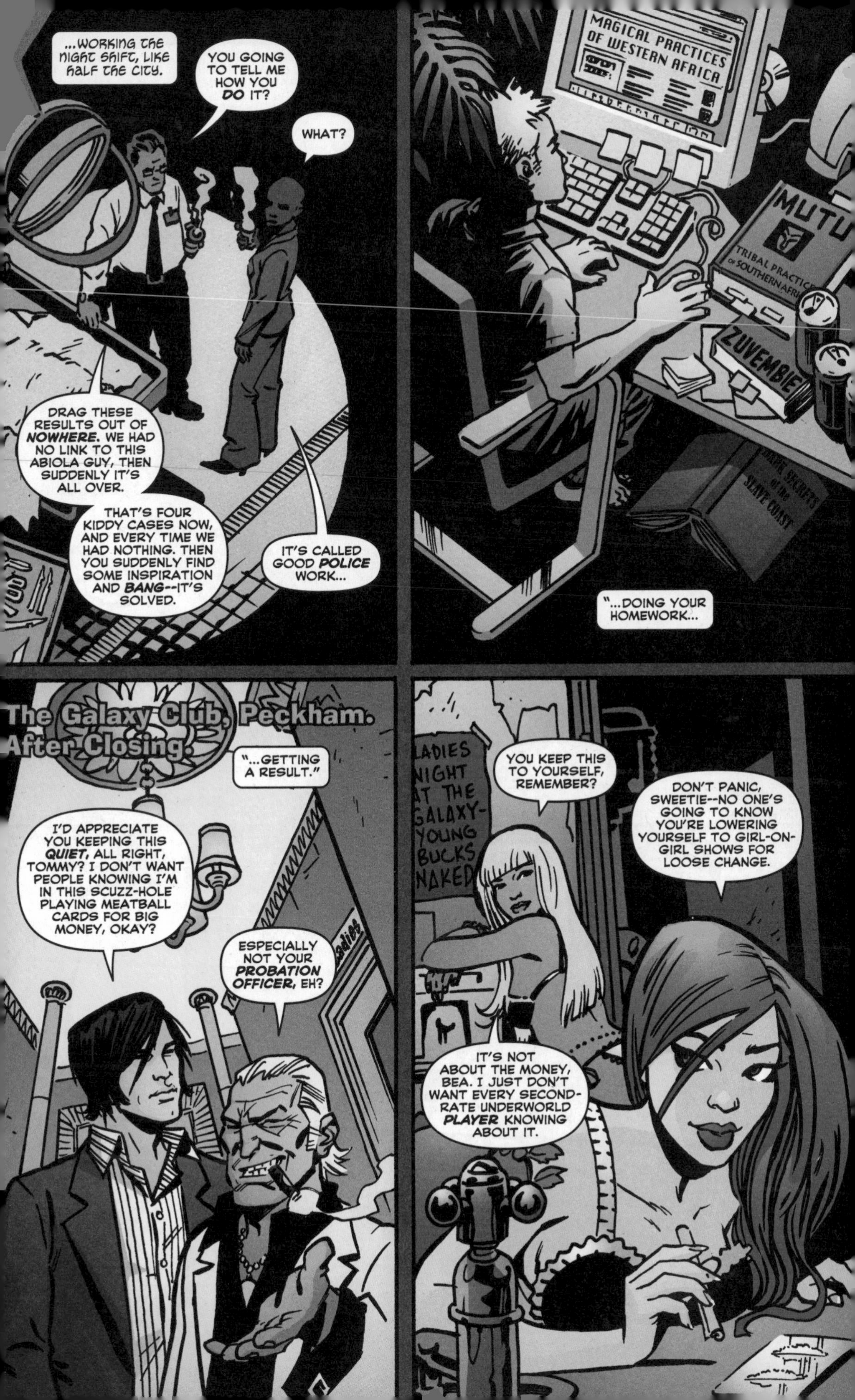
...WORKING THE NIGHT SHIFT, LIKE HALF THE CITY.
YOU GOING TO TELL ME HOW YOU DO IT?
WHAT?
DRAG THESE RESULTS OUT OF NOWHERE. WE HAD NO LINK TO THIS ABIOLA GUY, THEN SUDDENLY IT'S ALL OVER.
THAT'S FOUR KIDDY CASES NOW, AND EVERY TIME WE HAD NOTHING. THEN YOU SUDDENLY FIND SOME INSPIRATION AND BANG--IT'S SOLVED.
IT'S CALLED GOOD POLICE WORK...
MAGICAL PRACTICES OF WESTERN AFRICA
MUTU
TRIBAL PRACTICES OF SOUTHERN AFRI
ZUVEMBIE
SLAVE COAST
"...DOING YOUR HOMEWORK...
The Galaxy Club, Peckham. After Closing.
"...GETTING A RESULT."
I'D APPRECIATE YOU KEEPING THIS QUIET, ALL RIGHT, TOMMY? I DON'T WANT PEOPLE KNOWING I'M IN THIS SCUZZ-HOLE PLAYING MEATBALL CARDS FOR BIG MONEY, OKAY?
ESPECIALLY NOT YOUR PROBATION OFFICER, EH?
LADIES NIGHT AT THE GALAXY- YOUNG BUCKS NAKED
YOU KEEP THIS TO YOURSELF, REMEMBER?
DON'T PANIC, SWEETIE--NO ONE'S GOING TO KNOW YOU'RE LOWERING YOURSELF TO GIRL-ON-GIRL SHOWS FOR LOOSE CHANGE.
IT'S NOT ABOUT THE MONEY, BEA. I JUST DON'T WANT EVERY SECOND-RATE UNDERWORLD PLAYER KNOWING ABOUT IT.

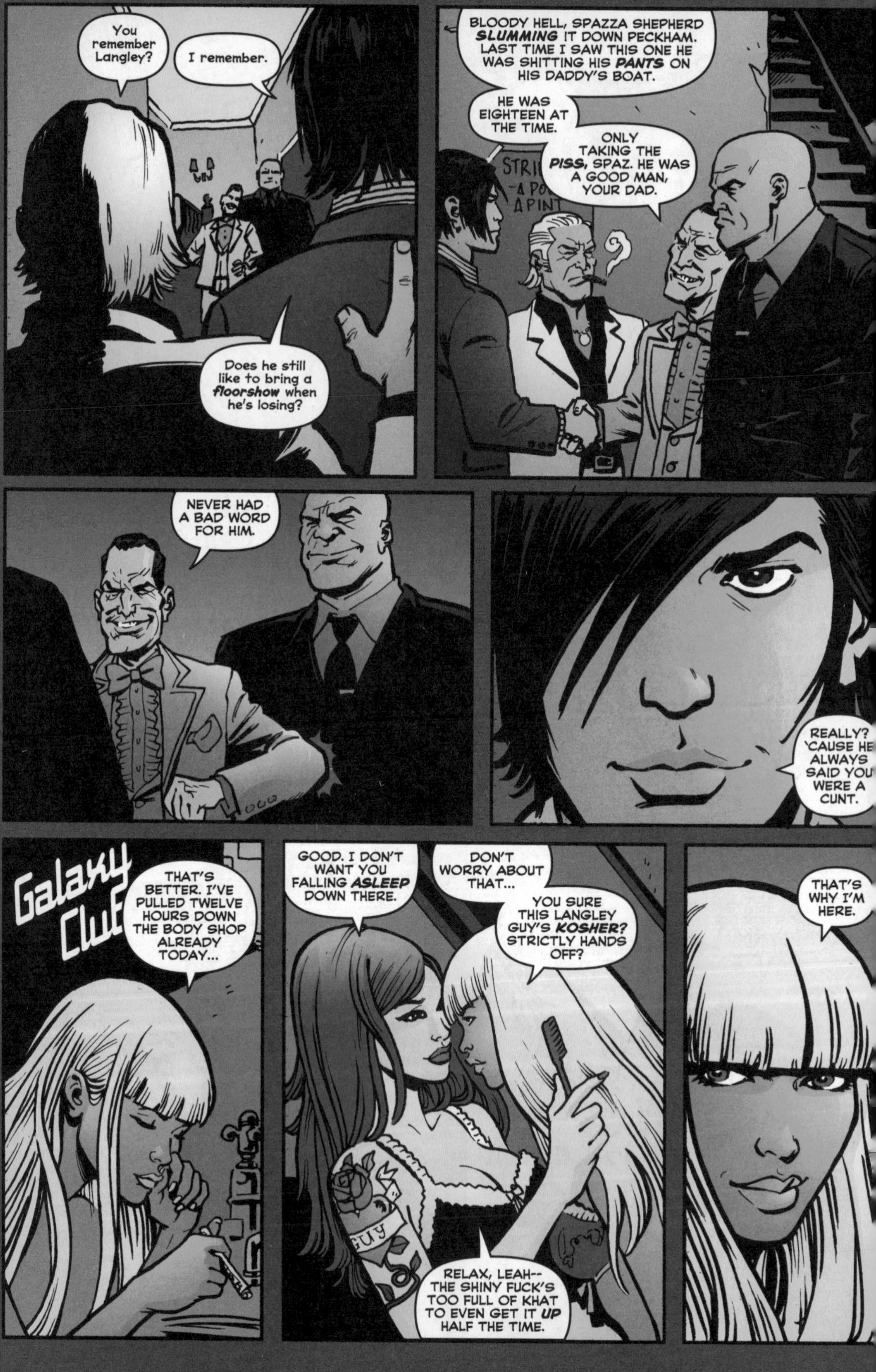
You remember Langley?
I remember.
Does he still like to bring a floorshow when he's losing?
BLOODY HELL, SPAZZA SHEPHERD SLUMMING IT DOWN PECKHAM. LAST TIME I SAW THIS ONE HE WAS SHITTING HIS PANTS ON HIS DADDY'S BOAT.
HE WAS EIGHTEEN AT THE TIME.
ONLY TAKING THE PISS, SPAZ. HE WAS A GOOD MAN, YOUR DAD.
NEVER HAD A BAD WORD FOR HIM.
REALLY? 'CAUSE HE ALWAYS SAID YOU WERE A CUNT.
Galaxy Club
THAT'S BETTER. I'VE PULLED TWELVE HOURS DOWN THE BODY SHOP ALREADY TODAY...
GOOD. I DON'T WANT YOU FALLING ASLEEP DOWN THERE.
DON'T WORRY ABOUT THAT...
YOU SURE THIS LANGLEY GUY'S KOSHER? STRICTLY HANDS OFF?
RELAX, LEAH-- THE SHINY FUCK'S TOO FULL OF KHAT TO EVEN GET IT UP HALF THE TIME.
THAT'S WHY I'M HERE.

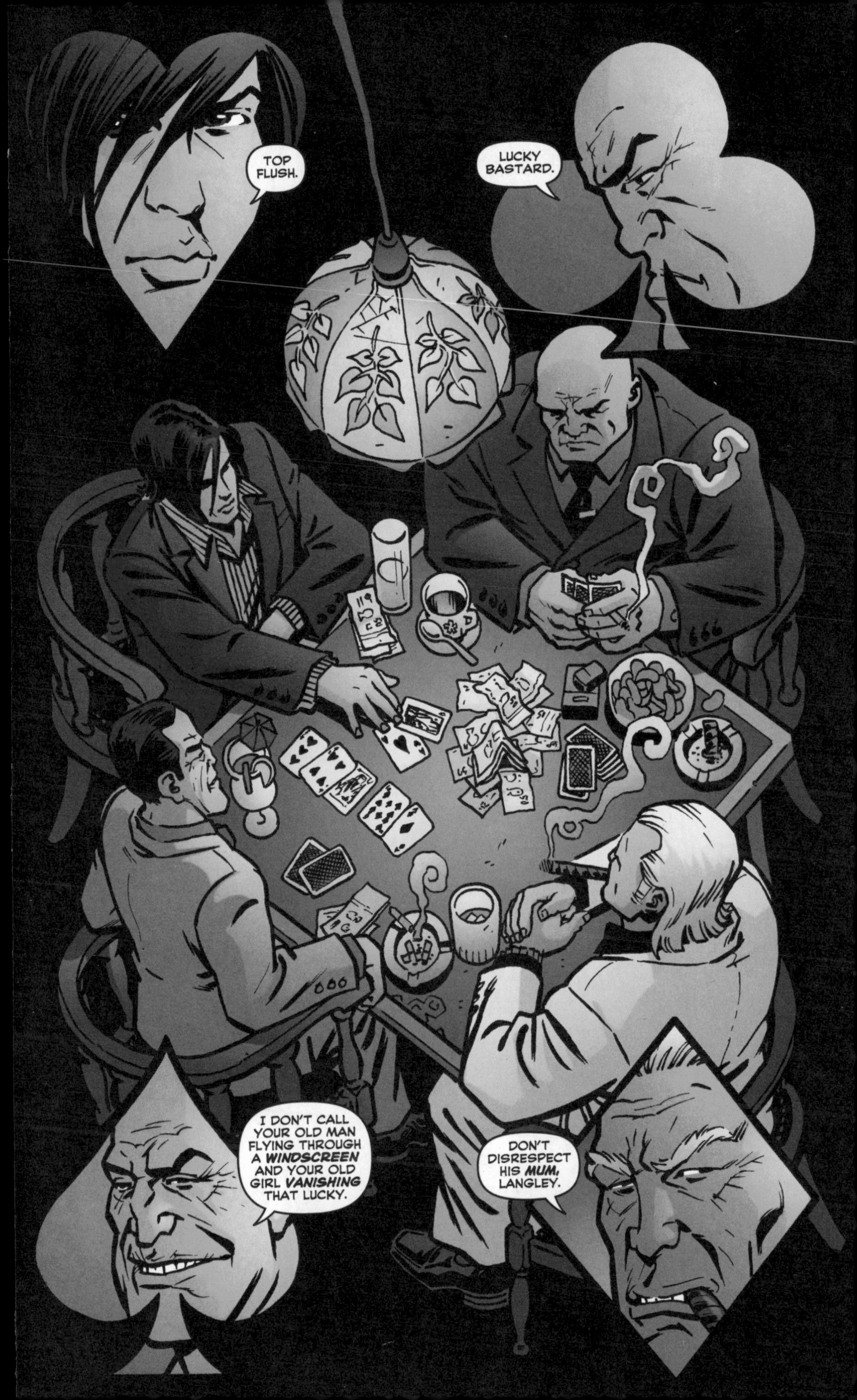
TOP FLUSH.
LUCKY BASTARD.
I DON'T CALL YOUR OLD MAN FLYING THROUGH A WINDSCREEN AND YOUR OLD GIRL VANISHING THAT LUCKY.
DON'T DISRESPECT HIS MUM, LANGLEY.

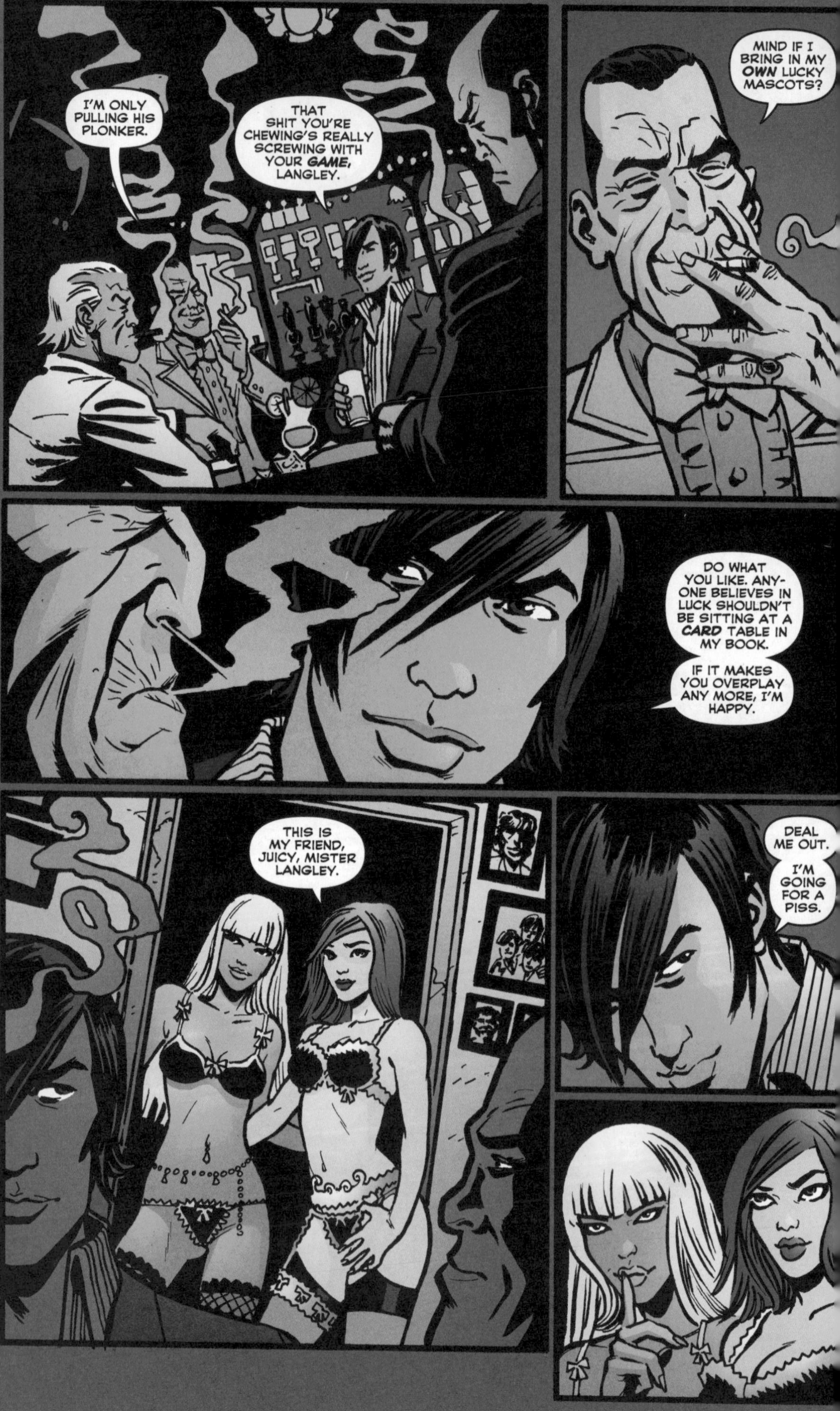
I'M ONLY PULLING HIS PLONKER.
THAT SHIT YOU'RE CHEWING'S REALLY SCREWING WITH YOUR GAME, LANGLEY.
MIND IF I BRING IN MY OWN LUCKY MASCOTS?
DO WHAT YOU LIKE. ANY-ONE BELIEVES IN LUCK SHOULDN'T BE SITTING AT A CARD TABLE IN MY BOOK.
IF IT MAKES YOU OVERPLAY ANY MORE, I'M HAPPY.
THIS IS MY FRIEND, JUICY, MISTER LANGLEY.
DEAL ME OUT.
I'M GOING FOR A PISS.

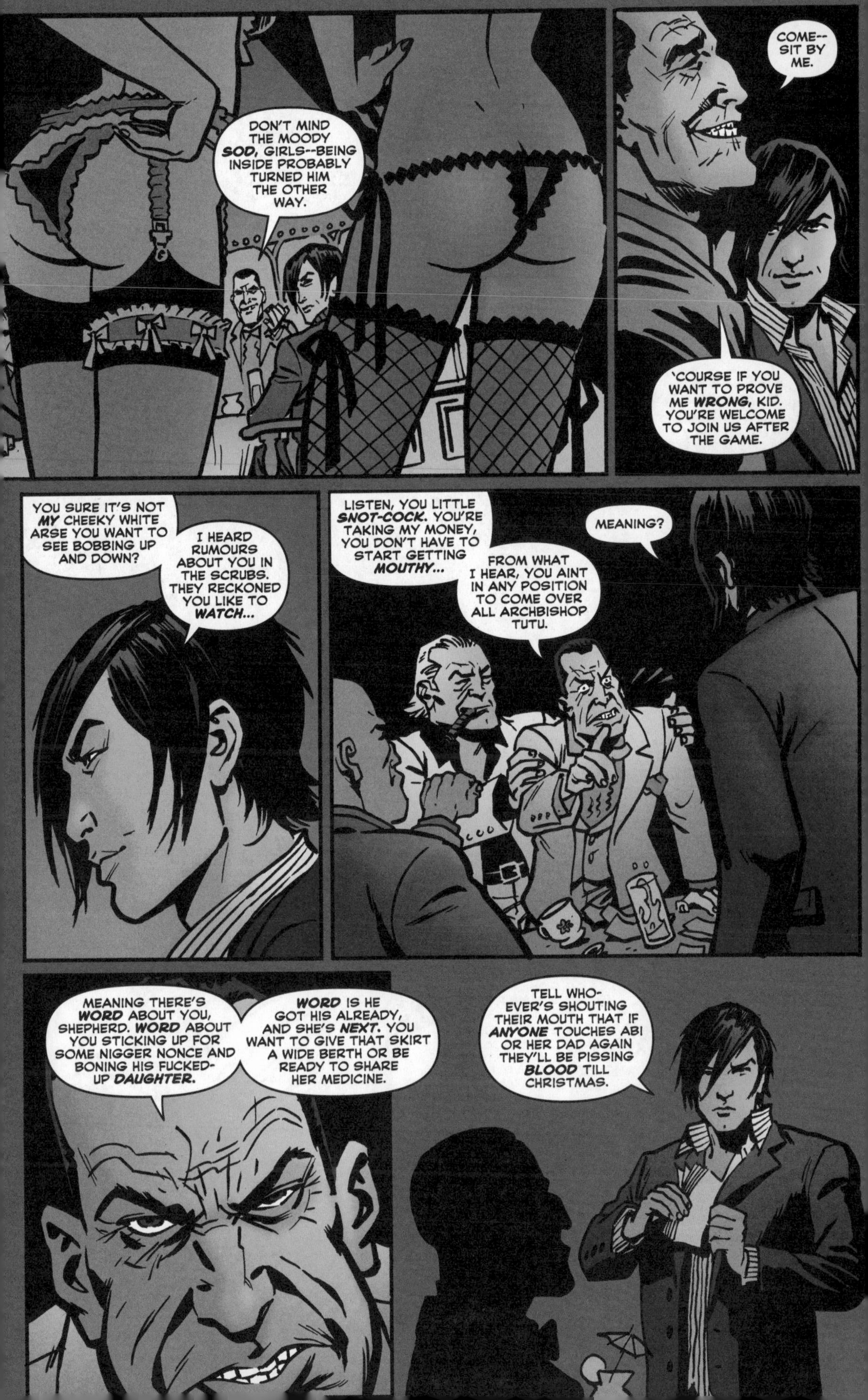

DON'T MIND THE MOODY SOD, GIRLS--BEING INSIDE PROBABLY TURNED HIM THE OTHER WAY.
COME--SIT BY ME.
'COURSE IF YOU WANT TO PROVE ME WRONG, KID. YOU'RE WELCOME TO JOIN US AFTER THE GAME.
YOU SURE IT'S NOT MY CHEEKY WHITE ARSE YOU WANT TO SEE BOBBING UP AND DOWN?
I HEARD RUMOURS ABOUT YOU IN THE SCRUBS. THEY RECKONED YOU LIKE TO WATCH...
LISTEN, YOU LITTLE SNOT-COCK. YOU'RE TAKING MY MONEY, YOU DON'T HAVE TO START GETTING MOUTHY...
FROM WHAT I HEAR, YOU AINT IN ANY POSITION TO COME OVER ALL ARCHBISHOP TUTU.
MEANING?
MEANING THERE'S WORD ABOUT YOU, SHEPHERD. WORD ABOUT YOU STICKING UP FOR SOME NIGGER NONCE AND BONING HIS FUCKED-UP DAUGHTER.
WORD IS HE GOT HIS ALREADY, AND SHE'S NEXT. YOU WANT TO GIVE THAT SKIRT A WIDE BERTH OR BE READY TO SHARE HER MEDICINE.
TELL WHO-EVER'S SHOUTING THEIR MOUTH THAT IF ANYONE TOUCHES ABI OR HER DAD AGAIN THEY'LL BE PISSING BLOOD TILL CHRISTMAS.

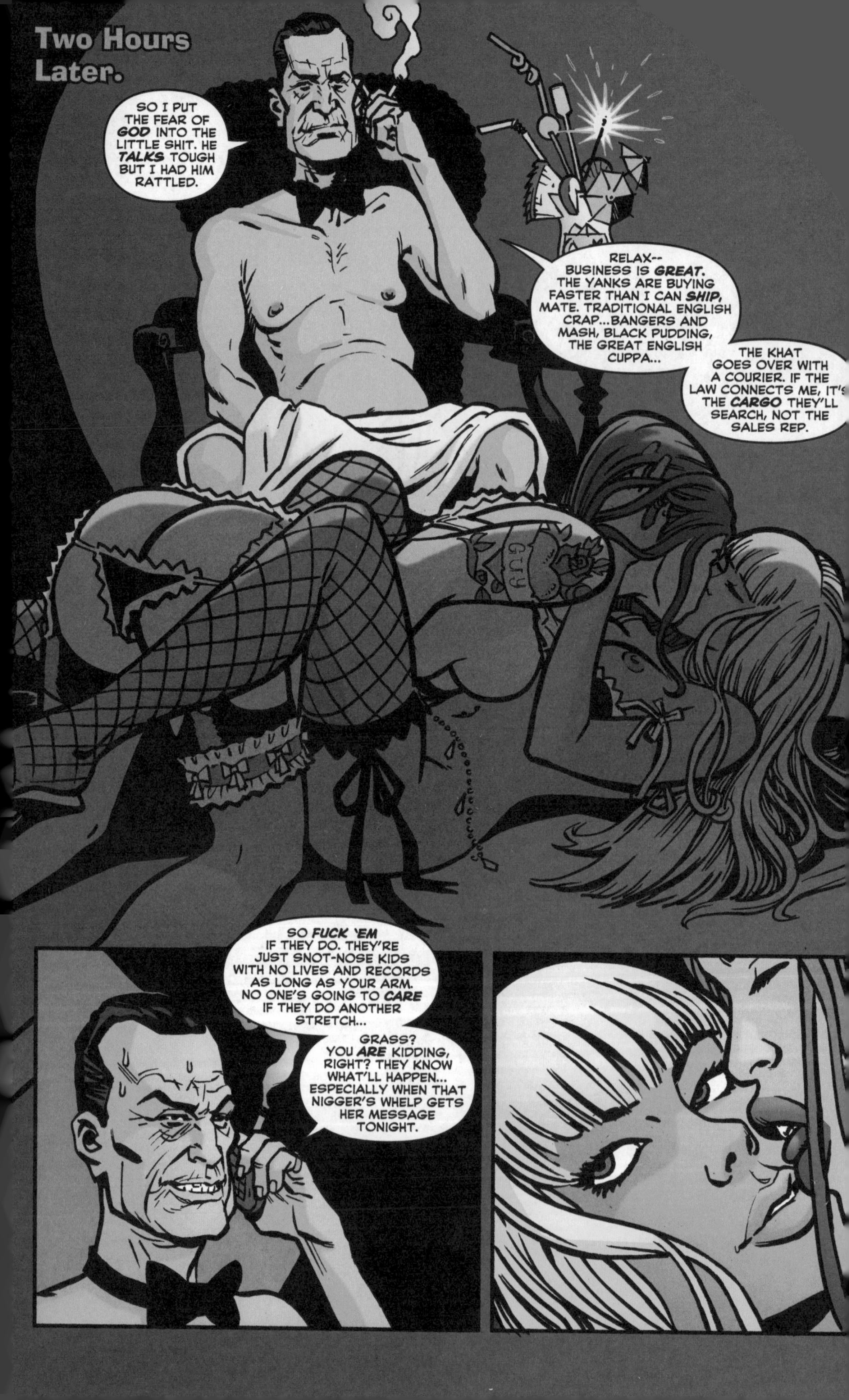
Two Hours Later.
SO I PUT THE FEAR OF GOD INTO THE LITTLE SHIT. HE TALKS TOUGH BUT I HAD HIM RATTLED.
RELAX-- BUSINESS IS GREAT. THE YANKS ARE BUYING FASTER THAN I CAN SHIP, MATE. TRADITIONAL ENGLISH CRAP...BANGERS AND MASH, BLACK PUDDING, THE GREAT ENGLISH CUPPA...
THE KHAT GOES OVER WITH A COURIER. IF THE LAW CONNECTS ME, IT'S THE CARGO THEY'LL SEARCH, NOT THE SALES REP.
GUY
SO FUCK 'EM IF THEY DO. THEY'RE JUST SNOT-NOSE KIDS WITH NO LIVES AND RECORDS AS LONG AS YOUR ARM. NO ONE'S GOING TO CARE IF THEY DO ANOTHER STRETCH...
GRASS? YOU ARE KIDDING, RIGHT? THEY KNOW WHAT'LL HAPPEN... ESPECIALLY WHEN THAT NIGGER'S WHELP GETS HER MESSAGE TONIGHT.

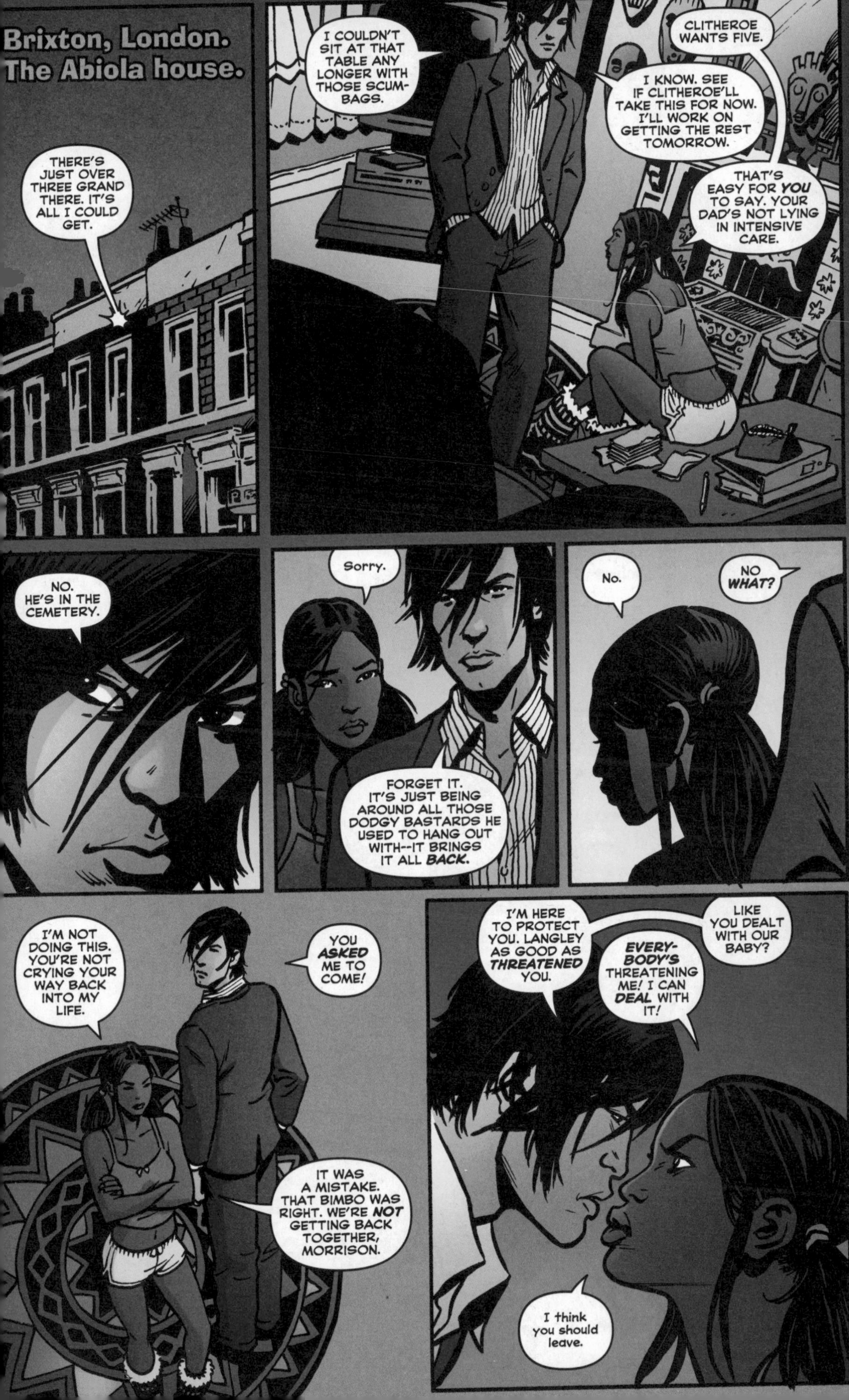
Brixton, London. The Abiola house.
THERE'S JUST OVER THREE GRAND THERE. IT'S ALL I COULD GET.
I COULDN'T SIT AT THAT TABLE ANY LONGER WITH THOSE SCUM-BAGS.
CLITHEROE WANTS FIVE.
I KNOW. SEE IF CLITHEROE'LL TAKE THIS FOR NOW. I'LL WORK ON GETTING THE REST TOMORROW.
THAT'S EASY FOR YOU TO SAY. YOUR DAD'S NOT LYING IN INTENSIVE CARE.
NO. HE'S IN THE CEMETERY.
Sorry.
FORGET IT. IT'S JUST BEING AROUND ALL THOSE DODGY BASTARDS HE USED TO HANG OUT WITH--IT BRINGS IT ALL BACK.
No.
NO WHAT?
I'M NOT DOING THIS. YOU'RE NOT CRYING YOUR WAY BACK INTO MY LIFE.
YOU ASKED ME TO COME!
IT WAS A MISTAKE. THAT BIMBO WAS RIGHT. WE'RE NOT GETTING BACK TOGETHER, MORRISON.
I'M HERE TO PROTECT YOU. LANGLEY AS GOOD AS THREATENED YOU.
LIKE YOU DEALT WITH OUR BABY?
EVERY-BODY'S THREATENING ME! I CAN DEAL WITH IT!
I think you should leave.

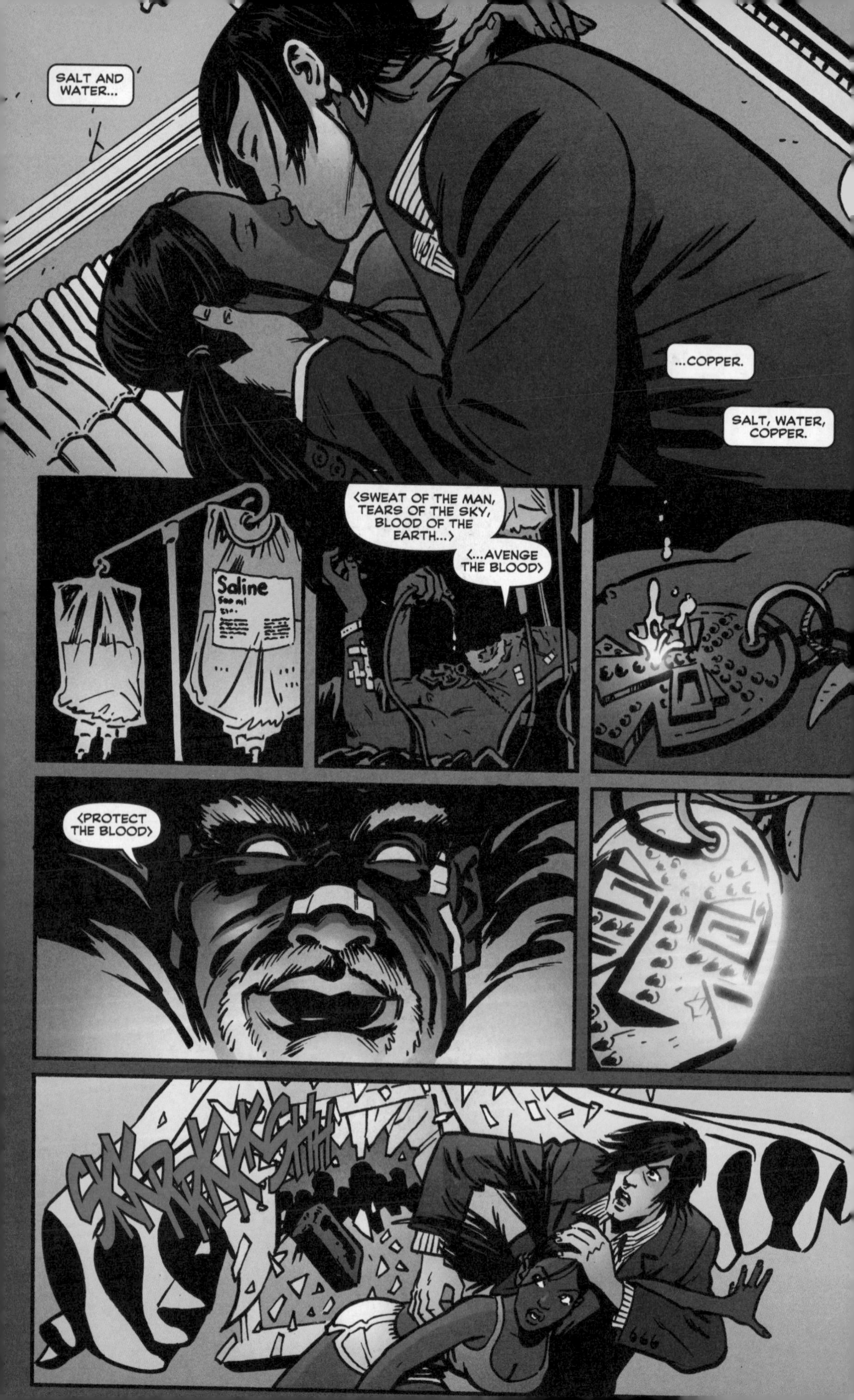
SALT AND WATER...
...COPPER.
SALT, WATER, COPPER.
Saline
<SWEAT OF THE MAN, TEARS OF THE SKY, BLOOD OF THE EARTH...>
<...AVENGE THE BLOOD>
<PROTECT THE BLOOD>

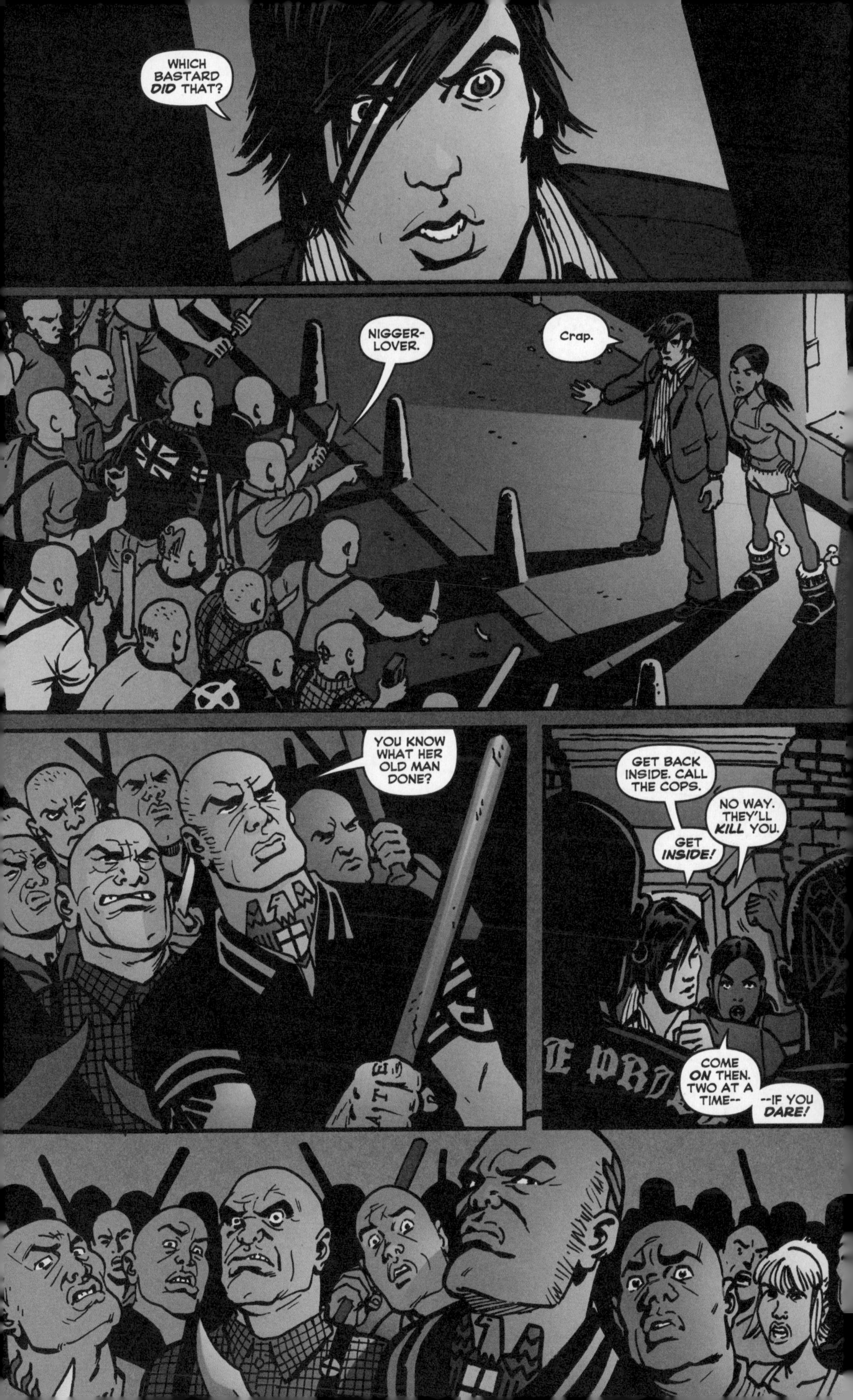
WHICH BASTARD DID THAT?
NIGGER-LOVER.
Crap.
YOU KNOW WHAT HER OLD MAN DONE?
GET BACK INSIDE. CALL THE COPS.
NO WAY. THEY'LL KILL YOU.
GET INSIDE!
COME ON THEN. TWO AT A TIME--
--IF YOU DARE!

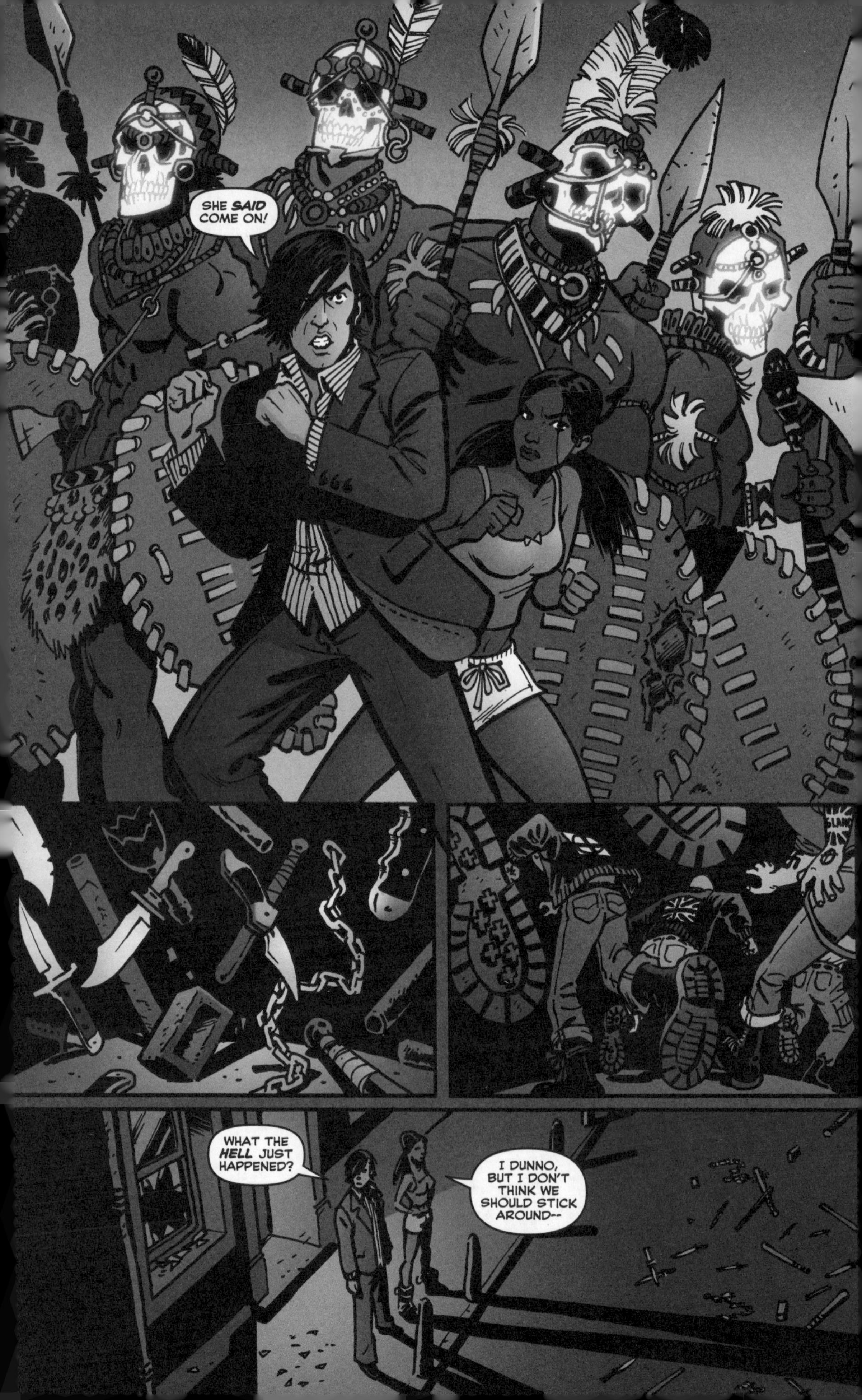
SHE SAID COME ON!
WHAT THE HELL JUST HAPPENED?
I DUNNO, BUT I DON'T THINK WE SHOULD STICK AROUND--

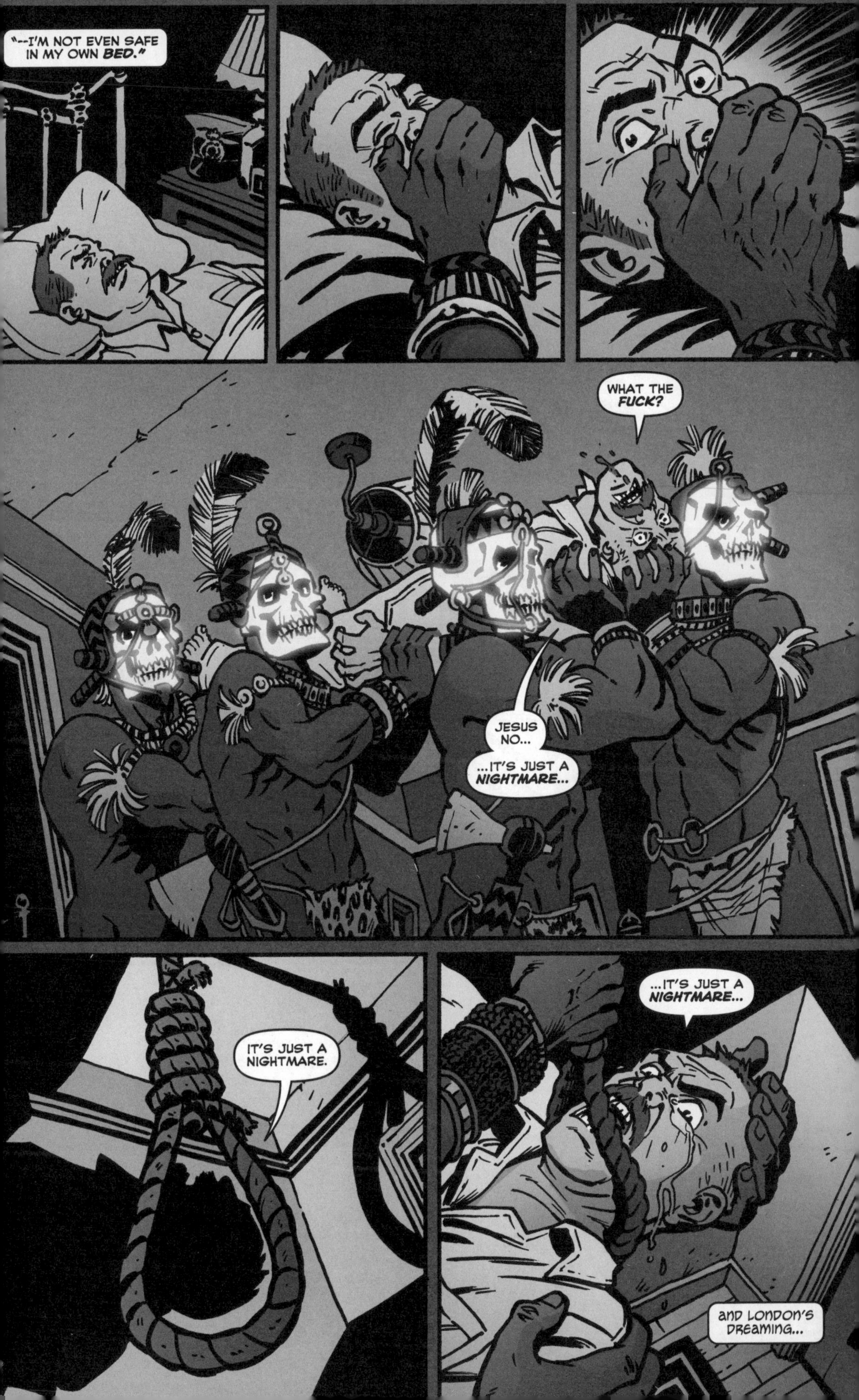
"--I'M NOT EVEN SAFE IN MY OWN *BED.*"
WHAT THE *FUCK?*
JESUS NO...
...IT'S JUST A *NIGHTMARE...*
IT'S JUST A NIGHTMARE.
...IT'S JUST A *NIGHTMARE...*
AND LONDON'S DREAMING...

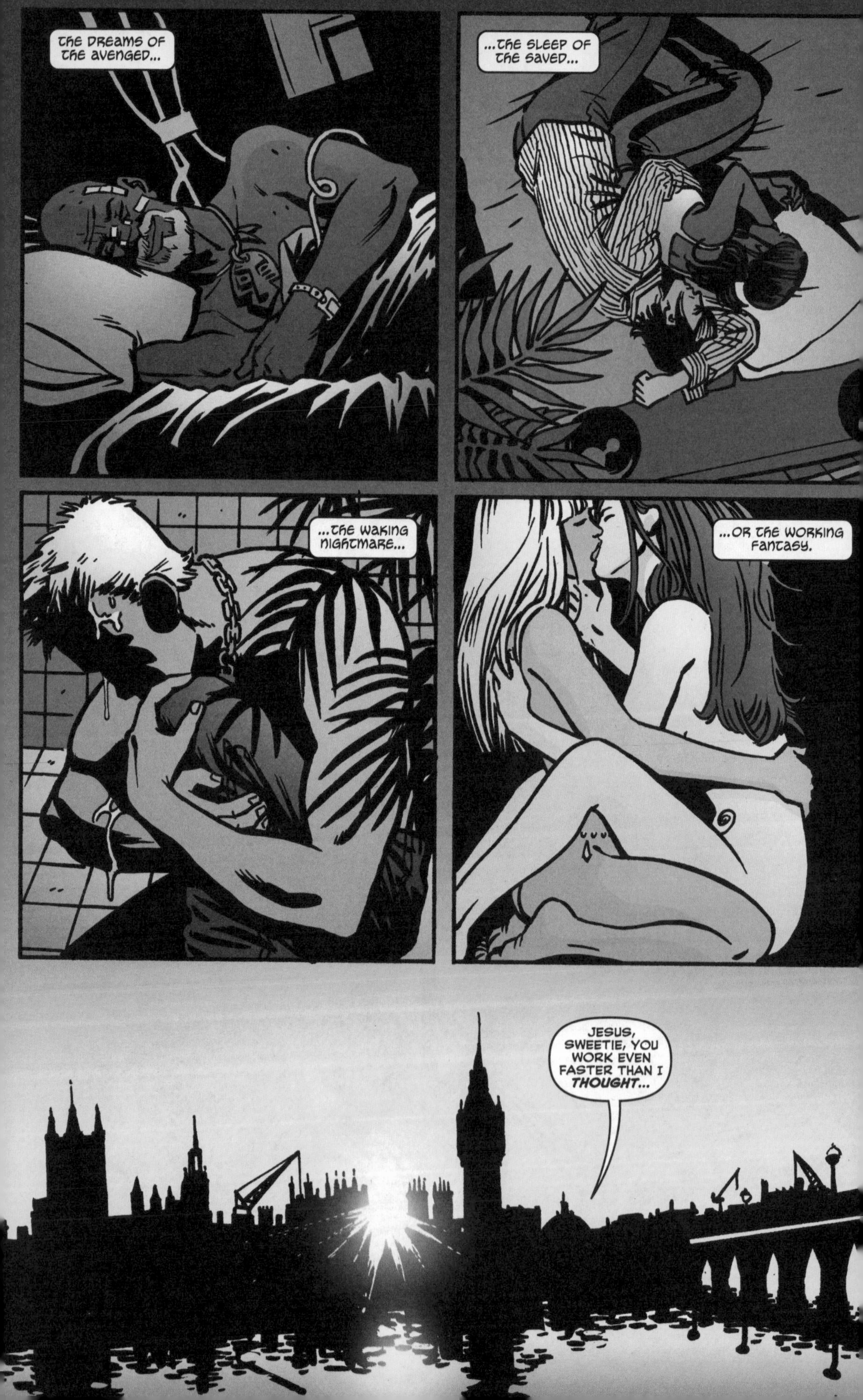
THE DREAMS OF THE AVENGED...
...THE SLEEP OF THE SAVED...
...THE WAKING NIGHTMARE...
...OR THE WORKING FANTASY.
JESUS, SWEETIE, YOU WORK EVEN FASTER THAN I *THOUGHT*...

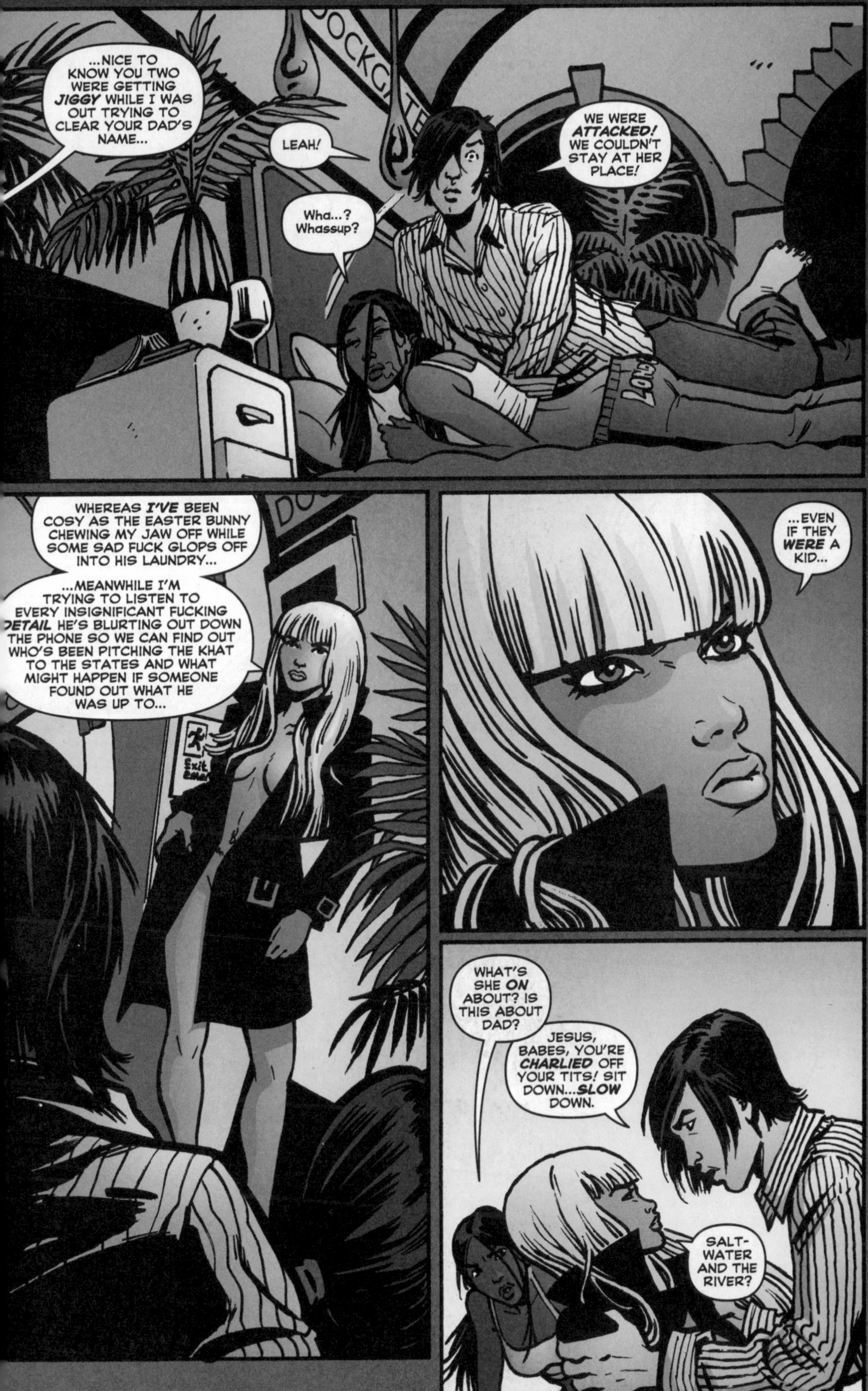
DOCKGATE
...NICE TO KNOW YOU TWO WERE GETTING JIGGY WHILE I WAS OUT TRYING TO CLEAR YOUR DAD'S NAME...
LEAH!
Wha...? Whassup?
WE WERE ATTACKED! WE COULDN'T STAY AT HER PLACE!
WHEREAS I'VE BEEN COSY AS THE EASTER BUNNY CHEWING MY JAW OFF WHILE SOME SAD FUCK GLOPS OFF INTO HIS LAUNDRY...
...MEANWHILE I'M TRYING TO LISTEN TO EVERY INSIGNIFICANT FUCKING DETAIL HE'S BLURTING OUT DOWN THE PHONE SO WE CAN FIND OUT WHO'S BEEN PITCHING THE KHAT TO THE STATES AND WHAT MIGHT HAPPEN IF SOMEONE FOUND OUT WHAT HE WAS UP TO...
...EVEN IF THEY WERE A KID...
WHAT'S SHE ON ABOUT? IS THIS ABOUT DAD?
JESUS, BABES, YOU'RE CHARLIED OFF YOUR TITS! SIT DOWN...SLOW DOWN.
SALT-WATER AND THE RIVER?

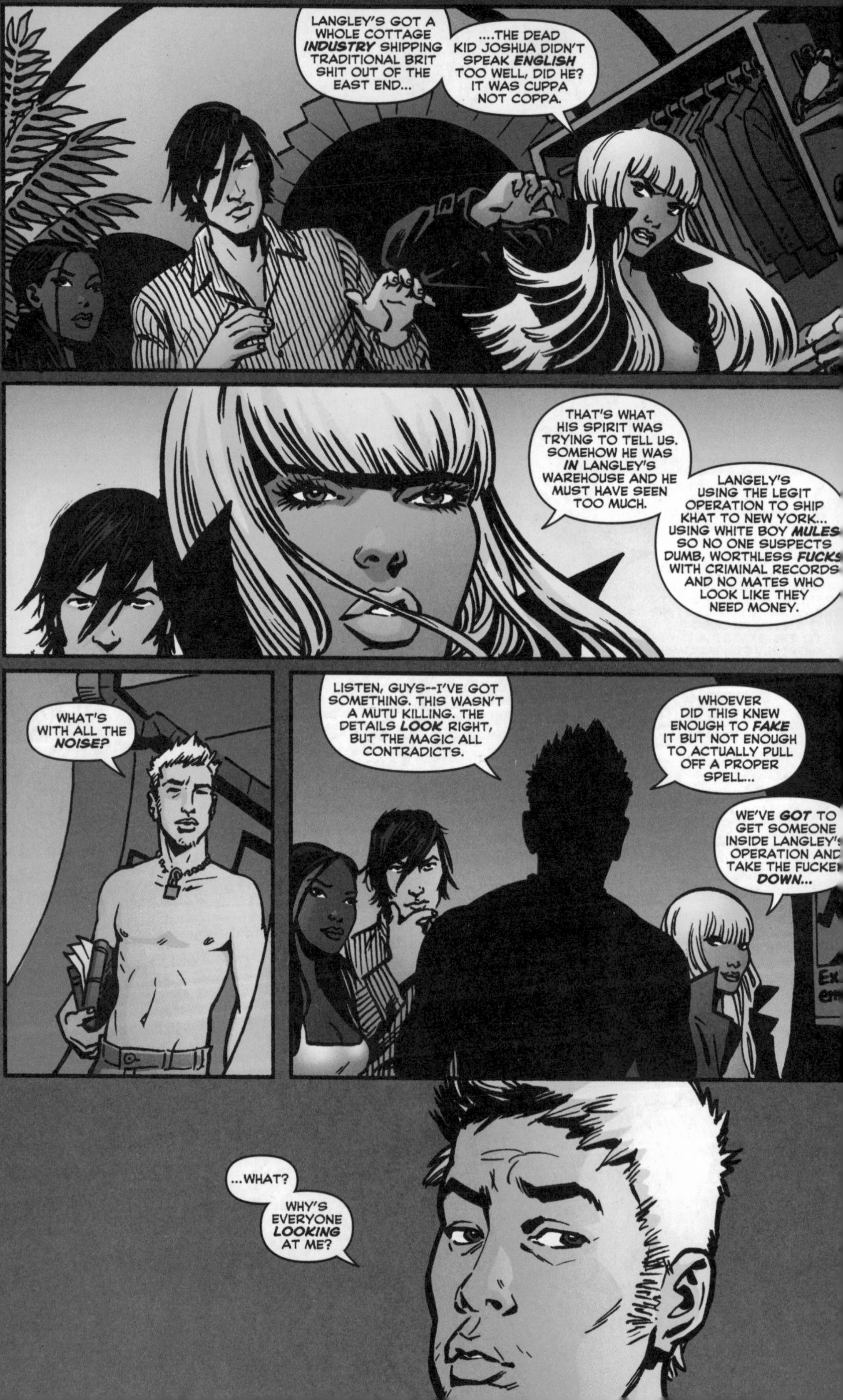
LANGLEY'S GOT A WHOLE COTTAGE INDUSTRY SHIPPING TRADITIONAL BRIT SHIT OUT OF THE EAST END...
....THE DEAD KID JOSHUA DIDN'T SPEAK ENGLISH TOO WELL, DID HE? IT WAS CUPPA NOT COPPA.
THAT'S WHAT HIS SPIRIT WAS TRYING TO TELL US. SOMEHOW HE WAS IN LANGLEY'S WAREHOUSE AND HE MUST HAVE SEEN TOO MUCH.
LANGELY'S USING THE LEGIT OPERATION TO SHIP KHAT TO NEW YORK... USING WHITE BOY MULES SO NO ONE SUSPECTS DUMB, WORTHLESS FUCKS WITH CRIMINAL RECORDS AND NO MATES WHO LOOK LIKE THEY NEED MONEY.
WHAT'S WITH ALL THE NOISE?
LISTEN, GUYS--I'VE GOT SOMETHING. THIS WASN'T A MUTU KILLING. THE DETAILS LOOK RIGHT, BUT THE MAGIC ALL CONTRADICTS.
WHOEVER DID THIS KNEW ENOUGH TO FAKE IT BUT NOT ENOUGH TO ACTUALLY PULL OFF A PROPER SPELL...
WE'VE GOT TO GET SOMEONE INSIDE LANGLEY'S OPERATION AND TAKE THE FUCKER DOWN...
...WHAT?
WHY'S EVERYONE LOOKING AT ME?

MULE TRAIN

4

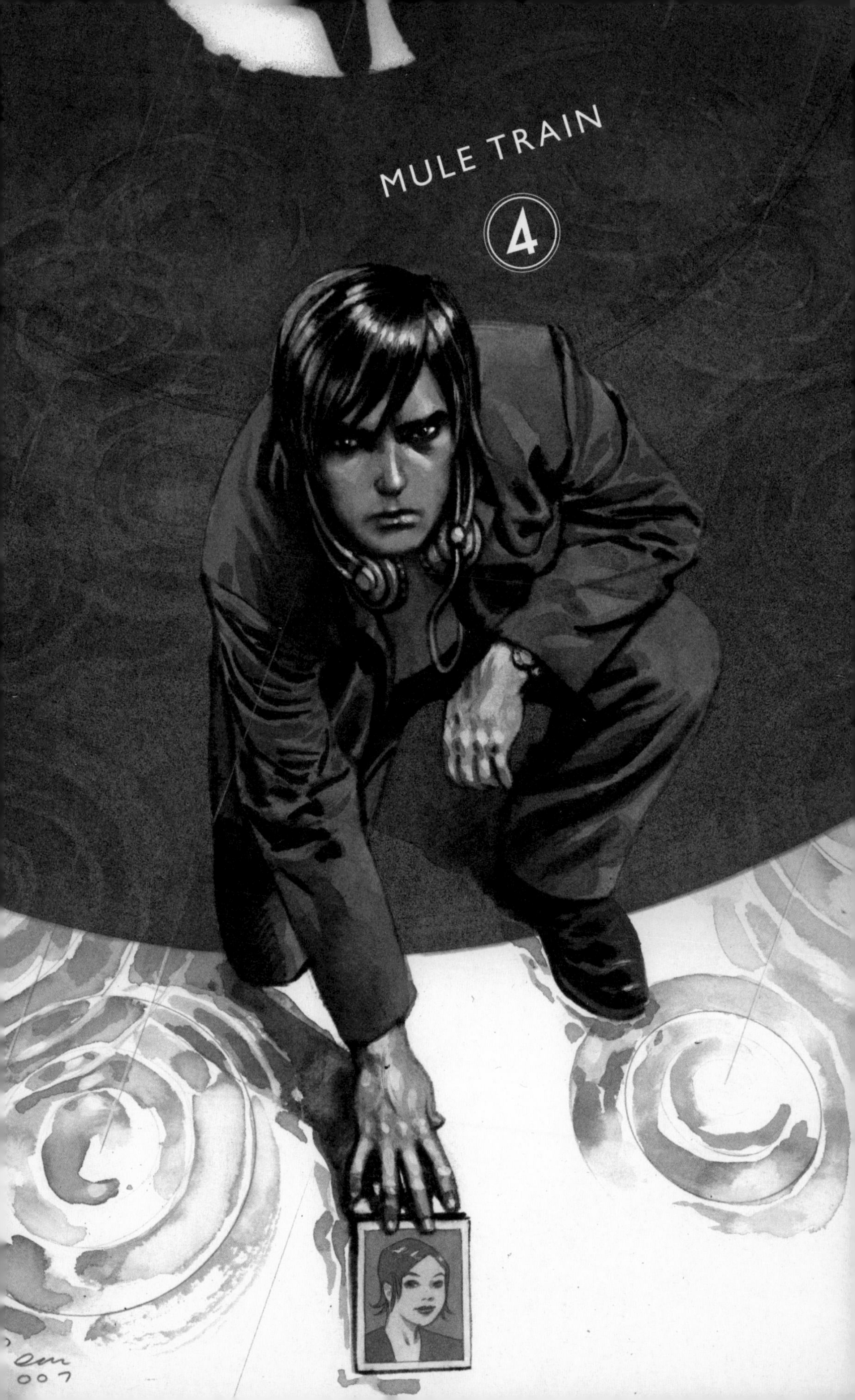

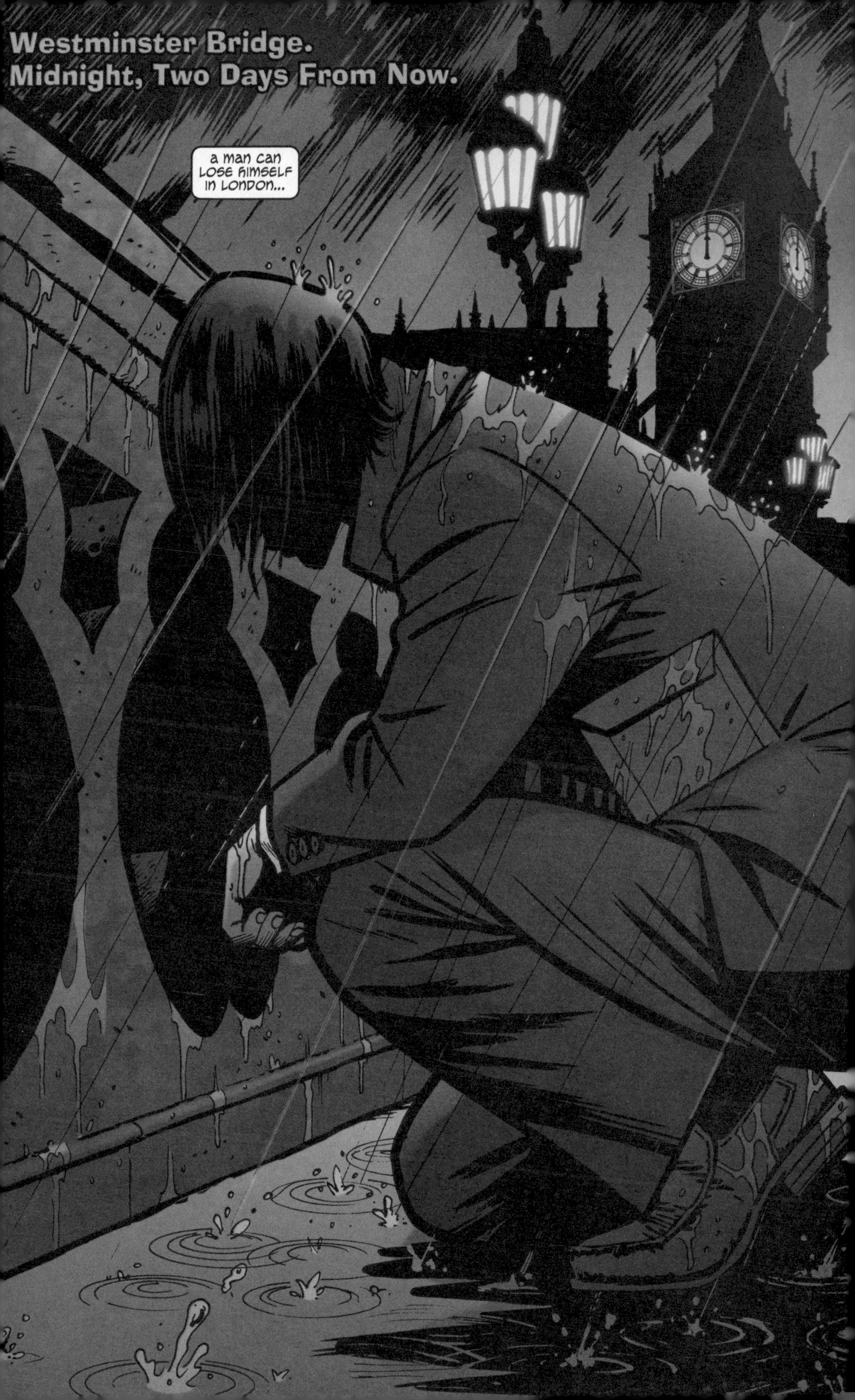
Westminster Bridge.
Midnight, Two Days From Now.
a man can lose himself in London...

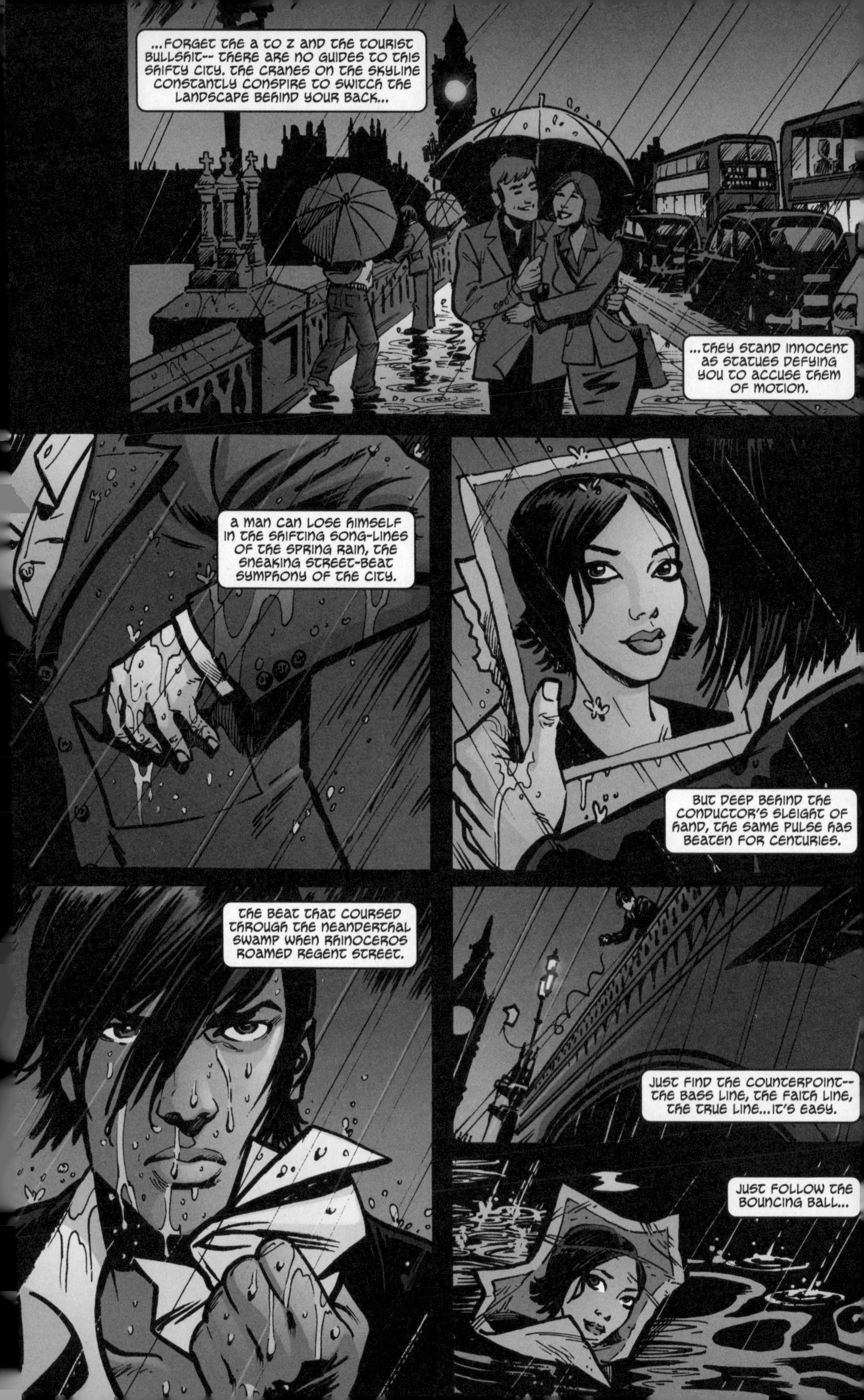
...FORGET THE A TO Z AND THE TOURIST BULLSHIT-- THERE ARE NO GUIDES TO THIS SHIFTY CITY. THE CRANES ON THE SKYLINE CONSTANTLY CONSPIRE TO SWITCH THE LANDSCAPE BEHIND YOUR BACK...
...THEY STAND INNOCENT AS STATUES DEFYING YOU TO ACCUSE THEM OF MOTION.
A MAN CAN LOSE HIMSELF IN THE SHIFTING SONG-LINES OF THE SPRING RAIN, THE SNEAKING STREET-BEAT SYMPHONY OF THE CITY.
BUT DEEP BEHIND THE CONDUCTOR'S SLEIGHT OF HAND, THE SAME PULSE HAS BEATEN FOR CENTURIES.
THE BEAT THAT COURSED THROUGH THE NEANDERTHAL SWAMP WHEN RHINOCEROS ROAMED REGENT STREET.
JUST FIND THE COUNTERPOINT-- THE BASS LINE, THE FAITH LINE, THE TRUE LINE...IT'S EASY.
JUST FOLLOW THE BOUNCING BALL...

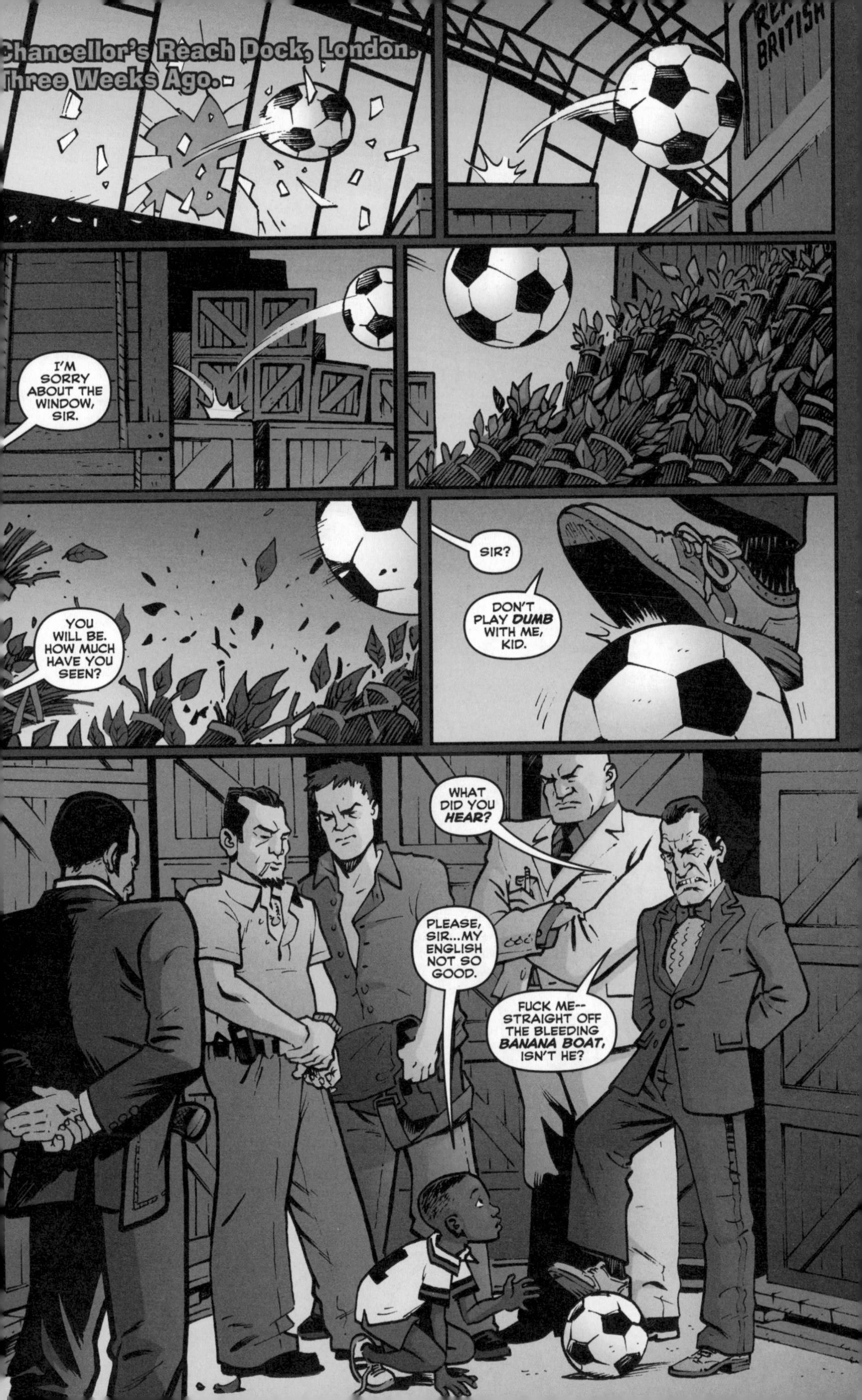
Chancellor's Reach Dock, London.
Three Weeks Ago.
I'M SORRY ABOUT THE WINDOW, SIR.
YOU WILL BE. HOW MUCH HAVE YOU SEEN?
SIR?
DON'T PLAY DUMB WITH ME, KID.
WHAT DID YOU HEAR?
PLEASE, SIR...MY ENGLISH NOT SO GOOD.
FUCK ME--STRAIGHT OFF THE BLEEDING BANANA BOAT, ISN'T HE?

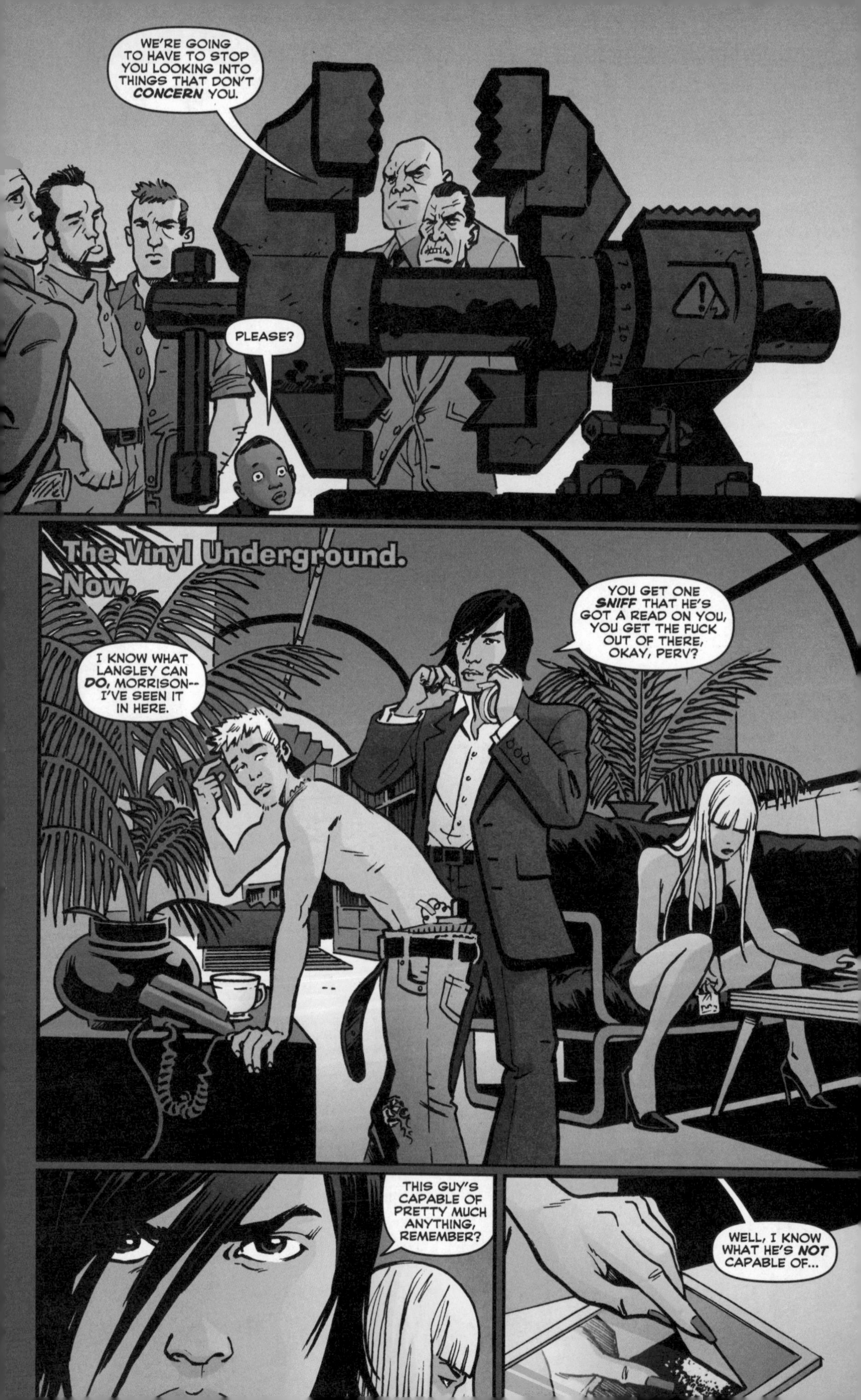

WE'RE GOING TO HAVE TO STOP YOU LOOKING INTO THINGS THAT DON'T *CONCERN* YOU.
PLEASE?
The Vinyl Underground. Now.
I KNOW WHAT LANGLEY CAN *DO*, MORRISON-- I'VE SEEN IT IN HERE.
YOU GET ONE *SNIFF* THAT HE'S GOT A READ ON YOU, YOU GET THE FUCK OUT OF THERE, OKAY, PERV?
THIS GUY'S CAPABLE OF PRETTY MUCH ANYTHING, REMEMBER?
WELL, I KNOW WHAT HE'S *NOT* CAPABLE OF...

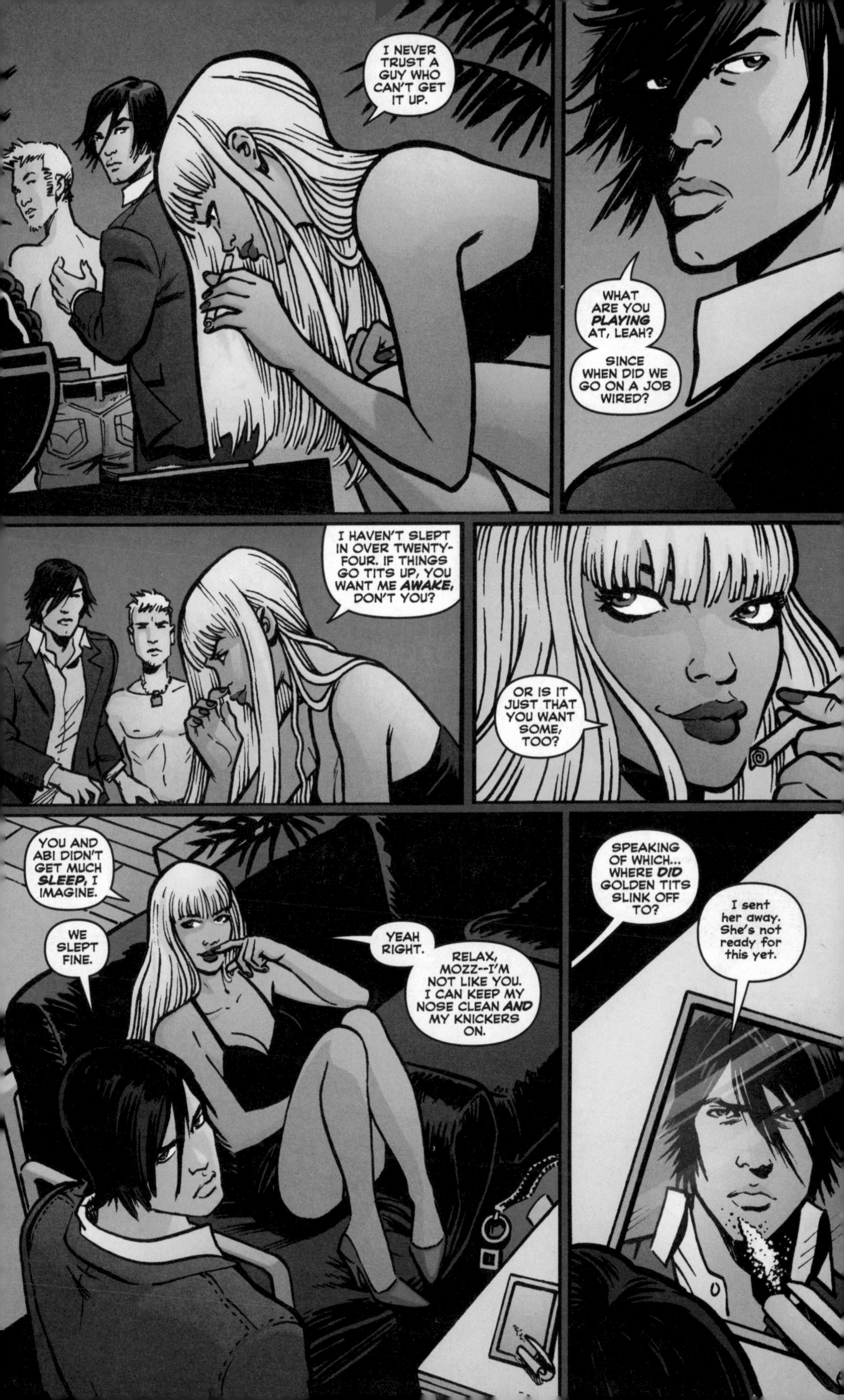
I NEVER TRUST A GUY WHO CAN'T GET IT UP.
WHAT ARE YOU PLAYING AT, LEAH?
SINCE WHEN DID WE GO ON A JOB WIRED?
I HAVEN'T SLEPT IN OVER TWENTY-FOUR. IF THINGS GO TITS UP, YOU WANT ME AWAKE, DON'T YOU?
OR IS IT JUST THAT YOU WANT SOME, TOO?
YOU AND ABI DIDN'T GET MUCH SLEEP, I IMAGINE.
WE SLEPT FINE.
YEAH RIGHT.
RELAX, MOZZ--I'M NOT LIKE YOU. I CAN KEEP MY NOSE CLEAN AND MY KNICKERS ON.
SPEAKING OF WHICH... WHERE DID GOLDEN TITS SLINK OFF TO?
I sent her away. She's not ready for this yet.

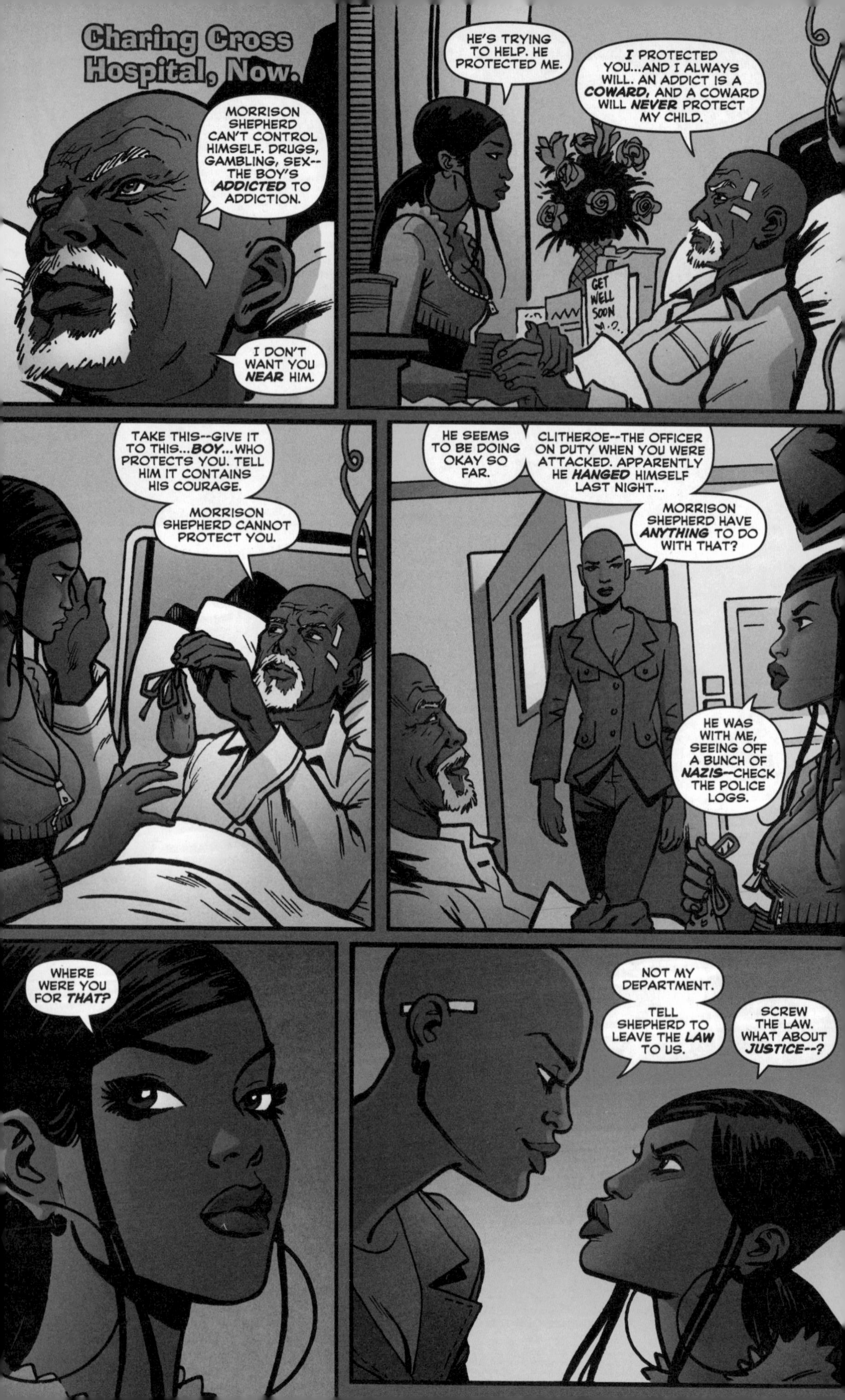
Charing Cross Hospital, Now.
MORRISON SHEPHERD CAN'T CONTROL HIMSELF. DRUGS, GAMBLING, SEX--THE BOY'S ADDICTED TO ADDICTION.
I DON'T WANT YOU NEAR HIM.
HE'S TRYING TO HELP. HE PROTECTED ME.
I PROTECTED YOU...AND I ALWAYS WILL. AN ADDICT IS A COWARD, AND A COWARD WILL NEVER PROTECT MY CHILD.
GET WELL SOON
TAKE THIS--GIVE IT TO THIS...BOY...WHO PROTECTS YOU. TELL HIM IT CONTAINS HIS COURAGE.
MORRISON SHEPHERD CANNOT PROTECT YOU.
HE SEEMS TO BE DOING OKAY SO FAR.
CLITHEROE--THE OFFICER ON DUTY WHEN YOU WERE ATTACKED. APPARENTLY HE HANGED HIMSELF LAST NIGHT...
MORRISON SHEPHERD HAVE ANYTHING TO DO WITH THAT?
HE WAS WITH ME, SEEING OFF A BUNCH OF NAZIS--CHECK THE POLICE LOGS.
WHERE WERE YOU FOR THAT?
NOT MY DEPARTMENT.
TELL SHEPHERD TO LEAVE THE LAW TO US.
SCREW THE LAW. WHAT ABOUT JUSTICE--?

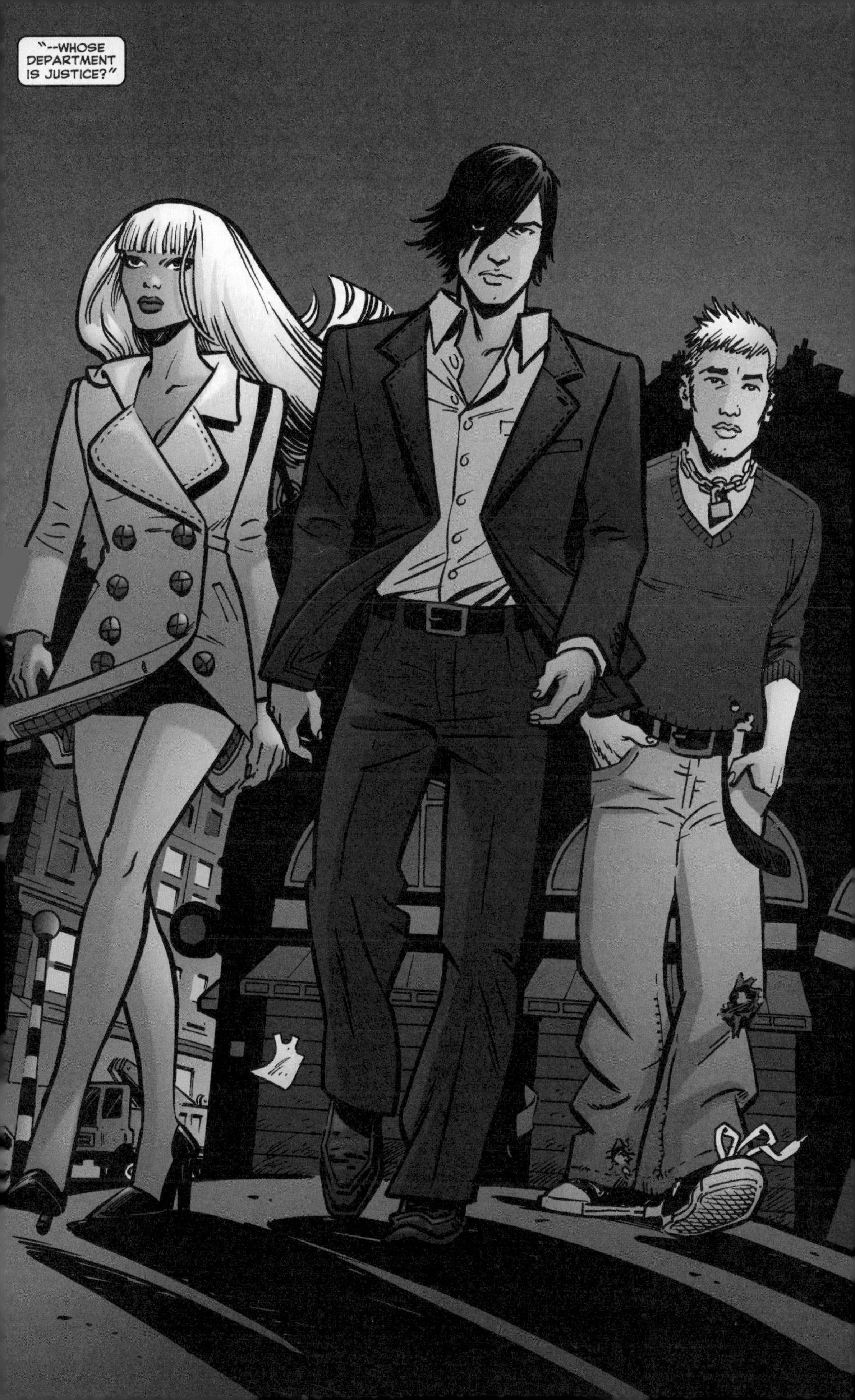
"--WHOSE DEPARTMENT IS JUSTICE?"

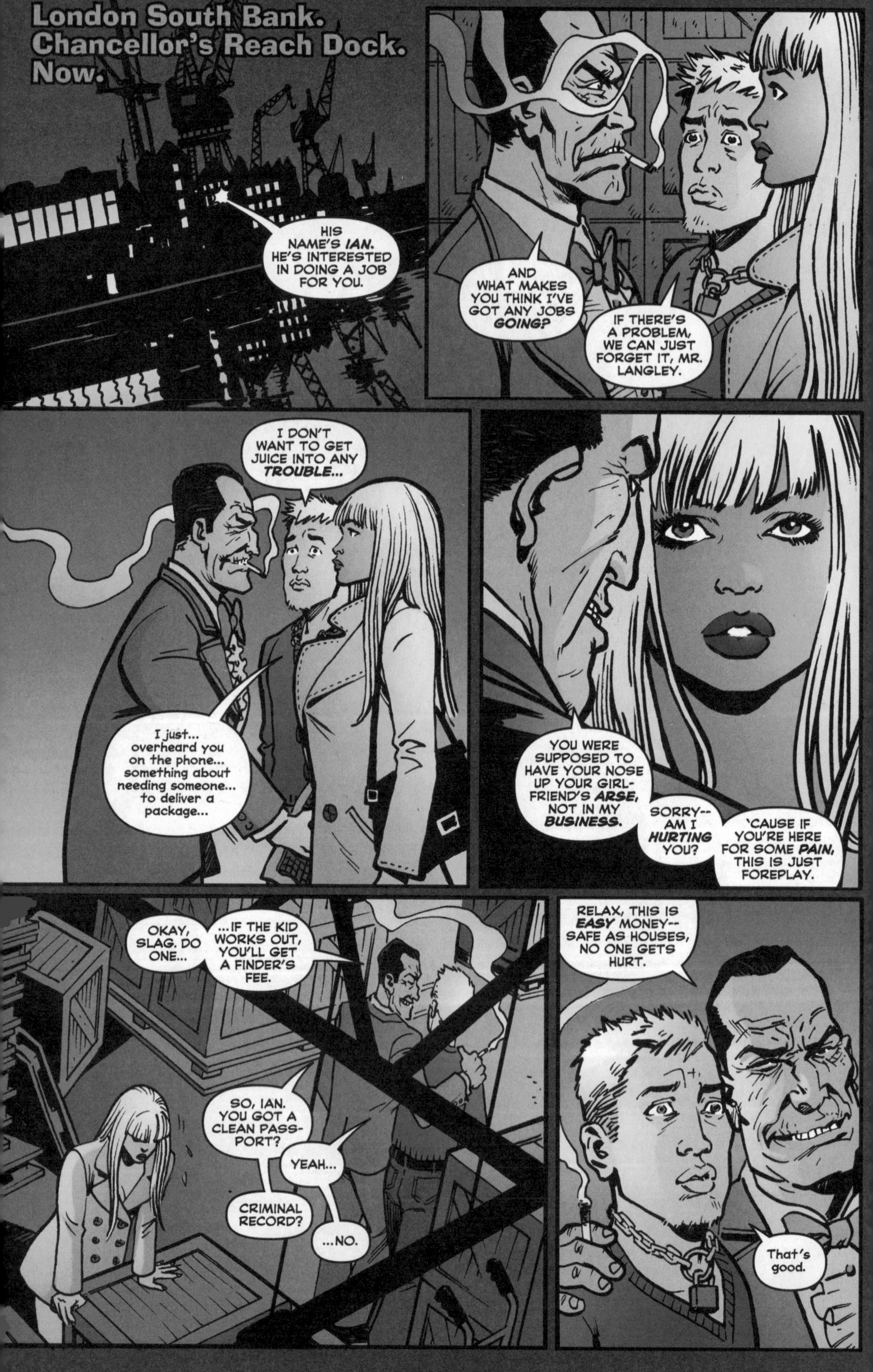
London South Bank. Chancellor's Reach Dock. Now.
HIS NAME'S IAN. HE'S INTERESTED IN DOING A JOB FOR YOU.
AND WHAT MAKES YOU THINK I'VE GOT ANY JOBS GOING?
IF THERE'S A PROBLEM, WE CAN JUST FORGET IT, MR. LANGLEY.
I DON'T WANT TO GET JUICE INTO ANY TROUBLE...
I just... overheard you on the phone... something about needing someone... to deliver a package...
YOU WERE SUPPOSED TO HAVE YOUR NOSE UP YOUR GIRL-FRIEND'S ARSE, NOT IN MY BUSINESS.
SORRY-- AM I HURTING YOU?
'CAUSE IF YOU'RE HERE FOR SOME PAIN, THIS IS JUST FOREPLAY.
OKAY, SLAG. DO ONE...
...IF THE KID WORKS OUT, YOU'LL GET A FINDER'S FEE.
SO, IAN. YOU GOT A CLEAN PASS-PORT?
YEAH...
CRIMINAL RECORD?
...NO.
RELAX, THIS IS EASY MONEY-- SAFE AS HOUSES, NO ONE GETS HURT.
That's good.

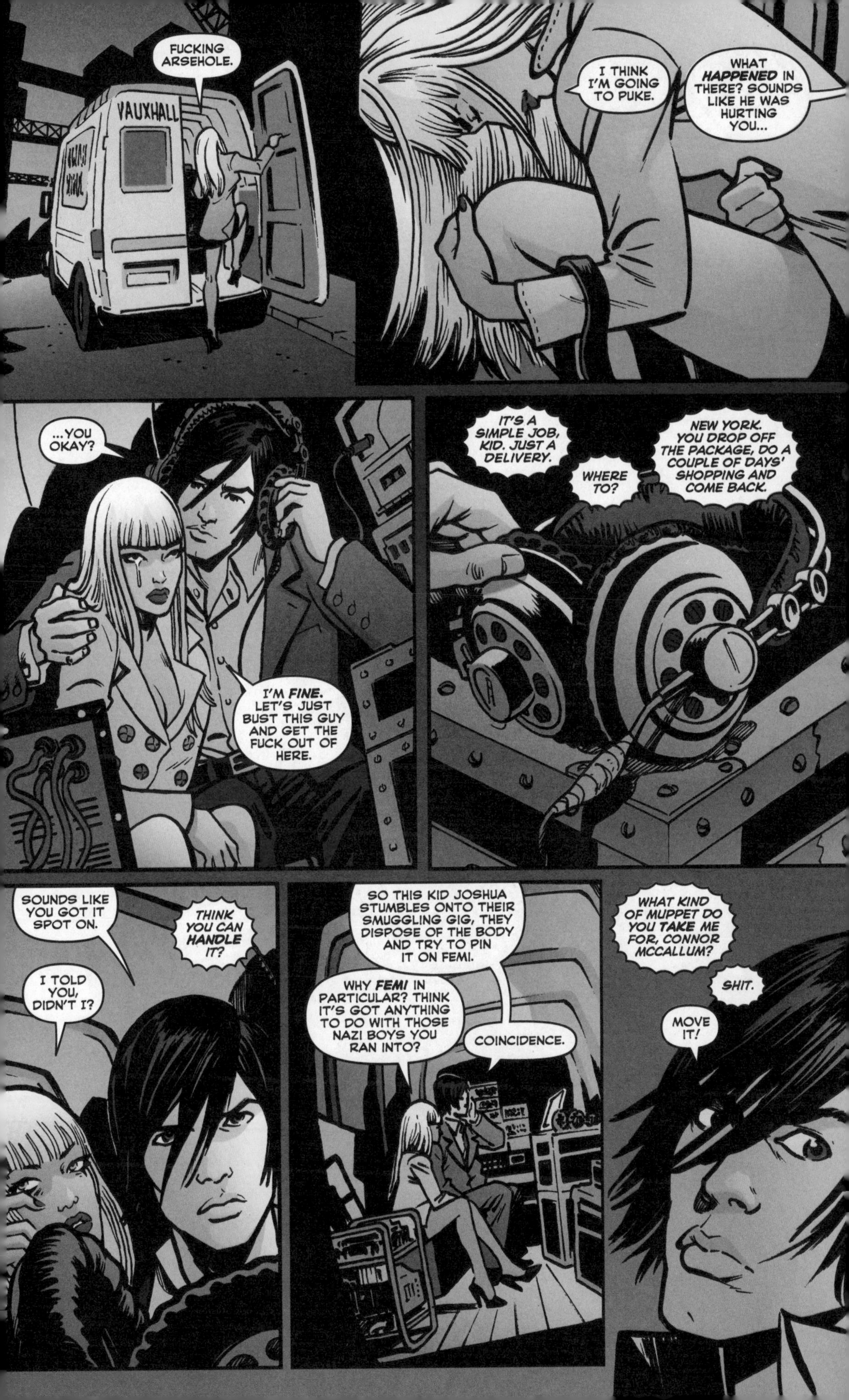
FUCKING ARSEHOLE.
VAUXHALL
I THINK I'M GOING TO PUKE.
WHAT HAPPENED IN THERE? SOUNDS LIKE HE WAS HURTING YOU...
...YOU OKAY?
I'M FINE. LET'S JUST BUST THIS GUY AND GET THE FUCK OUT OF HERE.
IT'S A SIMPLE JOB, KID. JUST A DELIVERY.
WHERE TO?
NEW YORK. YOU DROP OFF THE PACKAGE, DO A COUPLE OF DAYS' SHOPPING AND COME BACK.
SOUNDS LIKE YOU GOT IT SPOT ON.
THINK YOU CAN HANDLE IT?
I TOLD YOU, DIDN'T I?
SO THIS KID JOSHUA STUMBLES ONTO THEIR SMUGGLING GIG, THEY DISPOSE OF THE BODY AND TRY TO PIN IT ON FEMI.
WHY FEMI IN PARTICULAR? THINK IT'S GOT ANYTHING TO DO WITH THOSE NAZI BOYS YOU RAN INTO?
COINCIDENCE.
WHAT KIND OF MUPPET DO YOU TAKE ME FOR, CONNOR MCCALLUM?
SHIT.
MOVE IT!

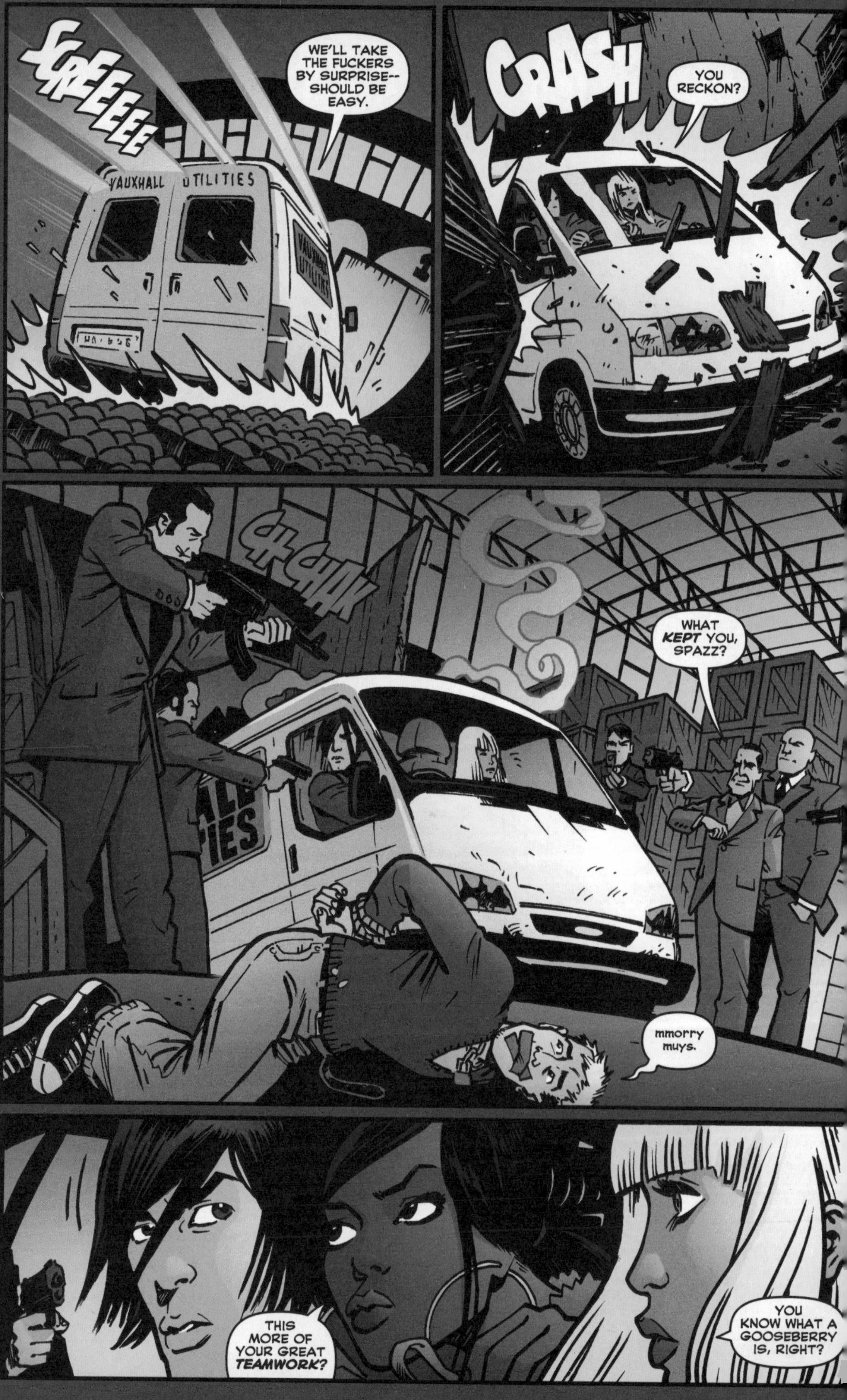
SCREEEEEE
WE'LL TAKE THE FUCKERS BY SURPRISE-- SHOULD BE EASY.
VAUXHALL UTILITIES
CRASH
YOU RECKON?
CH-CHUK
WHAT KEPT YOU, SPAZZ?
mmorry muys.
THIS MORE OF YOUR GREAT TEAMWORK?
YOU KNOW WHAT A GOOSEBERRY IS, RIGHT?

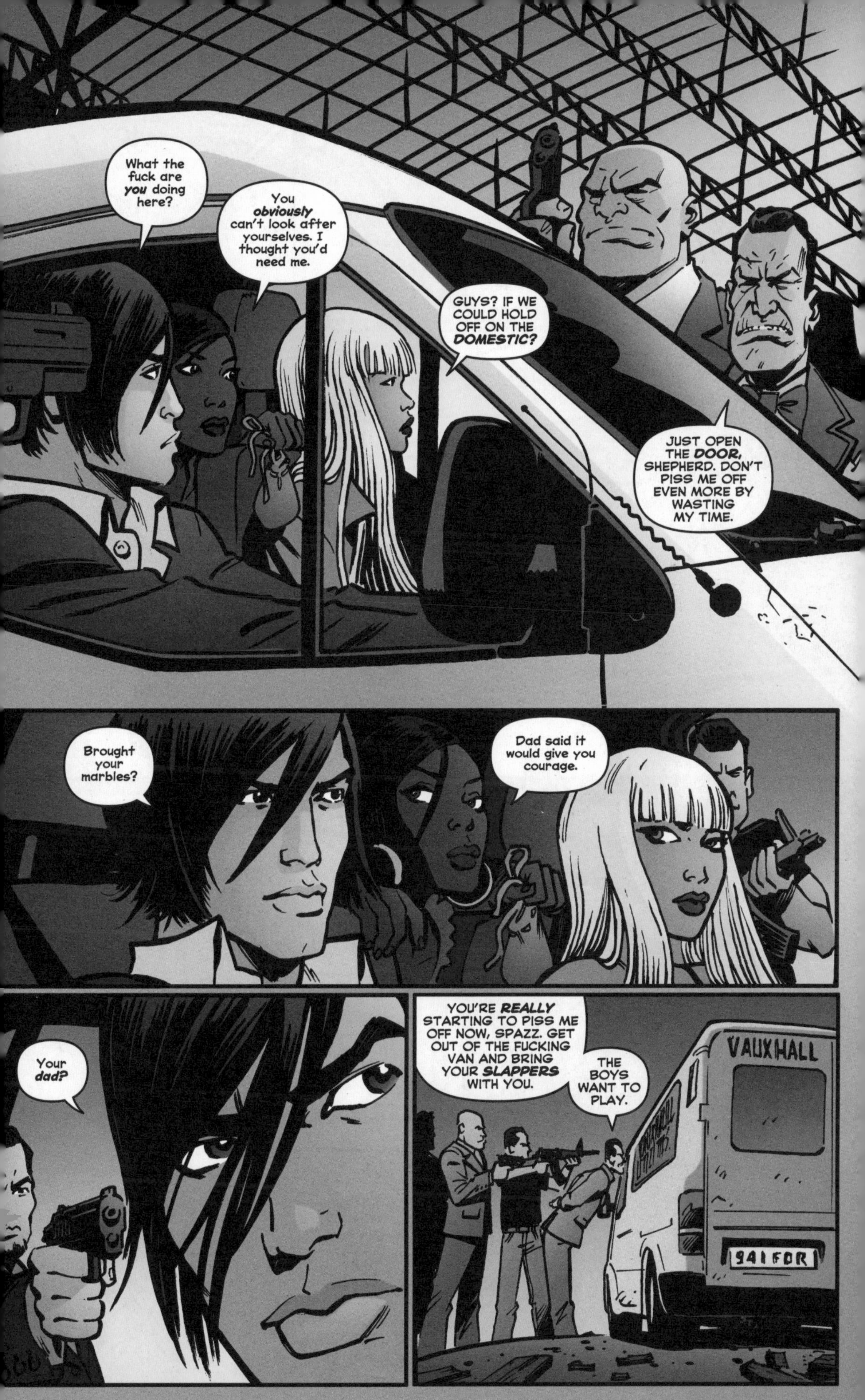
What the fuck are *you* doing here?
You *obviously* can't look after yourselves. I thought you'd need me.
GUYS? IF WE COULD HOLD OFF ON THE *DOMESTIC?*
JUST OPEN THE *DOOR,* SHEPHERD. DON'T PISS ME OFF EVEN MORE BY WASTING MY TIME.
Brought your marbles?
Dad said it would give you courage.
Your *dad?*
YOU'RE *REALLY* STARTING TO PISS ME OFF NOW, SPAZZ. GET OUT OF THE FUCKING VAN AND BRING YOUR *SLAPPERS* WITH YOU.
THE BOYS WANT TO PLAY.
VAUXHALL
941 FOR

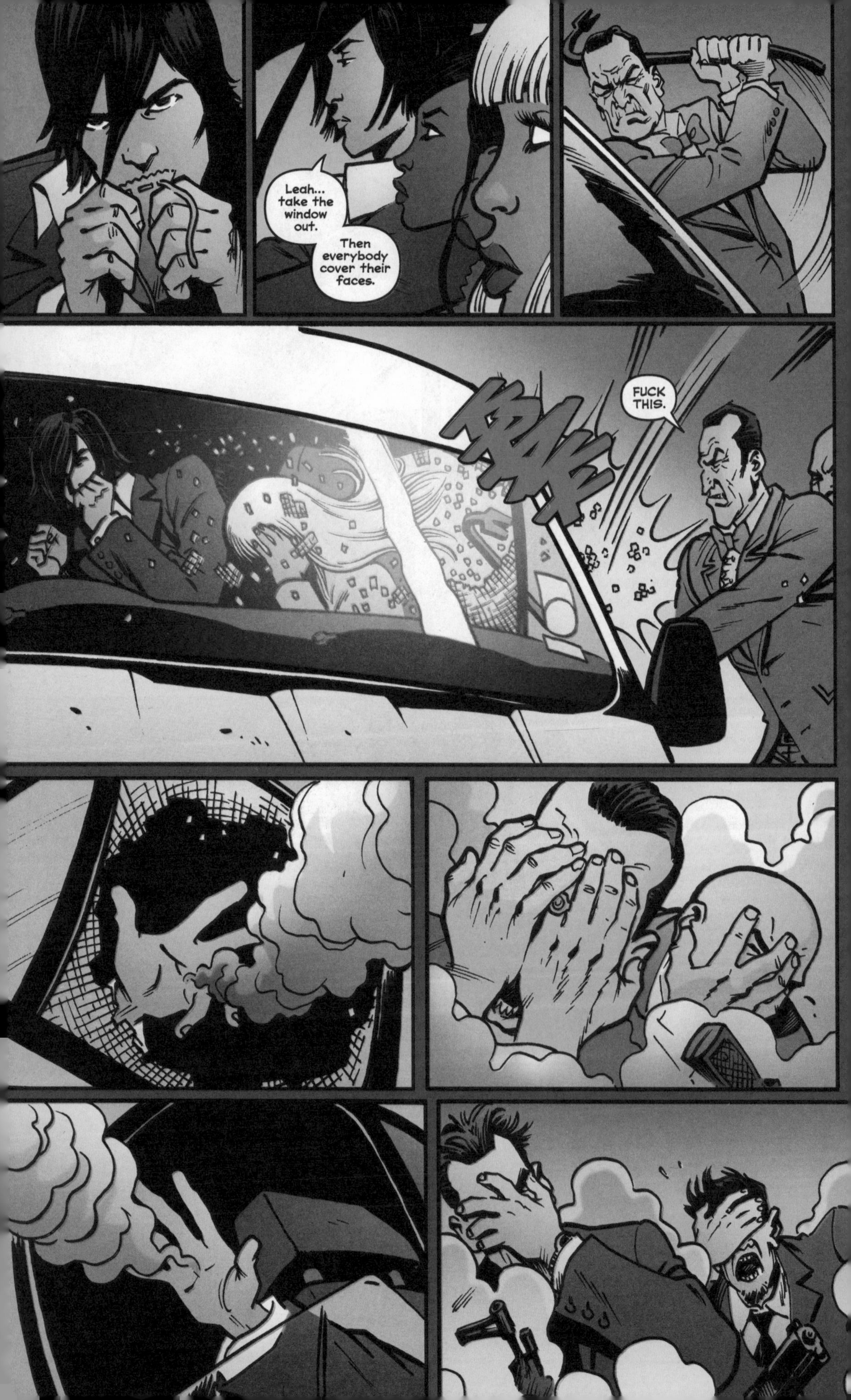
Leah... take the window out.
Then everybody cover their faces.
KRAK
FUCK THIS.

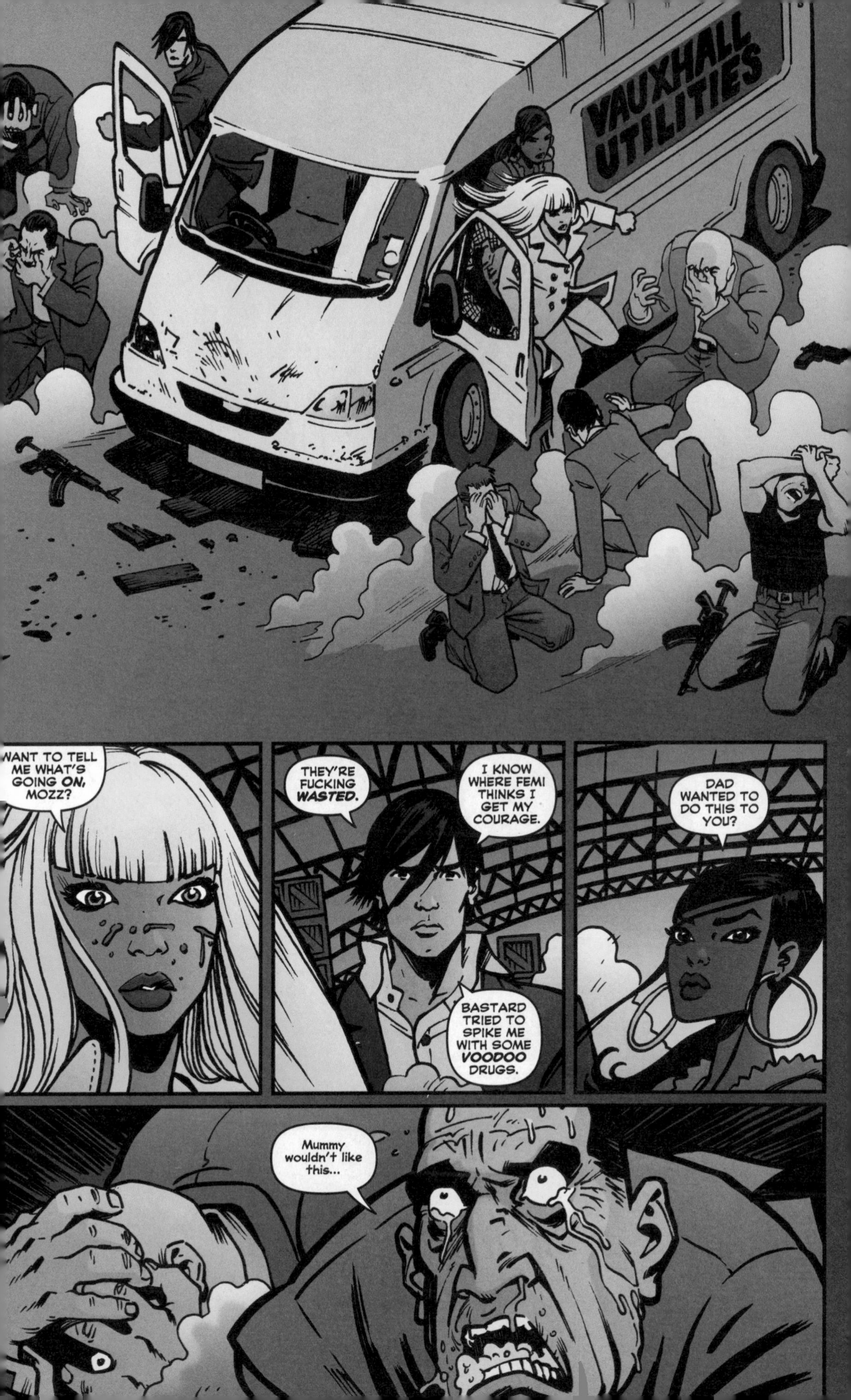
VAUXHALL UTILITIES
WANT TO TELL ME WHAT'S GOING ON, MOZZ?
THEY'RE FUCKING WASTED.
I KNOW WHERE FEMI THINKS I GET MY COURAGE.
BASTARD TRIED TO SPIKE ME WITH SOME VOODOO DRUGS.
DAD WANTED TO DO THIS TO YOU?
Mummy wouldn't like this...

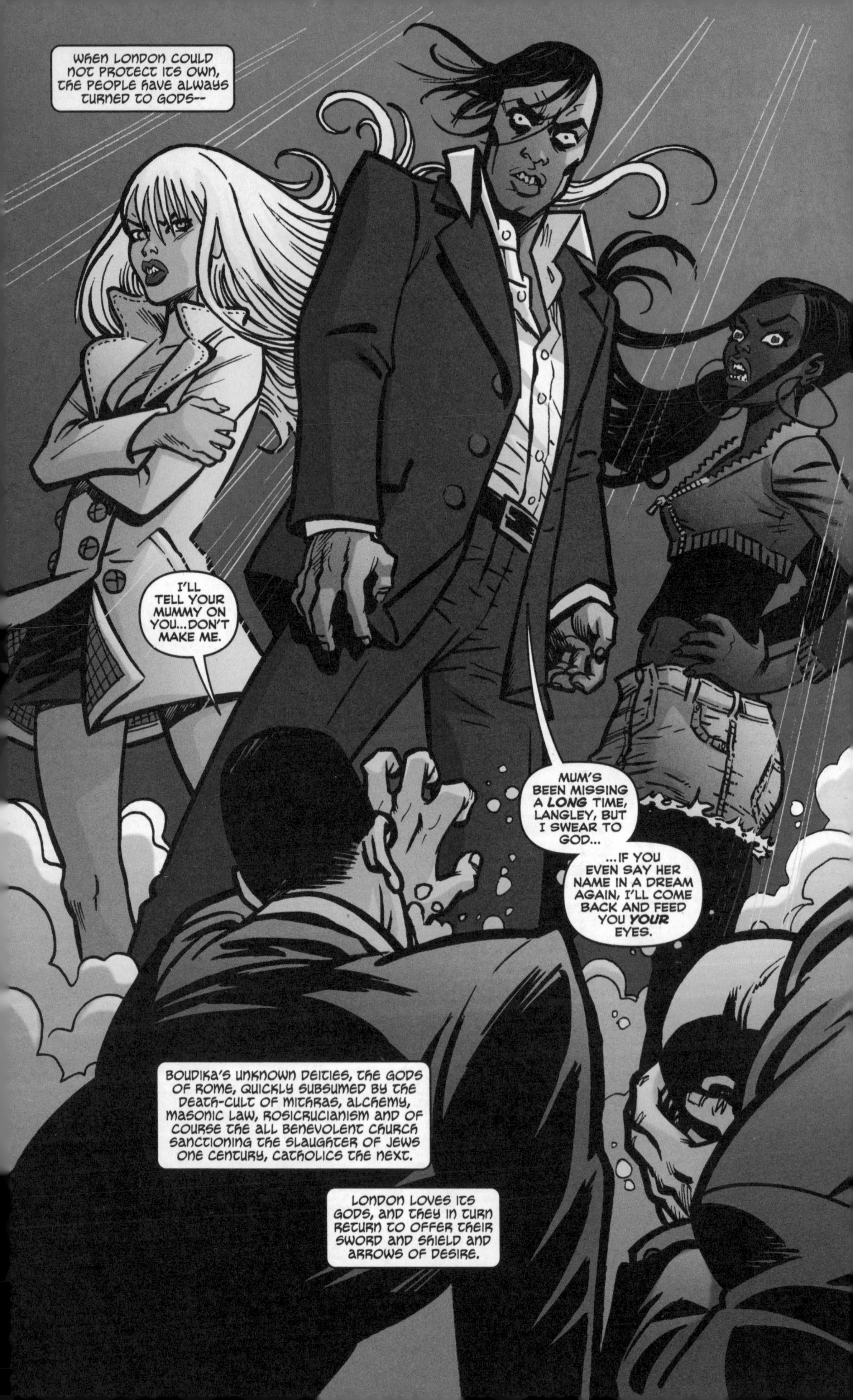
WHEN LONDON COULD NOT PROTECT ITS OWN, THE PEOPLE HAVE ALWAYS TURNED TO GODS--
I'LL TELL YOUR MUMMY ON YOU...DON'T MAKE ME.
MUM'S BEEN MISSING A LONG TIME, LANGLEY, BUT I SWEAR TO GOD...
...IF YOU EVEN SAY HER NAME IN A DREAM AGAIN, I'LL COME BACK AND FEED YOU YOUR EYES.
BOUDIKA'S UNKNOWN DEITIES, THE GODS OF ROME, QUICKLY SUBSUMED BY THE DEATH-CULT OF MITHRAS, ALCHEMY, MASONIC LAW, ROSICRUCIANISM AND OF COURSE THE ALL BENEVOLENT CHURCH SANCTIONING THE SLAUGHTER OF JEWS ONE CENTURY, CATHOLICS THE NEXT.
LONDON LOVES ITS GODS, AND THEY IN TURN RETURN TO OFFER THEIR SWORD AND SHIELD AND ARROWS OF DESIRE.

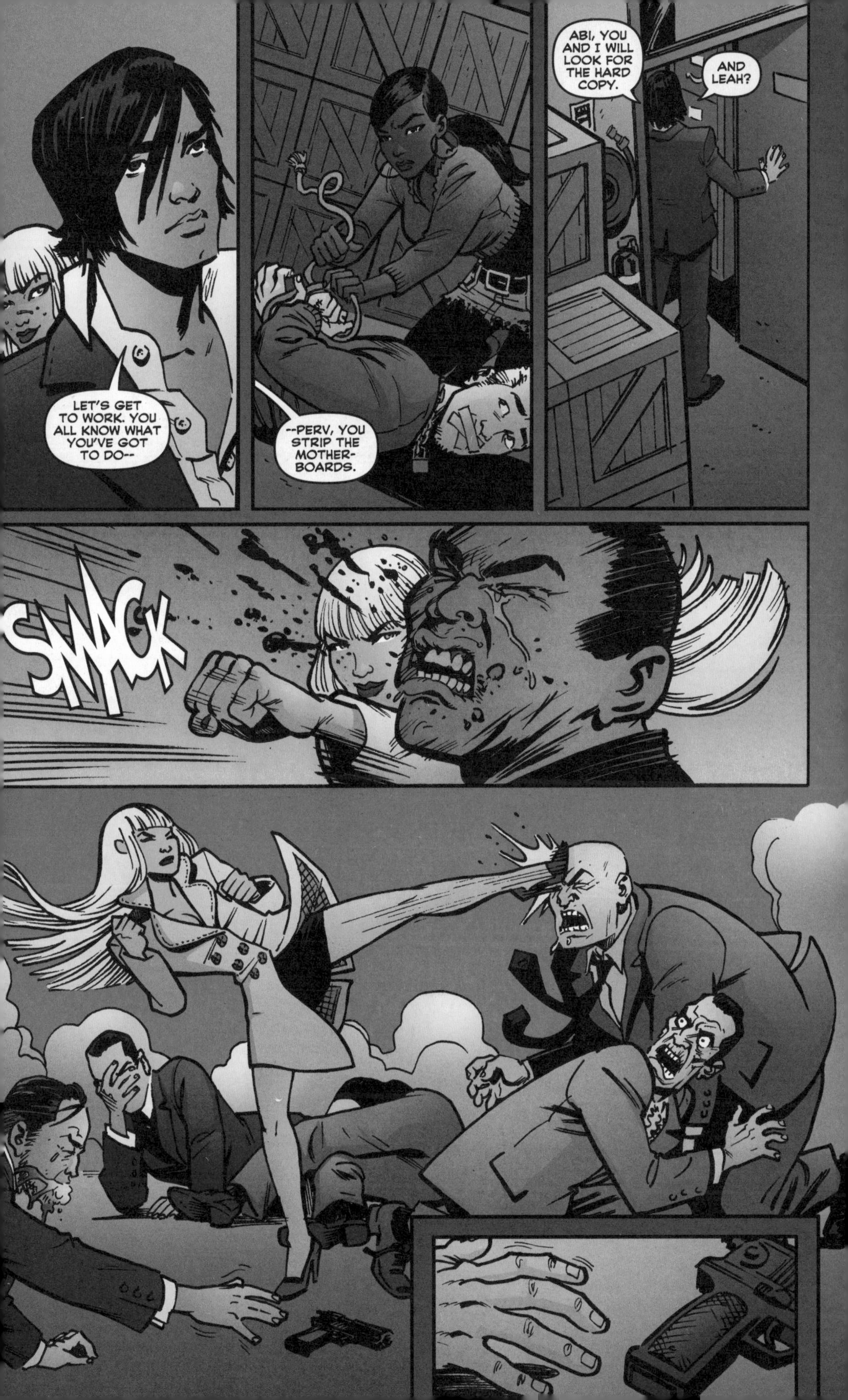
LET'S GET TO WORK. YOU ALL KNOW WHAT YOU'VE GOT TO DO--
--PERV, YOU STRIP THE MOTHER-BOARDS.
ABI, YOU AND I WILL LOOK FOR THE HARD COPY.
AND LEAH?
SMACK

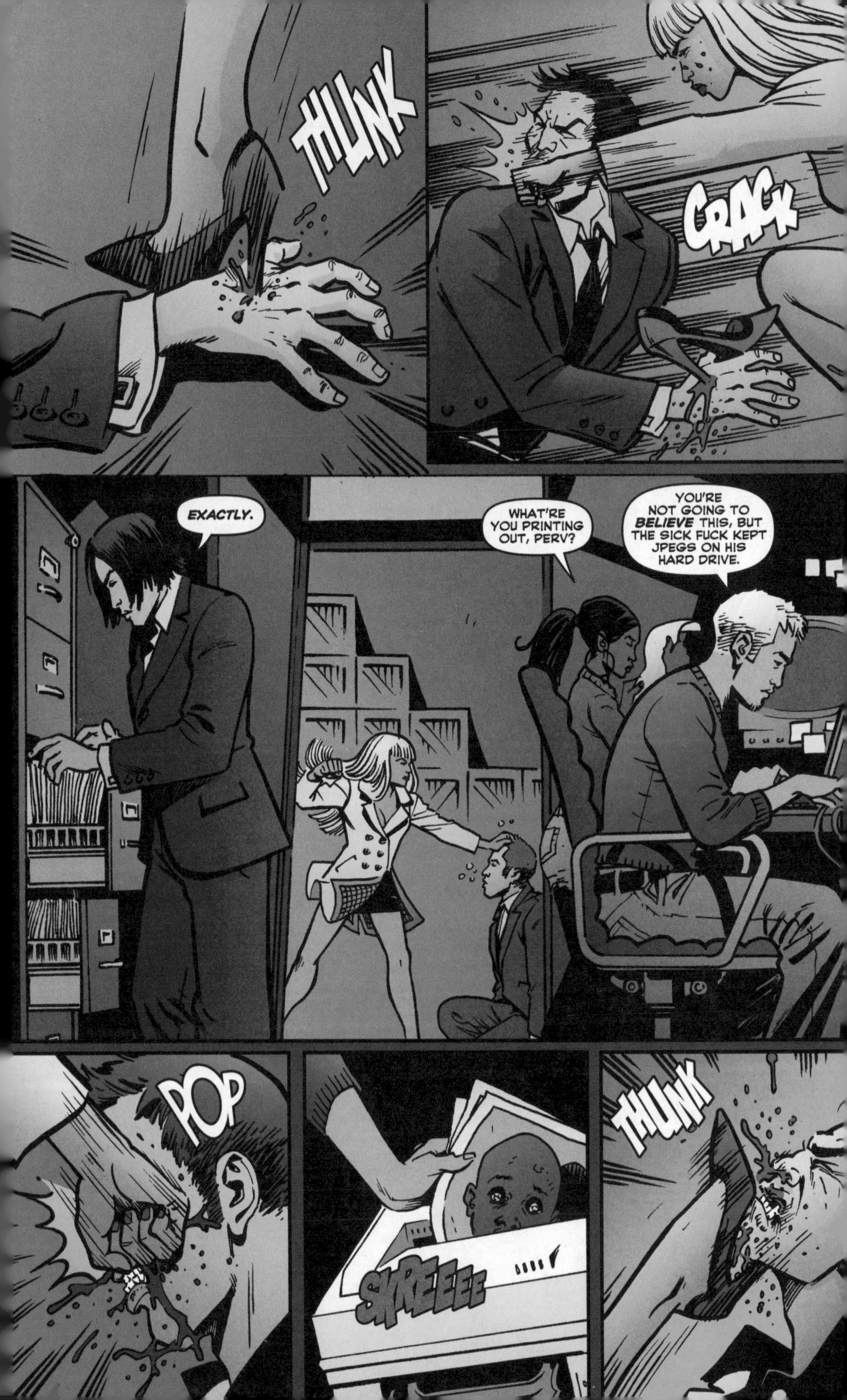
THUNK
CRACK
EXACTLY.
WHAT'RE YOU PRINTING OUT, PERV?
YOU'RE NOT GOING TO BELIEVE THIS, BUT THE SICK FUCK KEPT JPEGS ON HIS HARD DRIVE.
POP
SKREEEE
THUNK

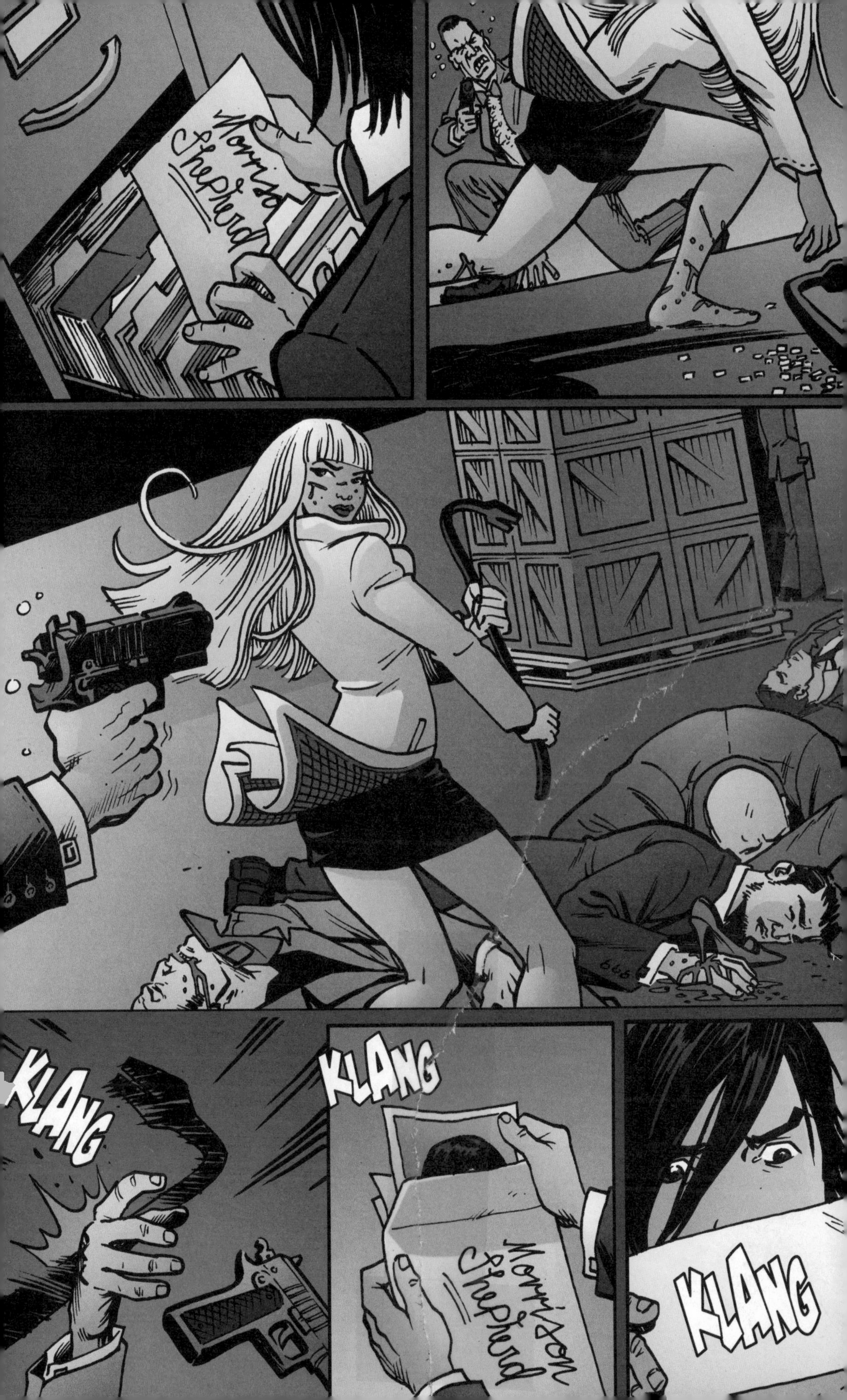
Morrison Shepherd
KLANG
KLANG
Morrison Shepherd
KLANG

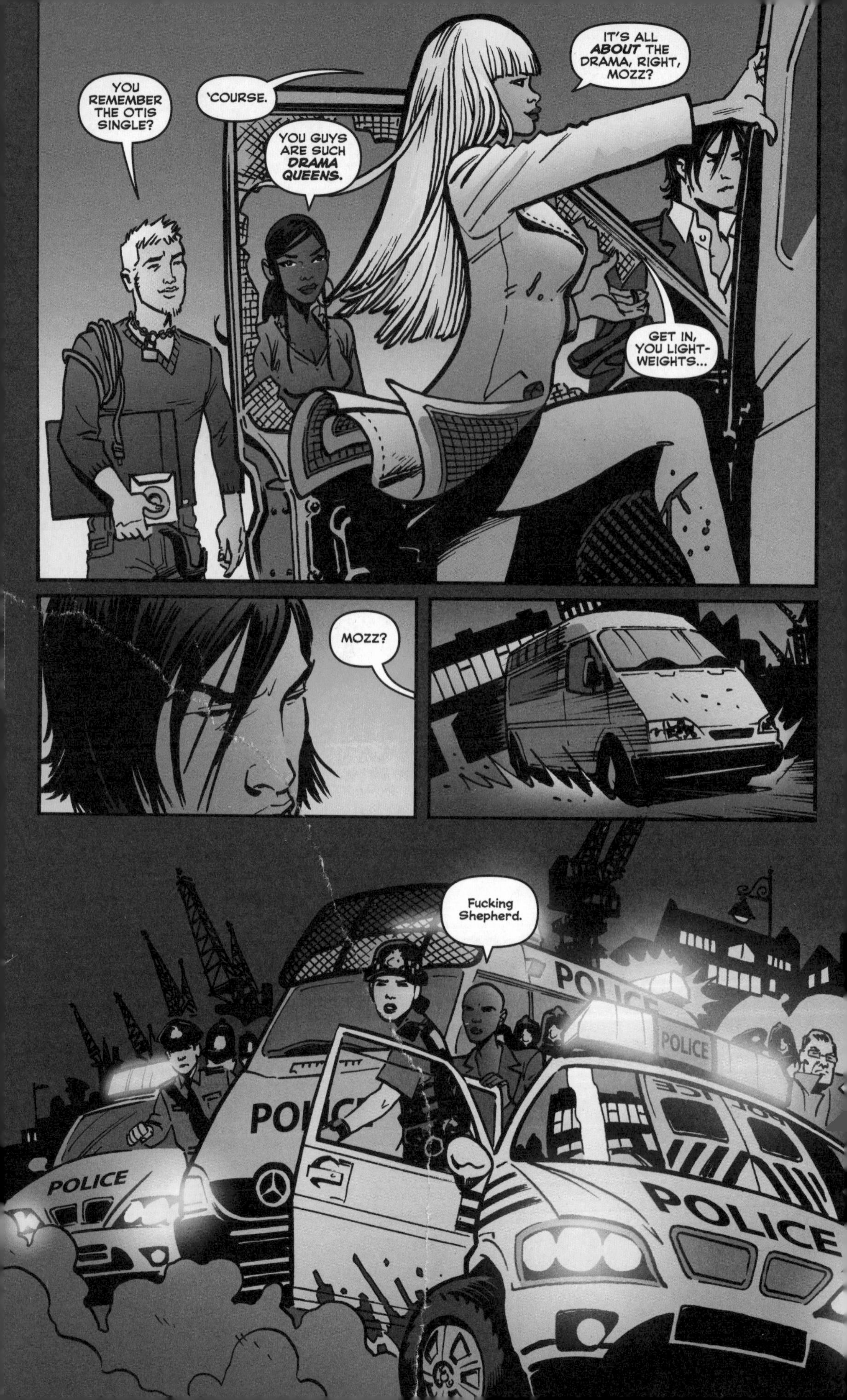

YOU REMEMBER THE OTIS SINGLE?
'COURSE.
YOU GUYS ARE SUCH DRAMA QUEENS.
IT'S ALL ABOUT THE DRAMA, RIGHT, MOZZ?
GET IN, YOU LIGHT-WEIGHTS...
MOZZ?
Fucking Shepherd.
POLICE
POLICE
POLICE
POLICE
POLICE

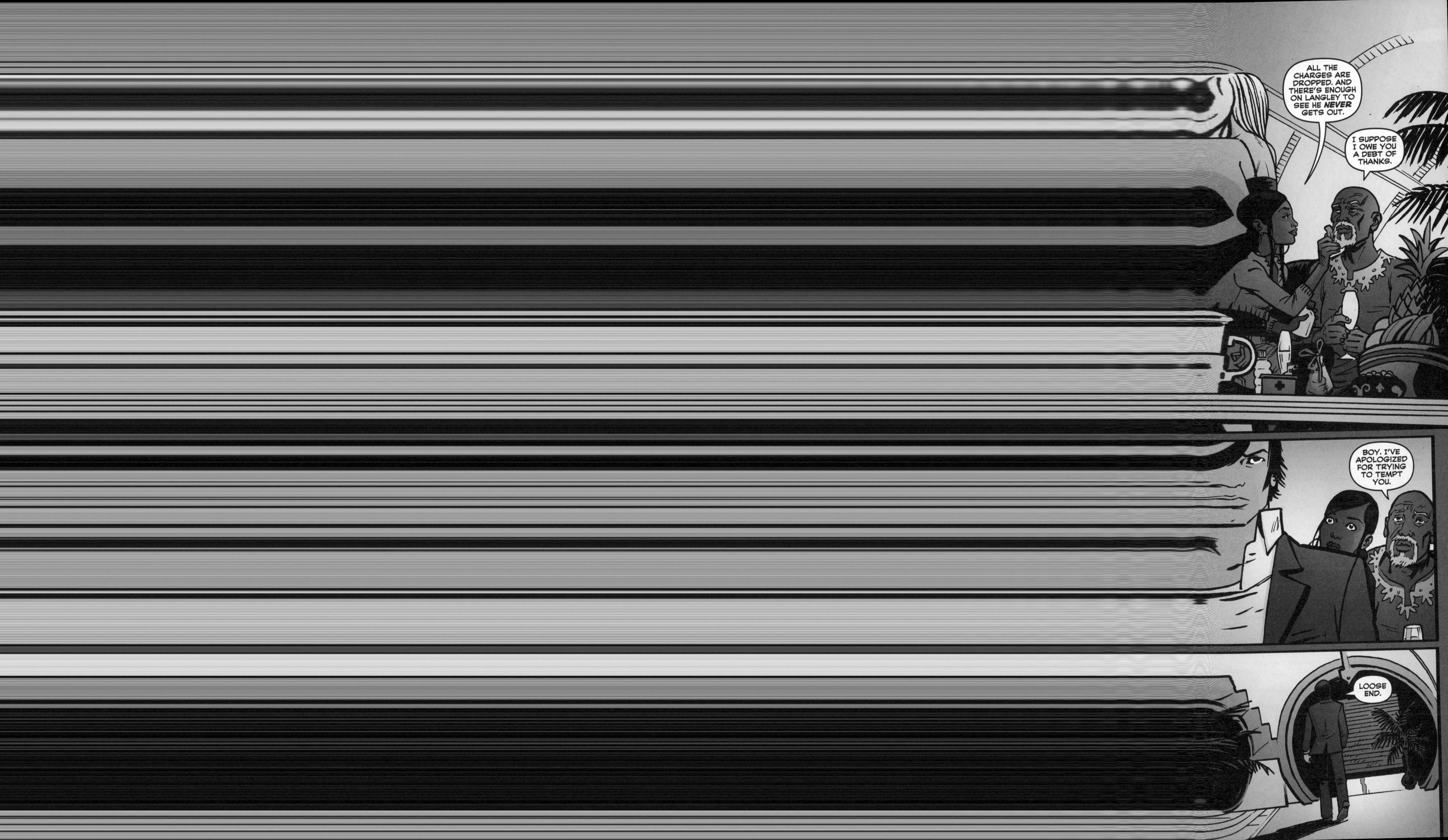
ALL THE CHARGES ARE DROPPED. AND THERE'S ENOUGH ON LANGLEY TO SEE HE *NEVER* GETS OUT.
I SUPPOSE I OWE YOU A DEBT OF THANKS.
BOY. I'VE APOLOGIZED FOR TRYING TO TEMPT YOU.
LOOSE END.

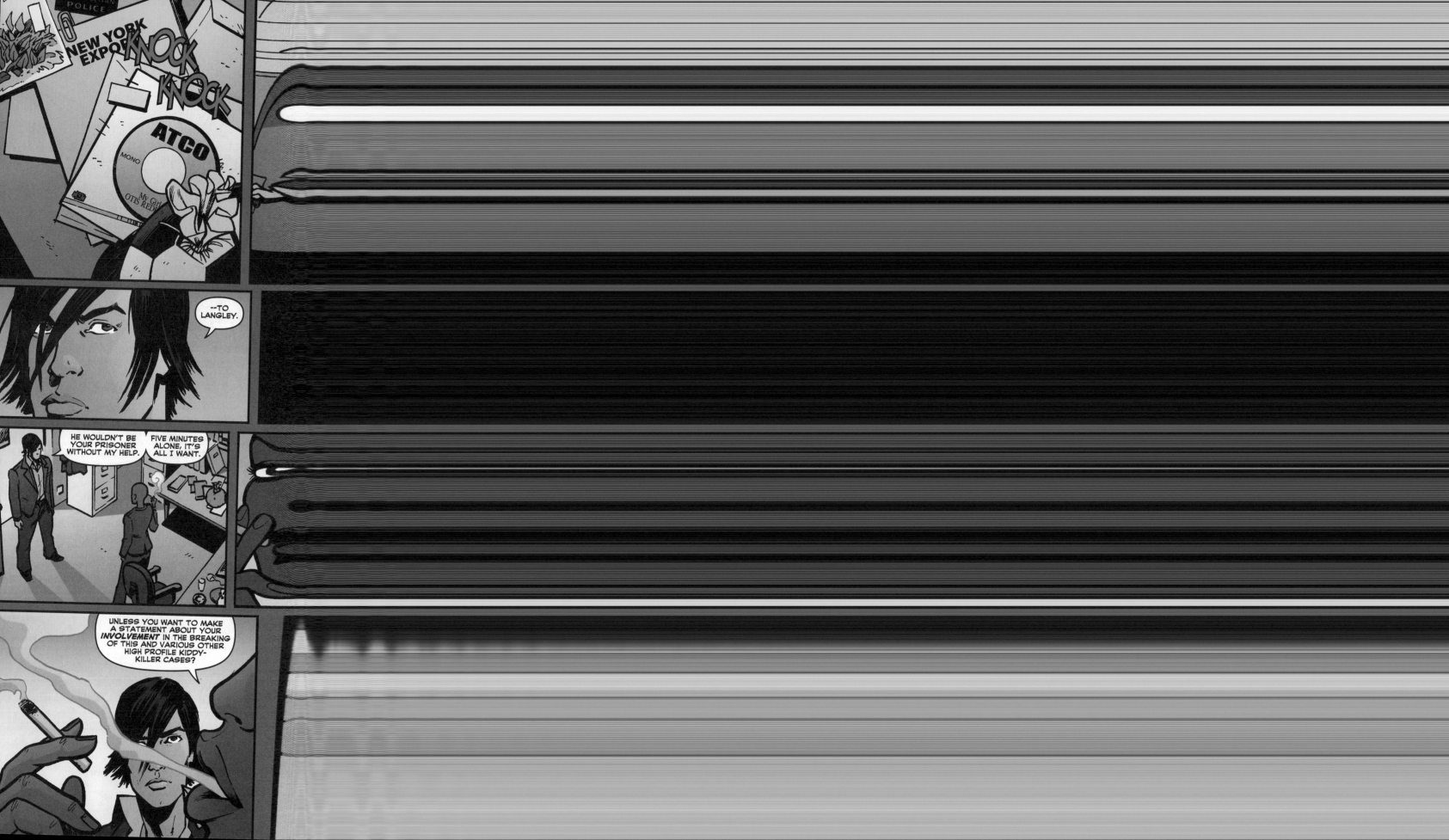

NEW YORK EXPO

KNOCK KNOCK

ATCO
MONO
My Girl
OTIS RED...

COME.

I WANT TO TALK--

--TO LANGLEY.

WE DON'T NORMALLY *ALLOW* PRISONERS ONE PHONE CALL AND A DJ.

HE WOULDN'T BE YOUR PRISONER WITHOUT MY HELP.

FIVE MINUTES ALONE, IT'S ALL I WANT.

YOU AND FEMI ABIOLA, HALF OF GANGLAND LONDON AND THE POOR KID'S PARENTS. THERE'S A *QUEUE*.

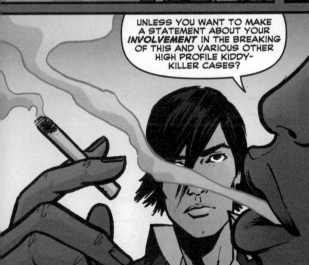

UNLESS YOU WANT TO MAKE A STATEMENT ABOUT YOUR *INVOLVEMENT* IN THE BREAKING OF THIS AND VARIOUS OTHER HIGH PROFILE KIDDY-KILLER CASES?

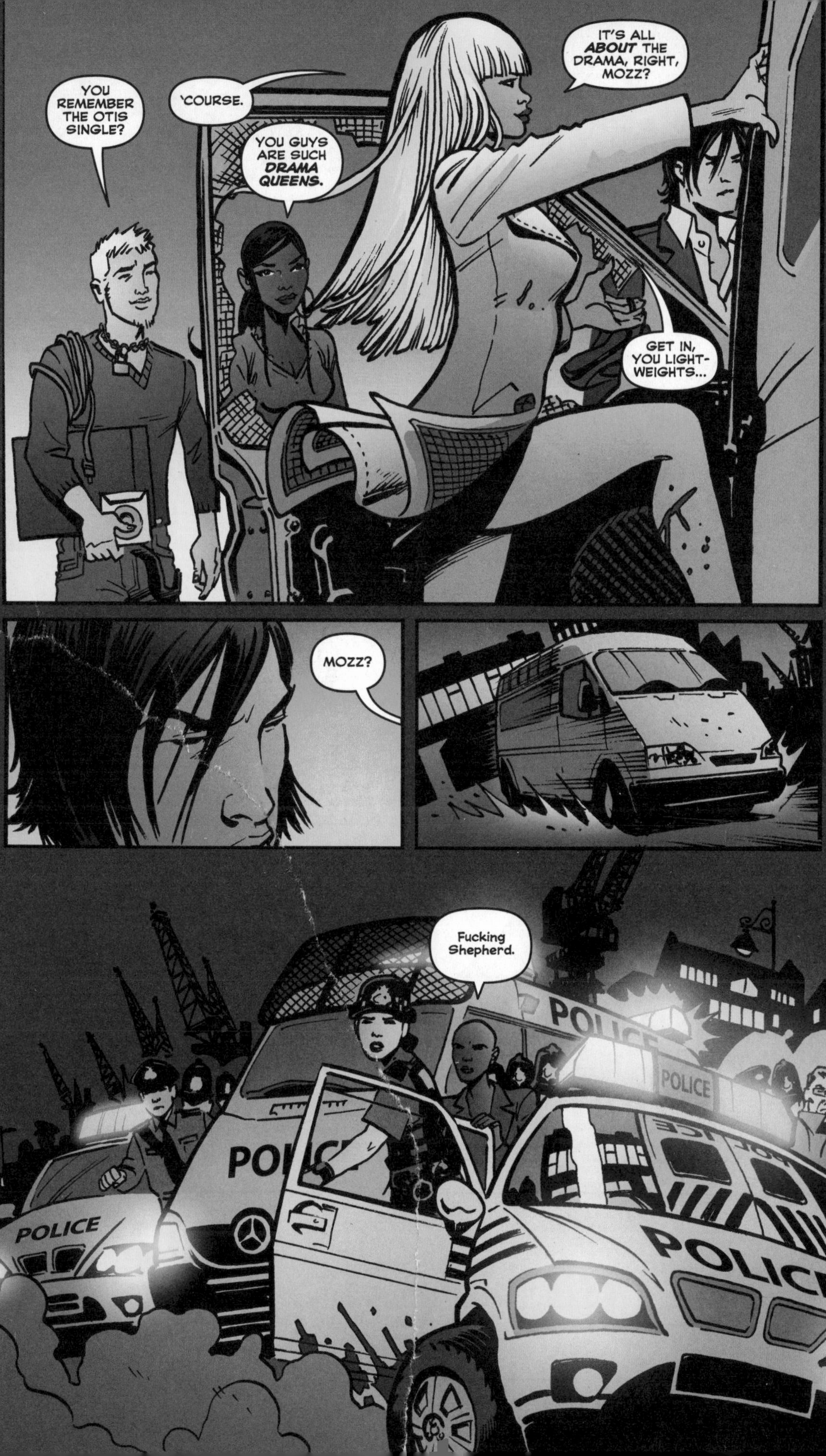
YOU REMEMBER THE OTIS SINGLE?
'COURSE.
IT'S ALL ABOUT THE DRAMA, RIGHT, MOZZ?
YOU GUYS ARE SUCH DRAMA QUEENS.
GET IN, YOU LIGHT-WEIGHTS...
MOZZ?
Fucking Shepherd.
POLICE
POLICE
POLICE
POLICE
POLICE

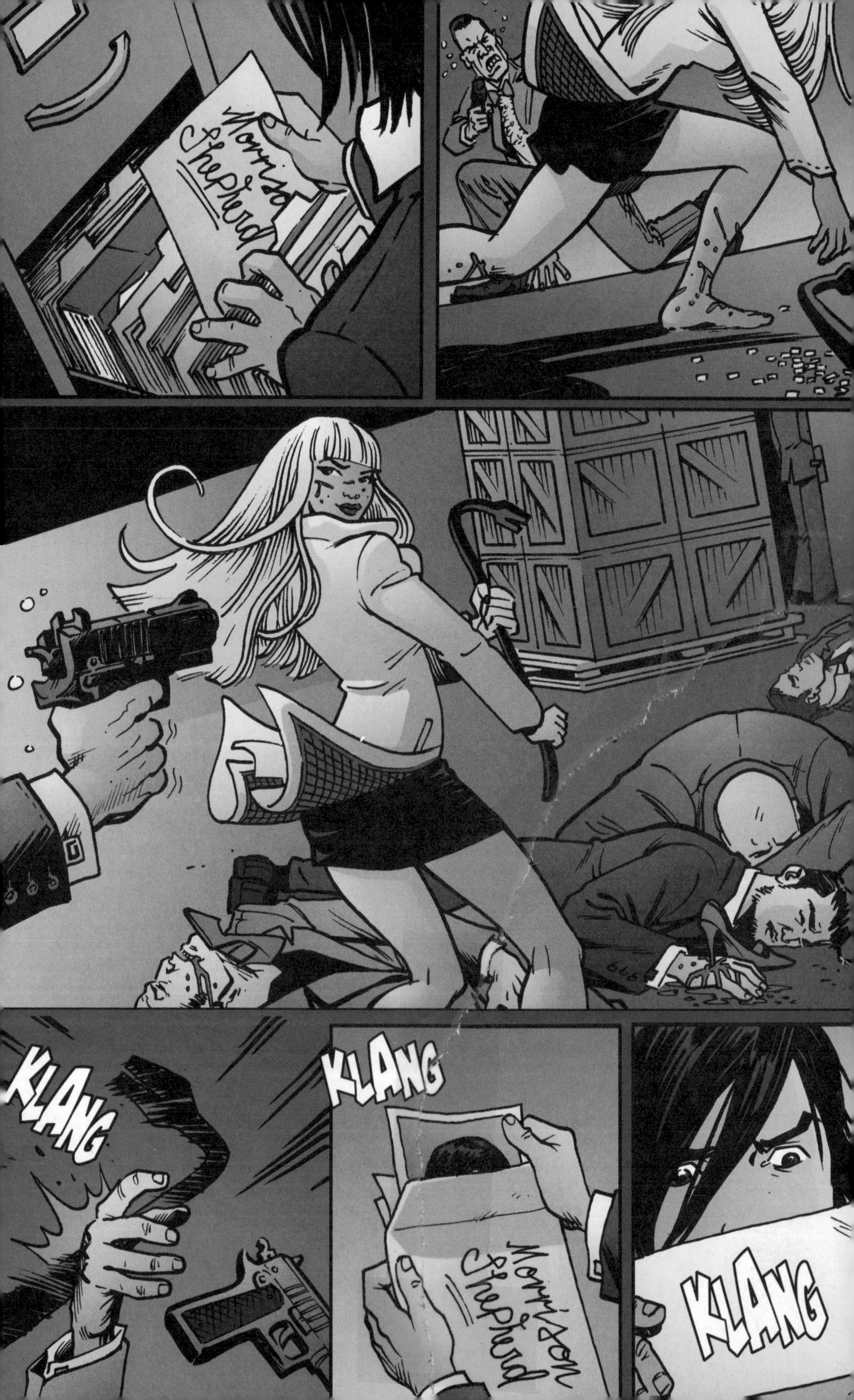
Morrison Shepherd
KLANG
KLANG
Morrison Shepherd
KLANG

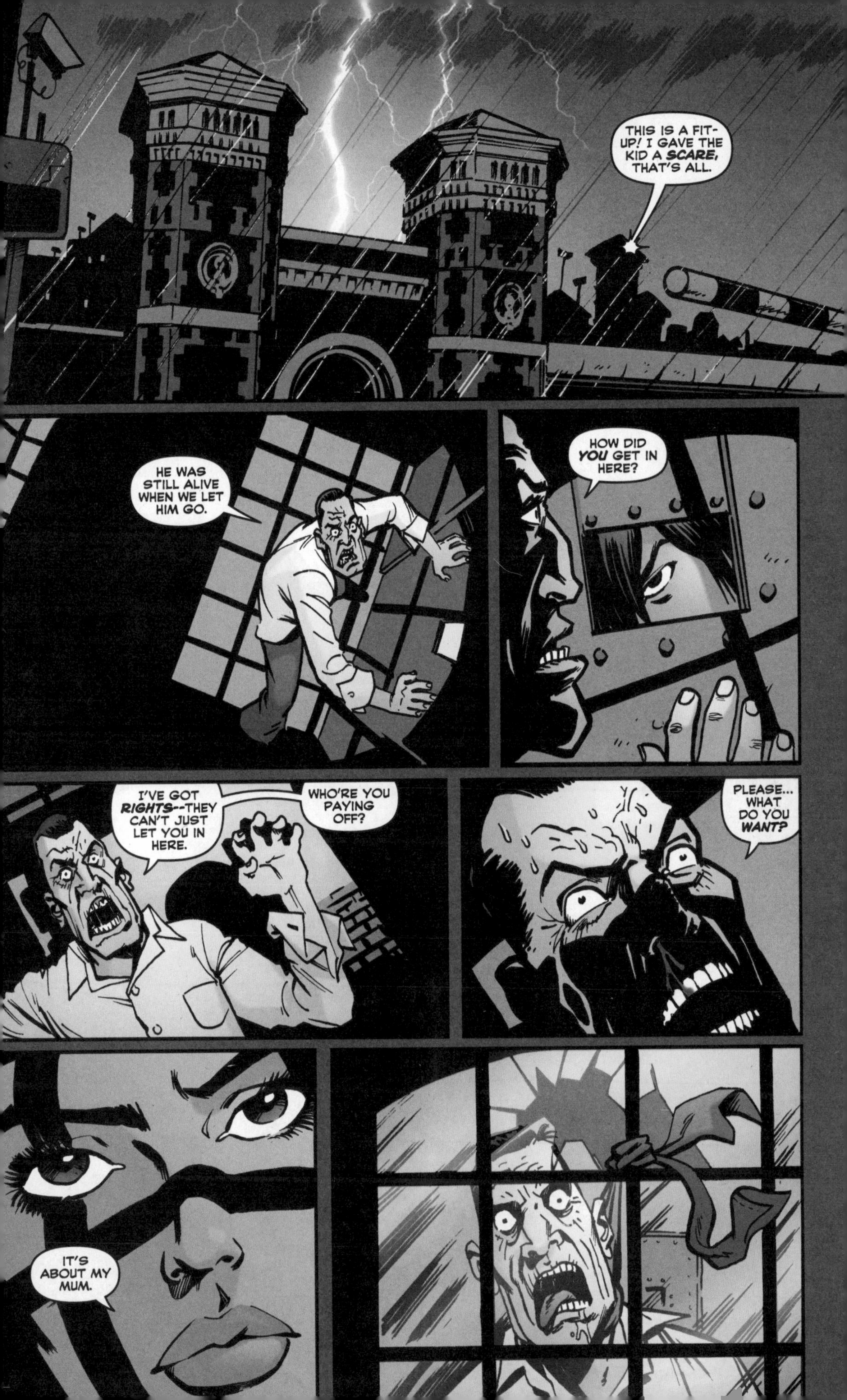
THIS IS A FIT-UP! I GAVE THE KID A SCARE, THAT'S ALL.
HE WAS STILL ALIVE WHEN WE LET HIM GO.
HOW DID YOU GET IN HERE?
I'VE GOT RIGHTS--THEY CAN'T JUST LET YOU IN HERE.
WHO'RE YOU PAYING OFF?
PLEASE... WHAT DO YOU WANT?
IT'S ABOUT MY MUM.

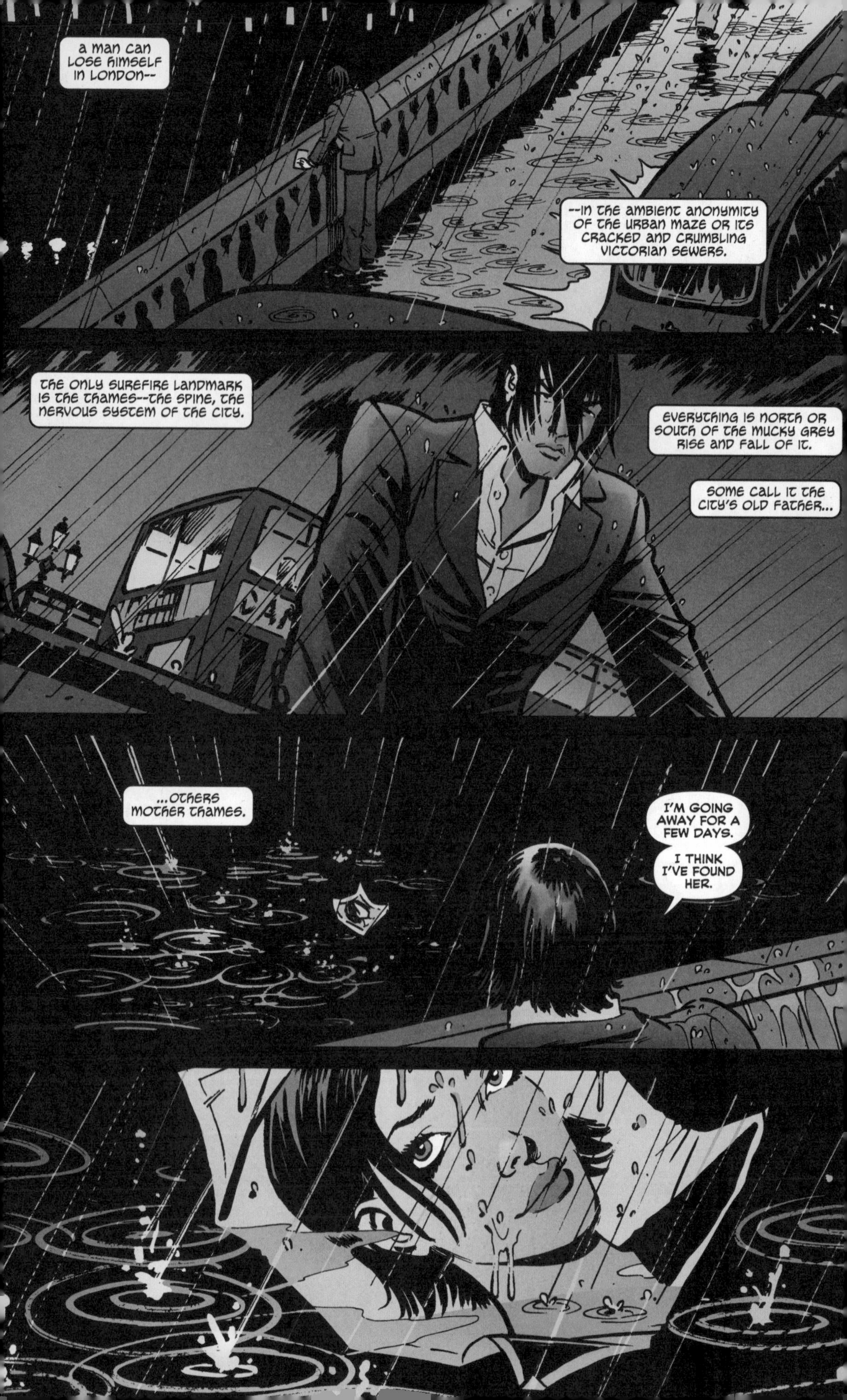
a man can lose himself in London--
--in the ambient anonymity of the urban maze or its cracked and crumbling Victorian sewers.
The only surefire landmark is the Thames--the spine, the nervous system of the city.
Everything is north or south of the mucky grey rise and fall of it.
Some call it the city's old father...
...others mother Thames.
I'M GOING AWAY FOR A FEW DAYS.
I THINK I'VE FOUND HER.

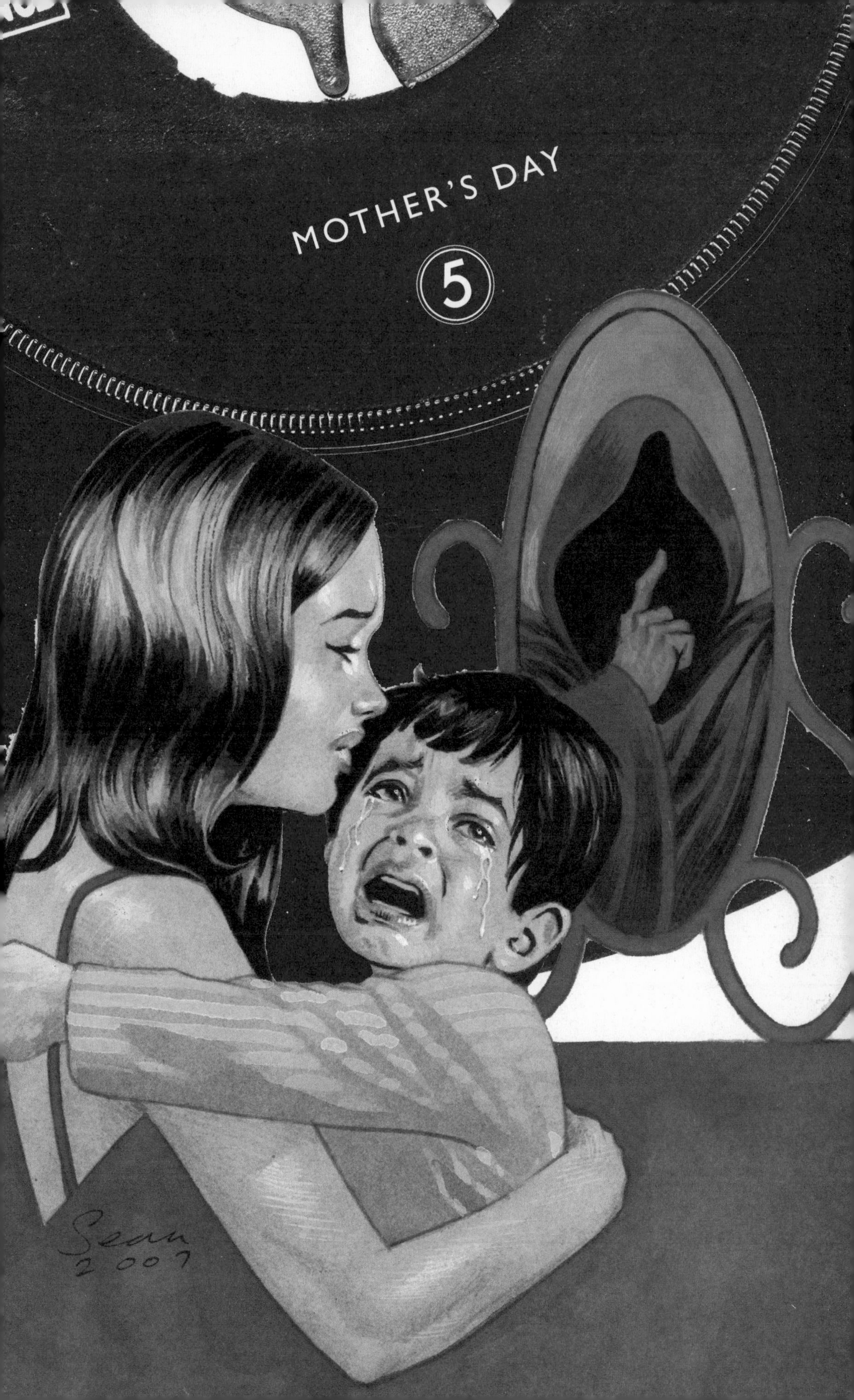
MOTHER'S DAY
5
Sean 2007

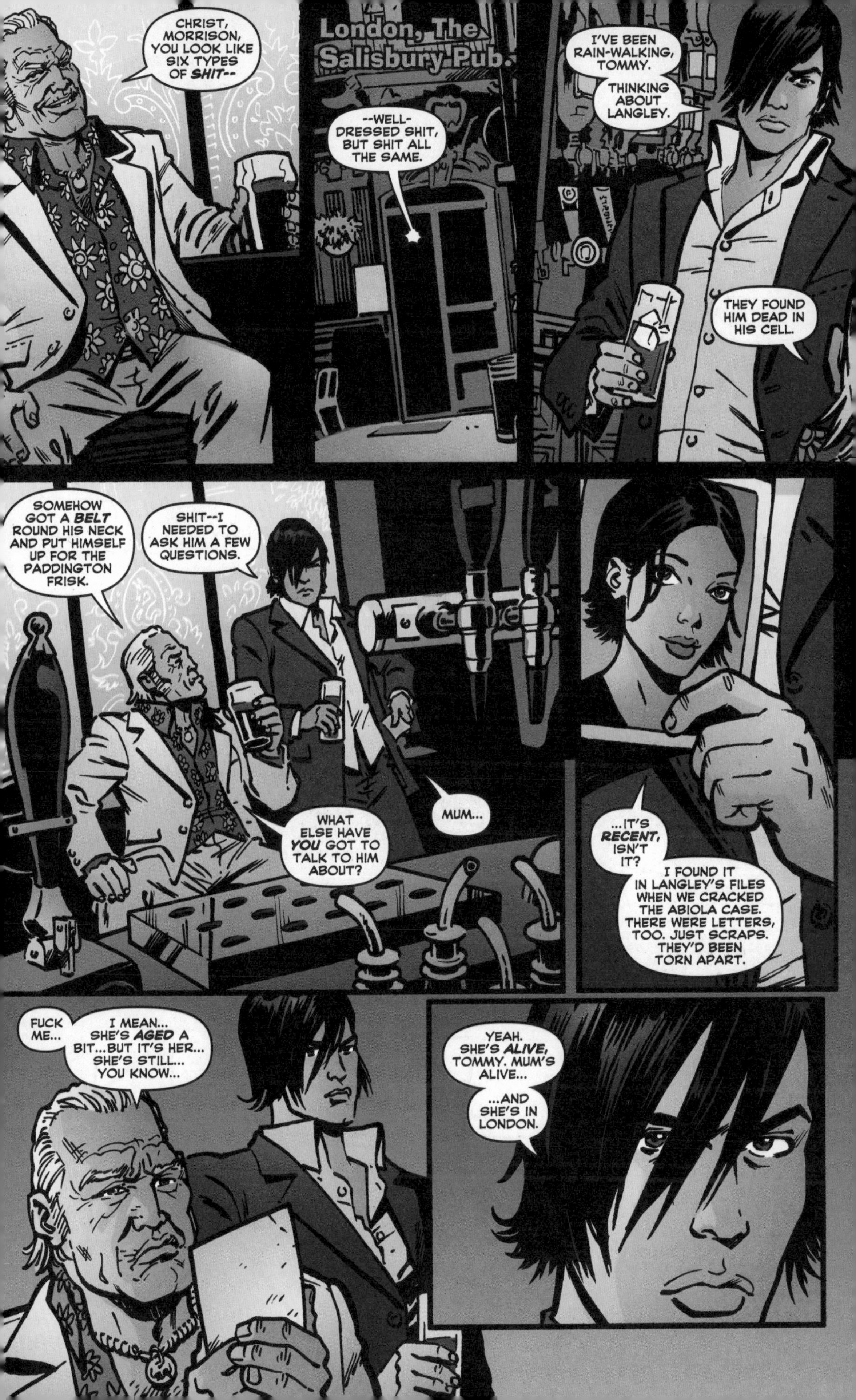
CHRIST, MORRISON, YOU LOOK LIKE SIX TYPES OF SHIT--
London, The Salisbury Pub.
--WELL-DRESSED SHIT, BUT SHIT ALL THE SAME.
I'VE BEEN RAIN-WALKING, TOMMY.
THINKING ABOUT LANGLEY.
THEY FOUND HIM DEAD IN HIS CELL.
SOMEHOW GOT A BELT ROUND HIS NECK AND PUT HIMSELF UP FOR THE PADDINGTON FRISK.
SHIT--I NEEDED TO ASK HIM A FEW QUESTIONS.
WHAT ELSE HAVE YOU GOT TO TALK TO HIM ABOUT?
MUM...
...IT'S RECENT, ISN'T IT?
I FOUND IT IN LANGLEY'S FILES WHEN WE CRACKED THE ABIOLA CASE. THERE WERE LETTERS, TOO. JUST SCRAPS. THEY'D BEEN TORN APART.
FUCK ME...
I MEAN... SHE'S AGED A BIT...BUT IT'S HER... SHE'S STILL... YOU KNOW...
YEAH. SHE'S ALIVE, TOMMY. MUM'S ALIVE...
...AND SHE'S IN LONDON.

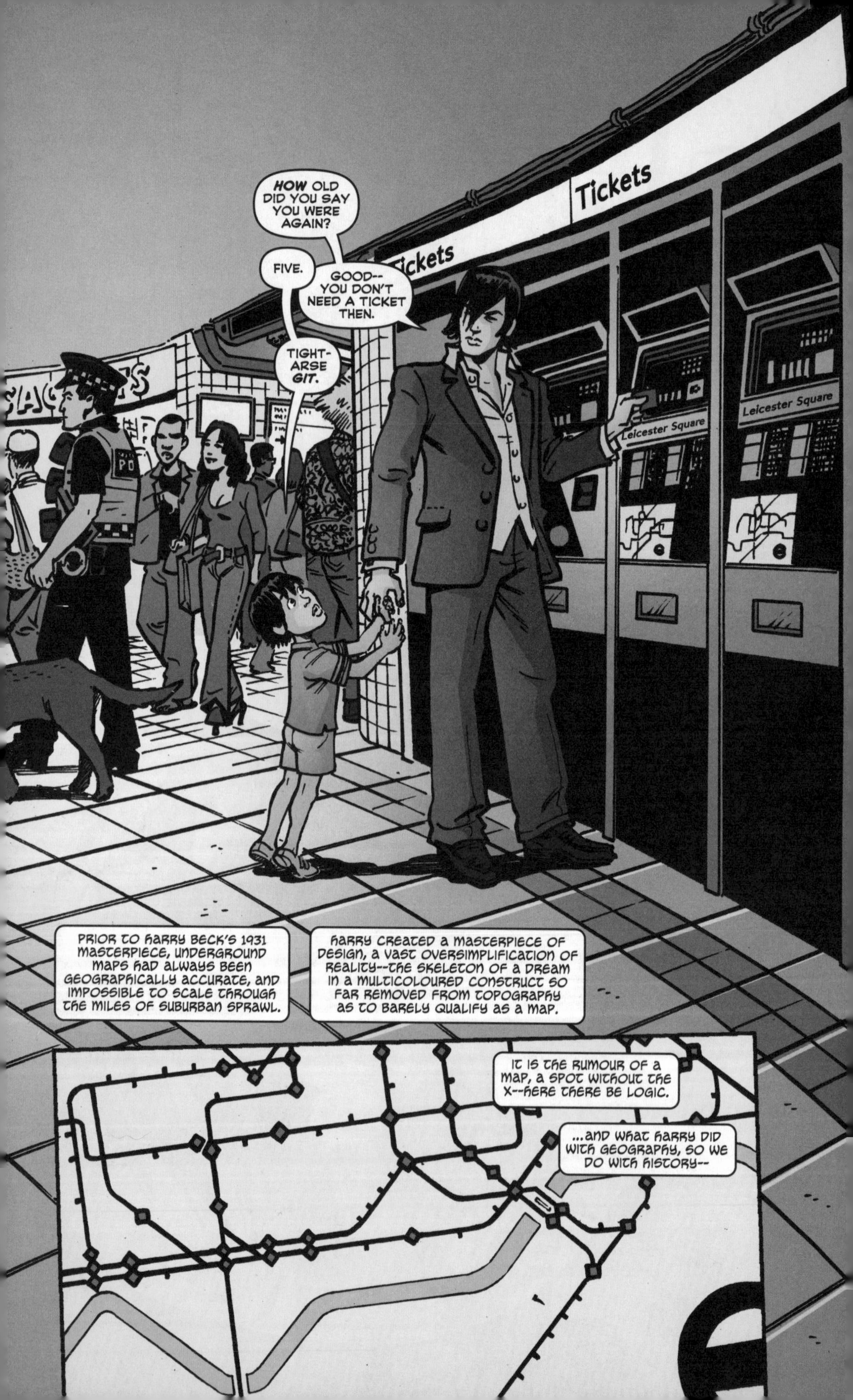

Tickets
Tickets
HOW OLD DID YOU SAY YOU WERE AGAIN?
FIVE.
GOOD-- YOU DON'T NEED A TICKET THEN.
TIGHT-ARSE GIT.
Leicester Square
Leicester Square
PRIOR TO HARRY BECK'S 1931 MASTERPIECE, UNDERGROUND MAPS HAD ALWAYS BEEN GEOGRAPHICALLY ACCURATE, AND IMPOSSIBLE TO SCALE THROUGH THE MILES OF SUBURBAN SPRAWL.
HARRY CREATED A MASTERPIECE OF DESIGN, A VAST OVERSIMPLIFICATION OF REALITY--THE SKELETON OF A DREAM IN A MULTICOLOURED CONSTRUCT SO FAR REMOVED FROM TOPOGRAPHY AS TO BARELY QUALIFY AS A MAP.
IT IS THE RUMOUR OF A MAP, A SPOT WITHOUT THE X--HERE THERE BE LOGIC.
...AND WHAT HARRY DID WITH GEOGRAPHY, SO WE DO WITH HISTORY--

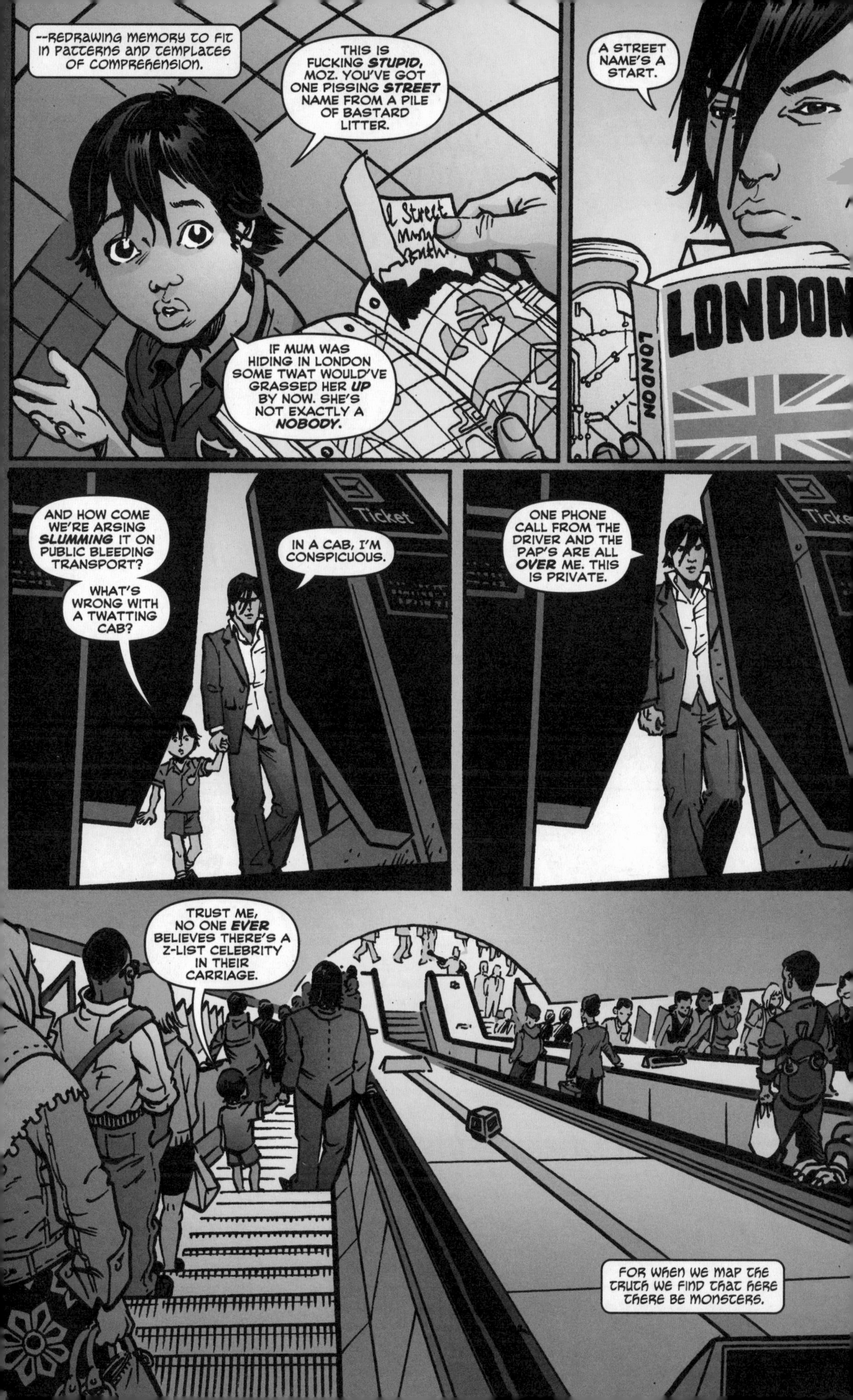
--REDRAWING MEMORY TO FIT IN PATTERNS AND TEMPLATES OF COMPREHENSION.
THIS IS FUCKING STUPID, MOZ. YOU'VE GOT ONE PISSING STREET NAME FROM A PILE OF BASTARD LITTER.
IF MUM WAS HIDING IN LONDON SOME TWAT WOULD'VE GRASSED HER UP BY NOW. SHE'S NOT EXACTLY A NOBODY.
A STREET NAME'S A START.
LONDON
LONDON
AND HOW COME WE'RE ARSING SLUMMING IT ON PUBLIC BLEEDING TRANSPORT?
WHAT'S WRONG WITH A TWATTING CAB?
Ticket
IN A CAB, I'M CONSPICUOUS.
ONE PHONE CALL FROM THE DRIVER AND THE PAP'S ARE ALL OVER ME. THIS IS PRIVATE.
TRUST ME, NO ONE EVER BELIEVES THERE'S A Z-LIST CELEBRITY IN THEIR CARRIAGE.
FOR WHEN WE MAP THE TRUTH WE FIND THAT HERE THERE BE MONSTERS.

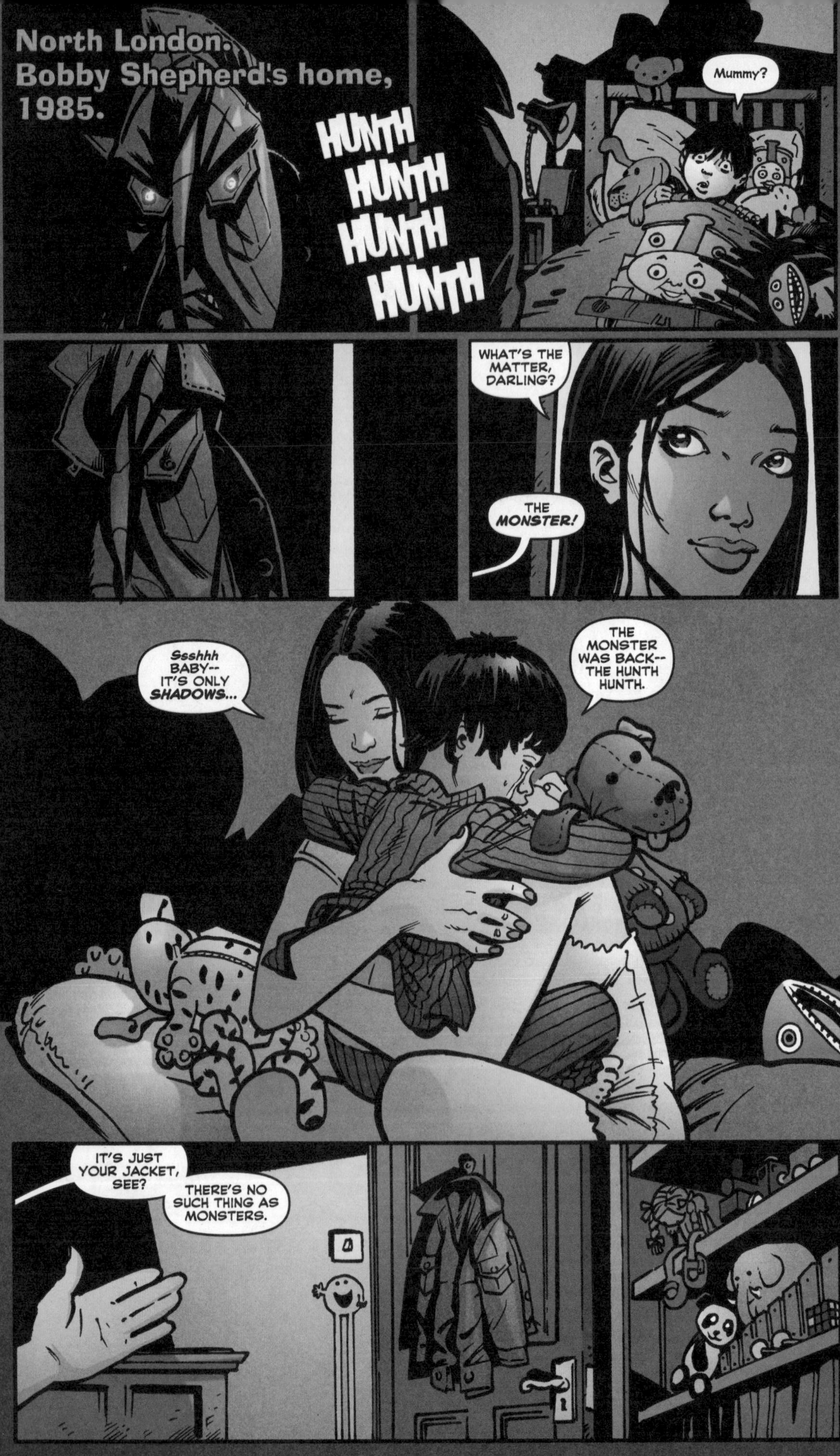
North London.
Bobby Shepherd's home, 1985.
HUNTH HUNTH HUNTH HUNTH
Mummy?
WHAT'S THE MATTER, DARLING?
THE MONSTER!
Ssshhh BABY-- IT'S ONLY SHADOWS...
THE MONSTER WAS BACK-- THE HUNTH HUNTH.
IT'S JUST YOUR JACKET, SEE?
THERE'S NO SUCH THING AS MONSTERS.

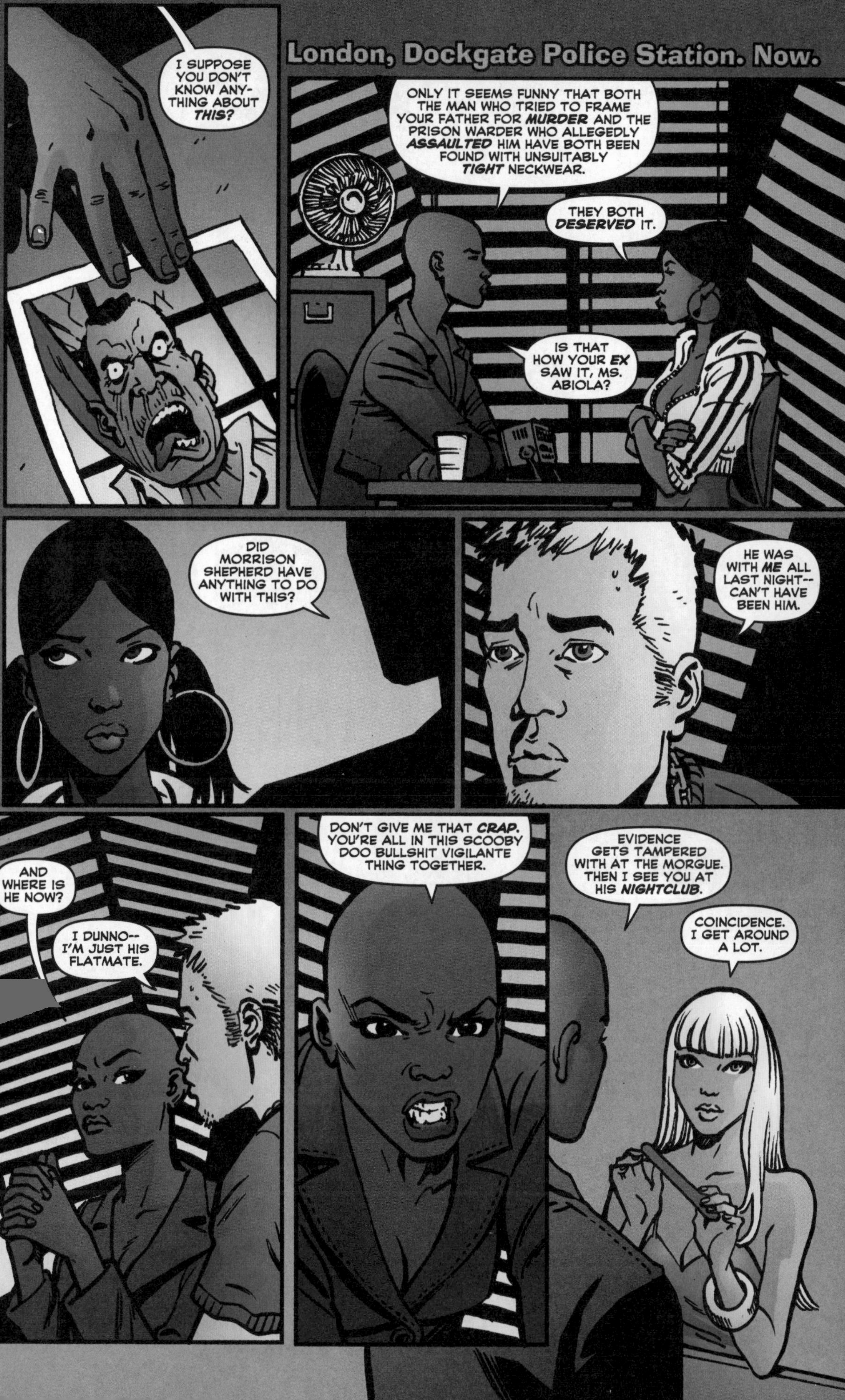
London, Dockgate Police Station. Now.
I SUPPOSE YOU DON'T KNOW ANYTHING ABOUT *THIS?*
ONLY IT SEEMS FUNNY THAT BOTH THE MAN WHO TRIED TO FRAME YOUR FATHER FOR *MURDER* AND THE PRISON WARDER WHO ALLEGEDLY *ASSAULTED* HIM HAVE BOTH BEEN FOUND WITH UNSUITABLY *TIGHT* NECKWEAR.
THEY BOTH *DESERVED* IT.
IS THAT HOW YOUR *EX* SAW IT, MS. ABIOLA?
DID MORRISON SHEPHERD HAVE ANYTHING TO DO WITH THIS?
HE WAS WITH *ME* ALL LAST NIGHT-- CAN'T HAVE BEEN HIM.
AND WHERE IS HE NOW?
I DUNNO-- I'M JUST HIS FLATMATE.
DON'T GIVE ME THAT *CRAP*. YOU'RE ALL IN THIS SCOOBY DOO BULLSHIT VIGILANTE THING TOGETHER.
EVIDENCE GETS TAMPERED WITH AT THE MORGUE. THEN I SEE YOU AT HIS *NIGHTCLUB*.
COINCIDENCE. I GET AROUND A LOT.

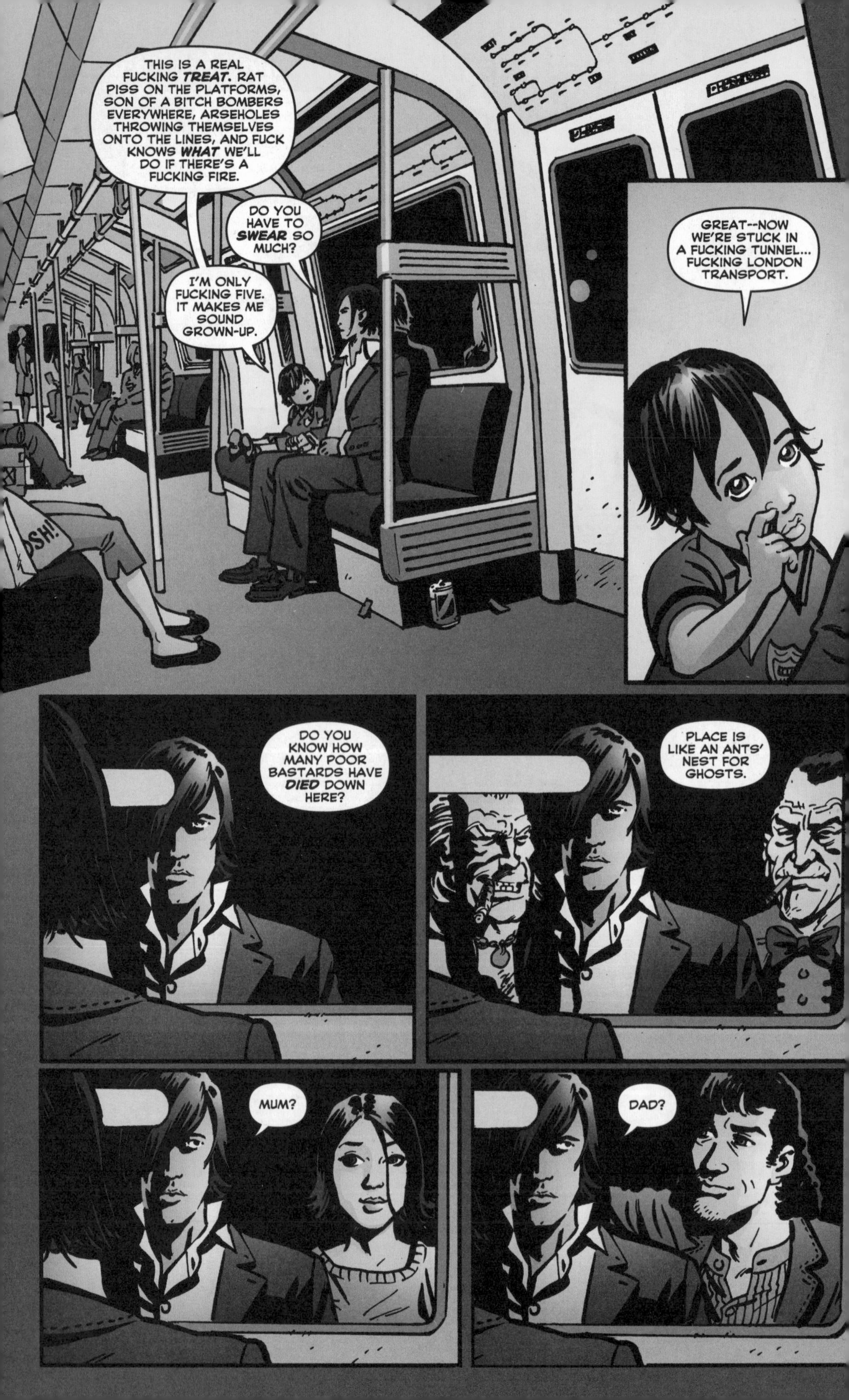
THIS IS A REAL FUCKING *TREAT.* RAT PISS ON THE PLATFORMS, SON OF A BITCH BOMBERS EVERYWHERE, ARSEHOLES THROWING THEMSELVES ONTO THE LINES, AND FUCK KNOWS *WHAT* WE'LL DO IF THERE'S A FUCKING FIRE.
DO YOU HAVE TO *SWEAR* SO MUCH?
I'M ONLY FUCKING FIVE. IT MAKES ME SOUND GROWN-UP.
GREAT--NOW WE'RE STUCK IN A FUCKING TUNNEL... FUCKING LONDON TRANSPORT.
DO YOU KNOW HOW MANY POOR BASTARDS HAVE *DIED* DOWN HERE?
PLACE IS LIKE AN ANTS' NEST FOR GHOSTS.
MUM?
DAD?

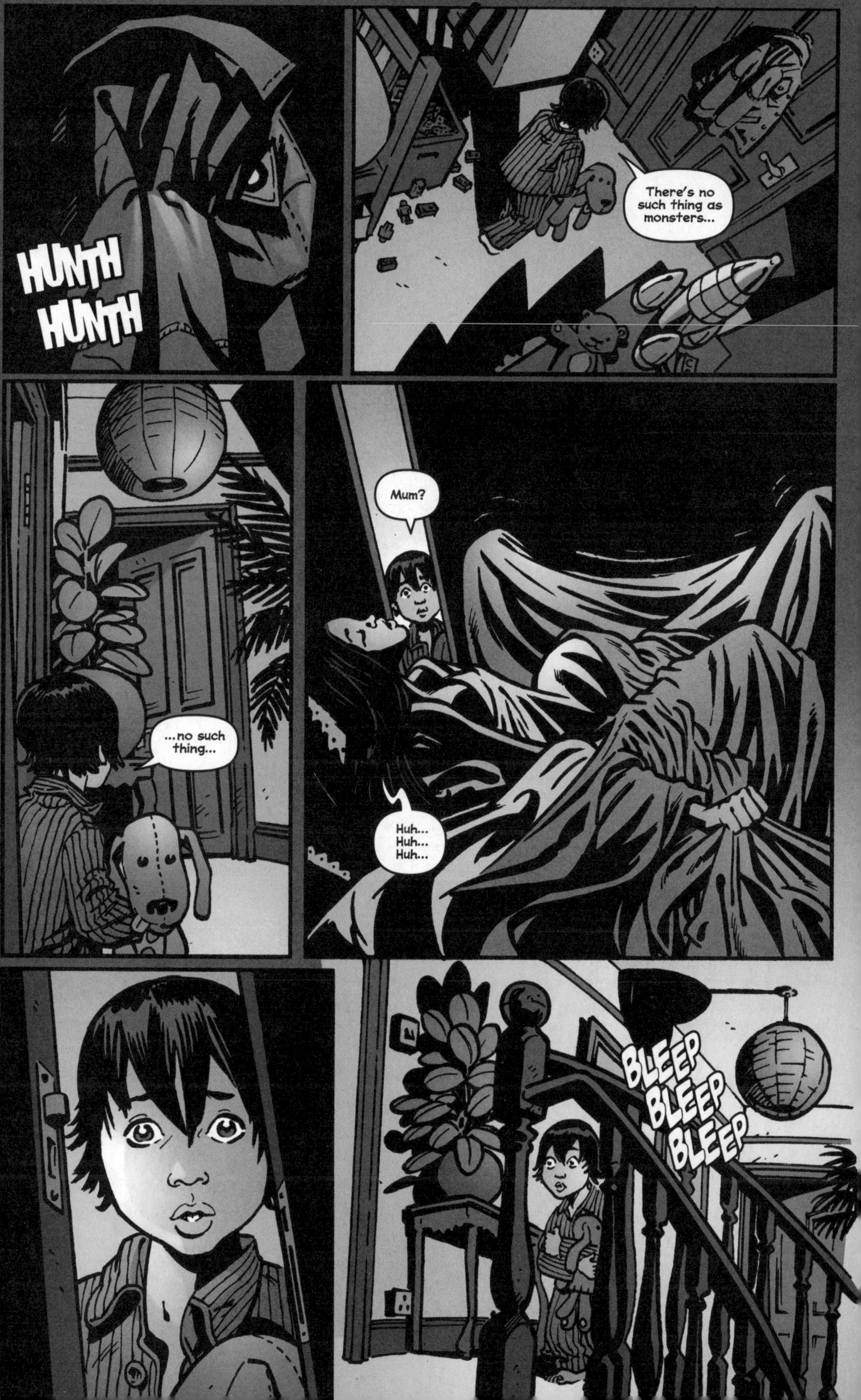
HUNTH
HUNTH
There's no such thing as monsters...
...no such thing...
Mum?
Huh... Huh... Huh...
BLEEP
BLEEP
BLEEP

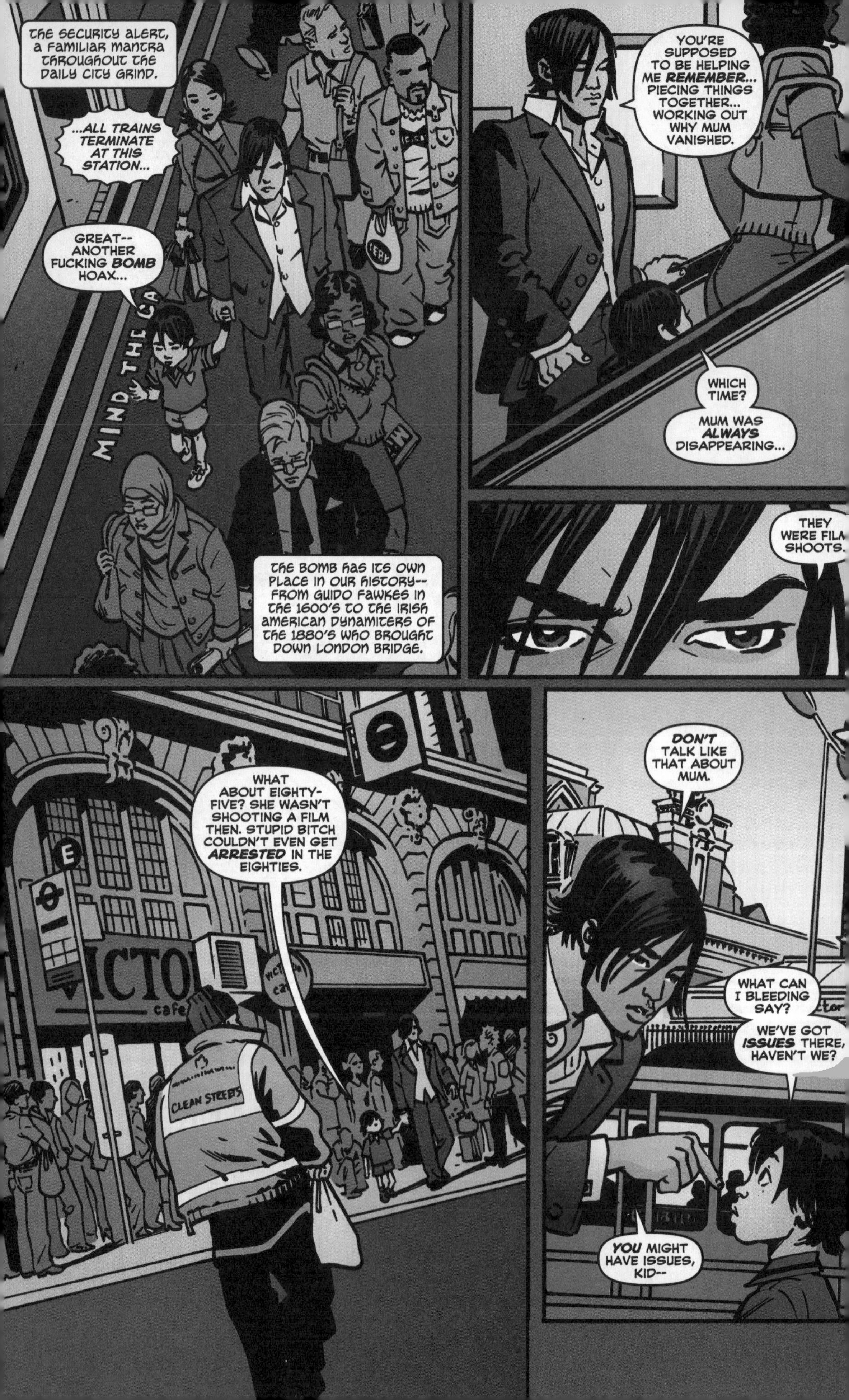
THE SECURITY ALERT, A FAMILIAR MANTRA THROUGHOUT THE DAILY CITY GRIND.
...ALL TRAINS TERMINATE AT THIS STATION...
GREAT-- ANOTHER FUCKING BOMB HOAX...
MIND THE GA
THE BOMB HAS ITS OWN PLACE IN OUR HISTORY-- FROM GUIDO FAWKES IN THE 1600'S TO THE IRISH AMERICAN DYNAMITERS OF THE 1880'S WHO BROUGHT DOWN LONDON BRIDGE.
YOU'RE SUPPOSED TO BE HELPING ME REMEMBER... PIECING THINGS TOGETHER... WORKING OUT WHY MUM VANISHED.
WHICH TIME?
MUM WAS ALWAYS DISAPPEARING...
THEY WERE FILM SHOOTS.
WHAT ABOUT EIGHTY-FIVE? SHE WASN'T SHOOTING A FILM THEN. STUPID BITCH COULDN'T EVEN GET ARRESTED IN THE EIGHTIES.
E
VICTO
cafe
CLEAN STREETS
DON'T TALK LIKE THAT ABOUT MUM.
WHAT CAN I BLEEDING SAY?
WE'VE GOT ISSUES THERE, HAVEN'T WE?
YOU MIGHT HAVE ISSUES, KID--

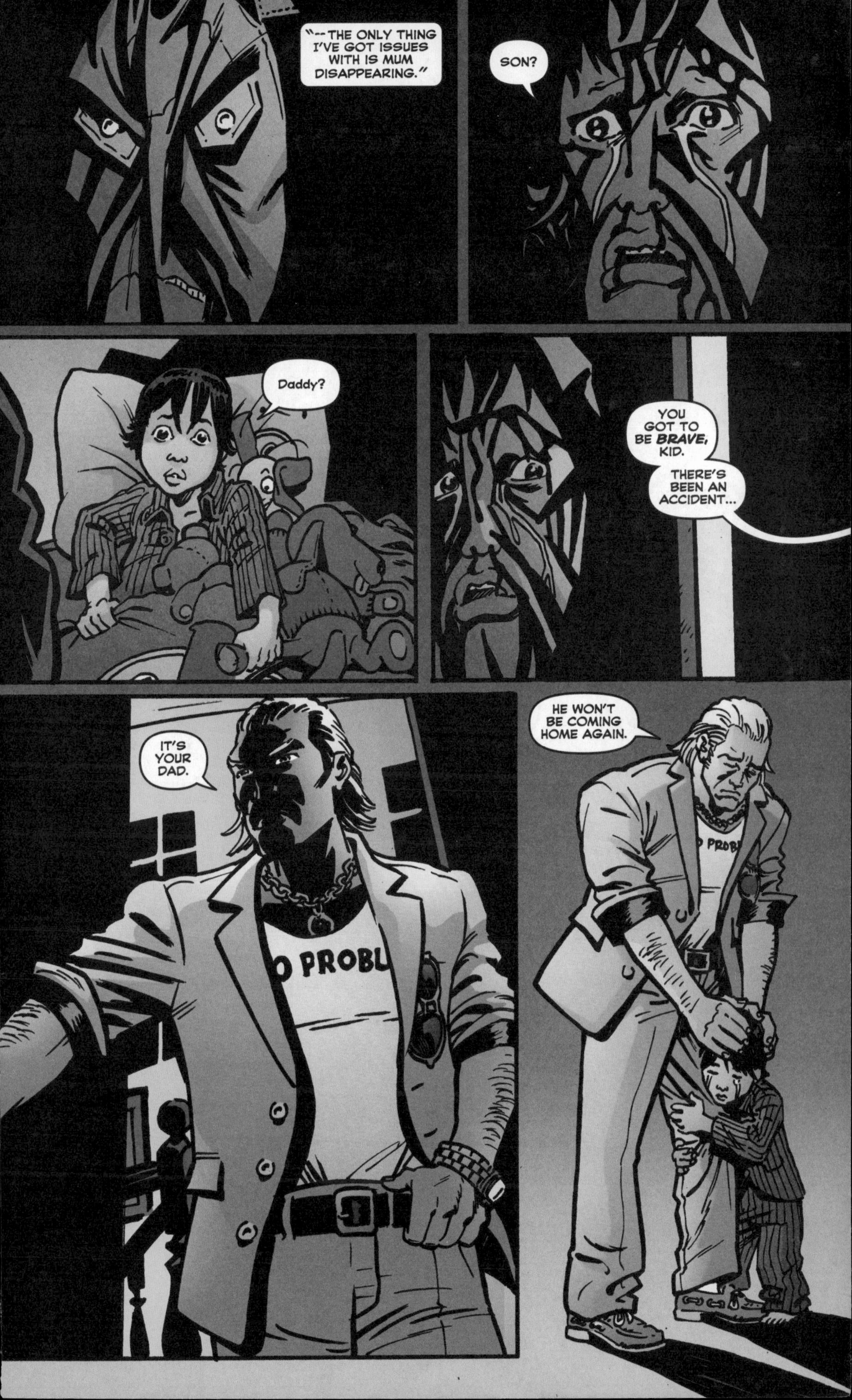
"--THE ONLY THING I'VE GOT ISSUES WITH IS MUM DISAPPEARING."
SON?
Daddy?
YOU GOT TO BE *BRAVE,* KID.
THERE'S BEEN AN ACCIDENT...
IT'S YOUR DAD.
HE WON'T BE COMING HOME AGAIN.
O PROBL
O PROB

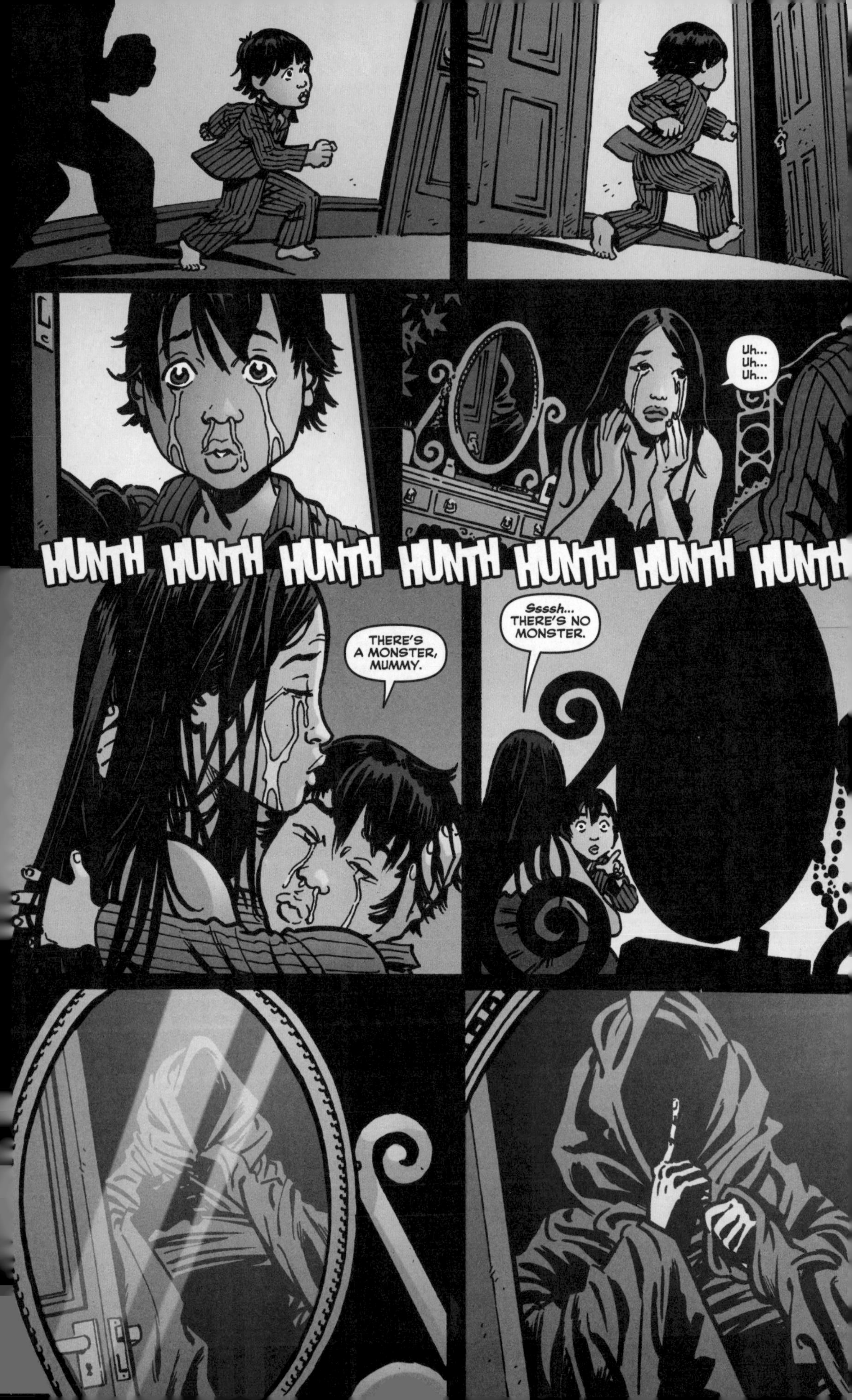
Uh...
Uh...
Uh...
HUNTH HUNTH HUNTH HUNTH HUNTH HUNTH HUNTH
THERE'S A MONSTER, MUMMY.
Ssssh... THERE'S NO MONSTER.

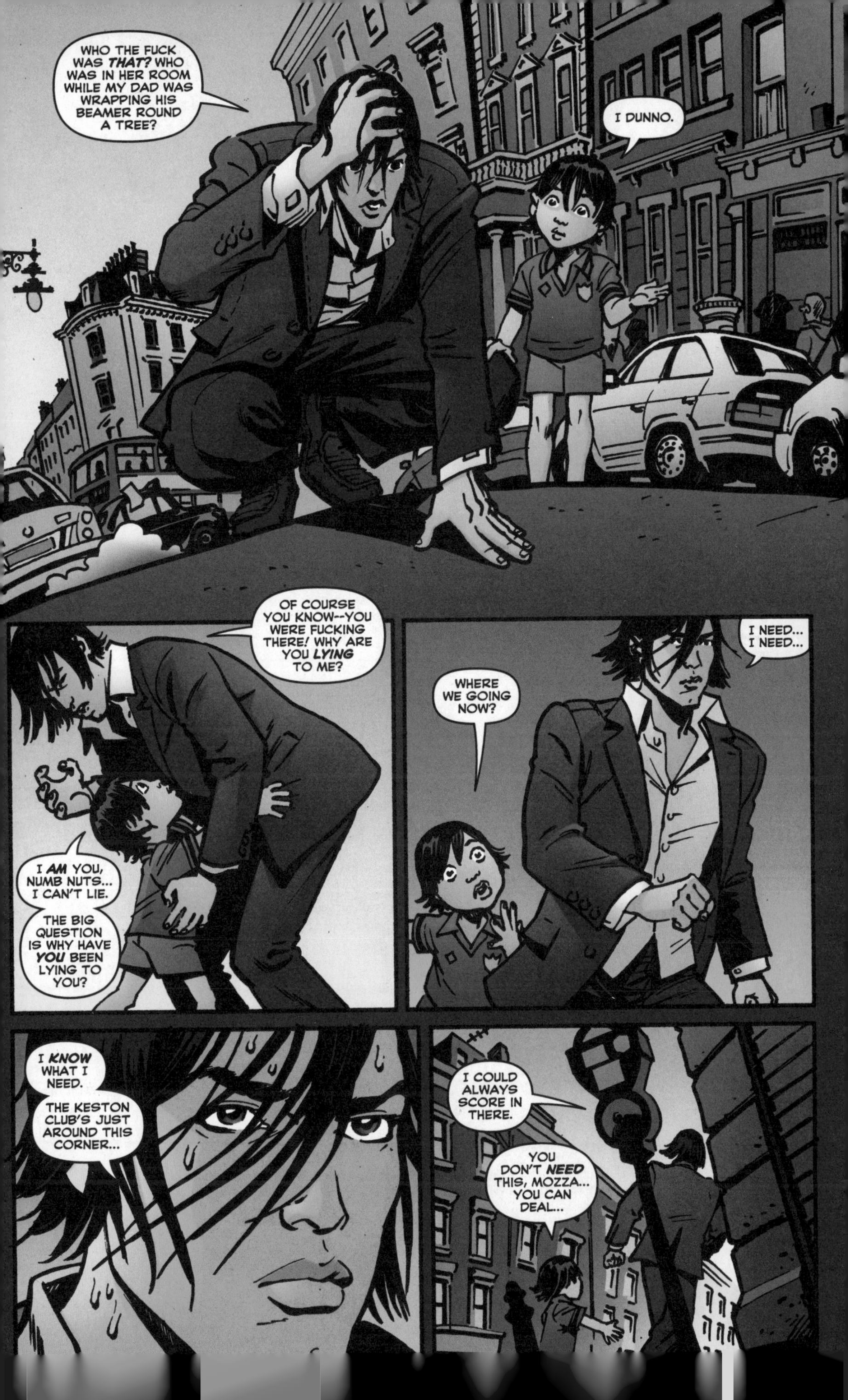
WHO THE FUCK WAS *THAT?* WHO WAS IN HER ROOM WHILE MY DAD WAS WRAPPING HIS BEAMER ROUND A TREE?
I DUNNO.
OF COURSE YOU KNOW--YOU WERE FUCKING THERE! WHY ARE YOU *LYING* TO ME?
I *AM* YOU, NUMB NUTS... I CAN'T LIE.
THE BIG QUESTION IS WHY HAVE *YOU* BEEN LYING TO YOU?
I NEED... I NEED...
WHERE WE GOING NOW?
I *KNOW* WHAT I NEED.
THE KESTON CLUB'S JUST AROUND THIS CORNER...
I COULD ALWAYS SCORE IN THERE.
YOU DON'T *NEED* THIS, MOZZA... YOU CAN DEAL...

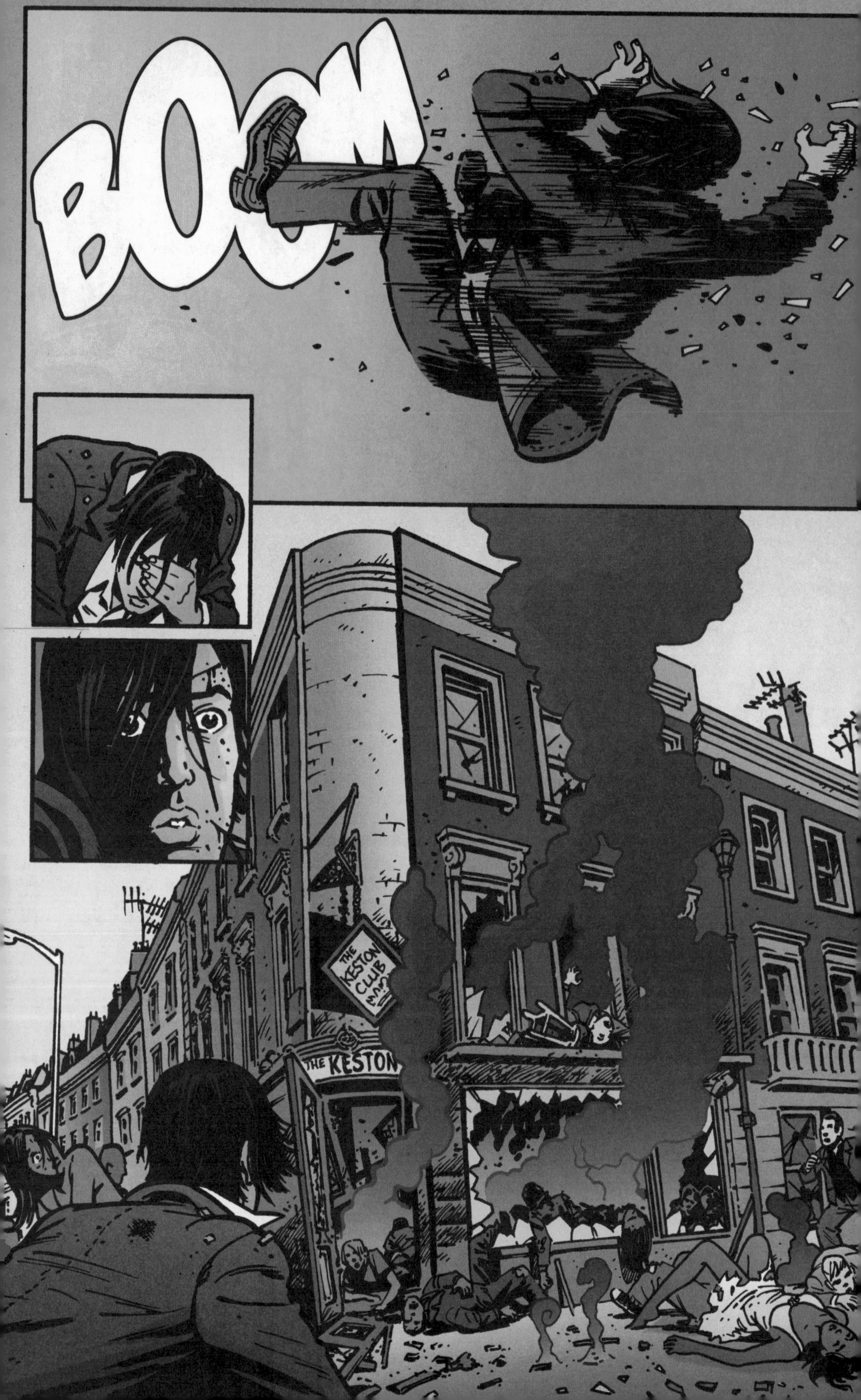
BOOM
THE KESTON CLUB
THE KESTON

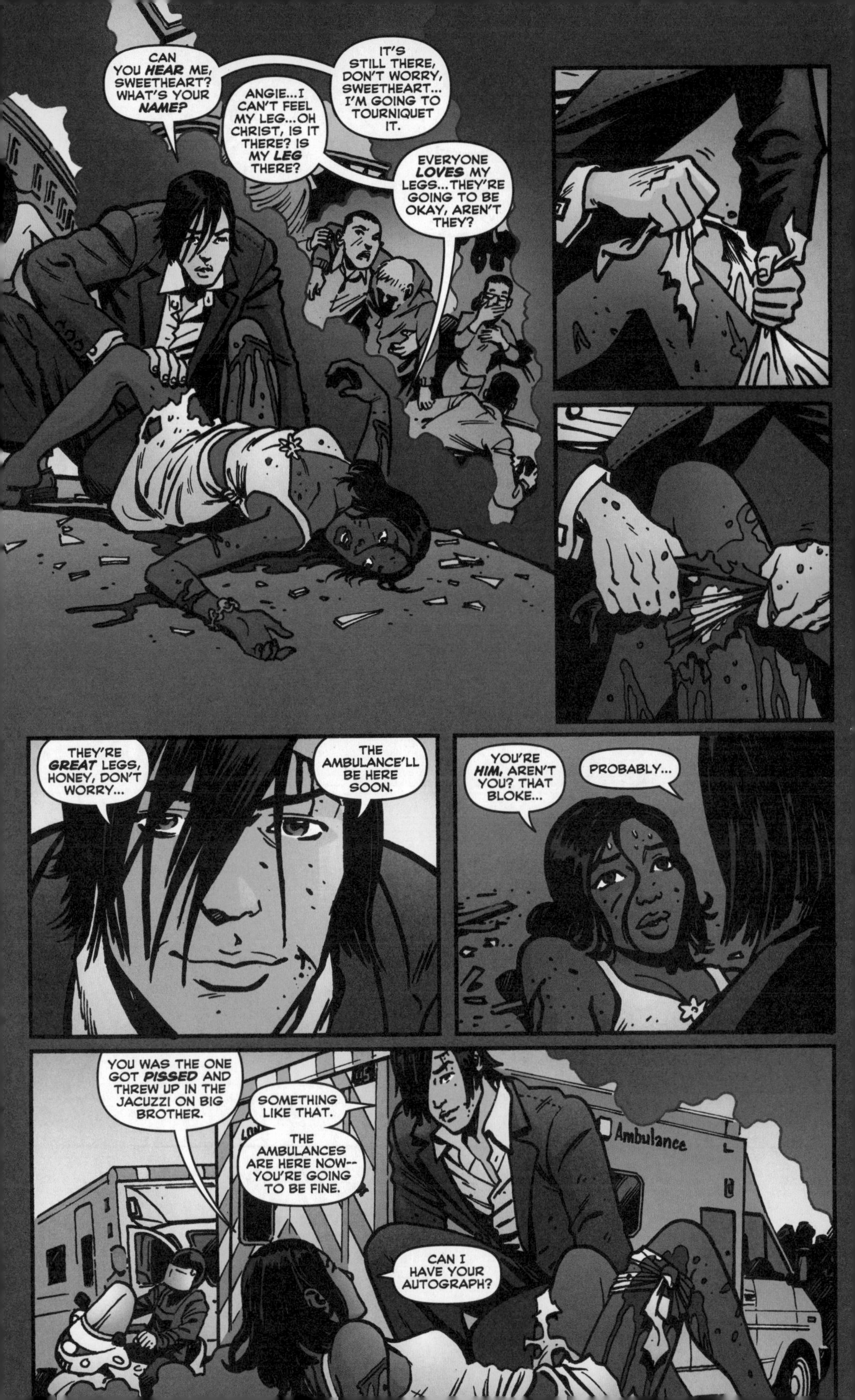
CAN YOU HEAR ME, SWEETHEART? WHAT'S YOUR NAME?
ANGIE...I CAN'T FEEL MY LEG...OH CHRIST, IS IT THERE? IS MY LEG THERE?
IT'S STILL THERE, DON'T WORRY, SWEETHEART... I'M GOING TO TOURNIQUET IT.
EVERYONE LOVES MY LEGS...THEY'RE GOING TO BE OKAY, AREN'T THEY?
THEY'RE GREAT LEGS, HONEY, DON'T WORRY...
THE AMBULANCE'LL BE HERE SOON.
YOU'RE HIM, AREN'T YOU? THAT BLOKE...
PROBABLY...
YOU WAS THE ONE GOT PISSED AND THREW UP IN THE JACUZZI ON BIG BROTHER.
SOMETHING LIKE THAT.
THE AMBULANCES ARE HERE NOW-- YOU'RE GOING TO BE FINE.
Ambulance
CAN I HAVE YOUR AUTOGRAPH?

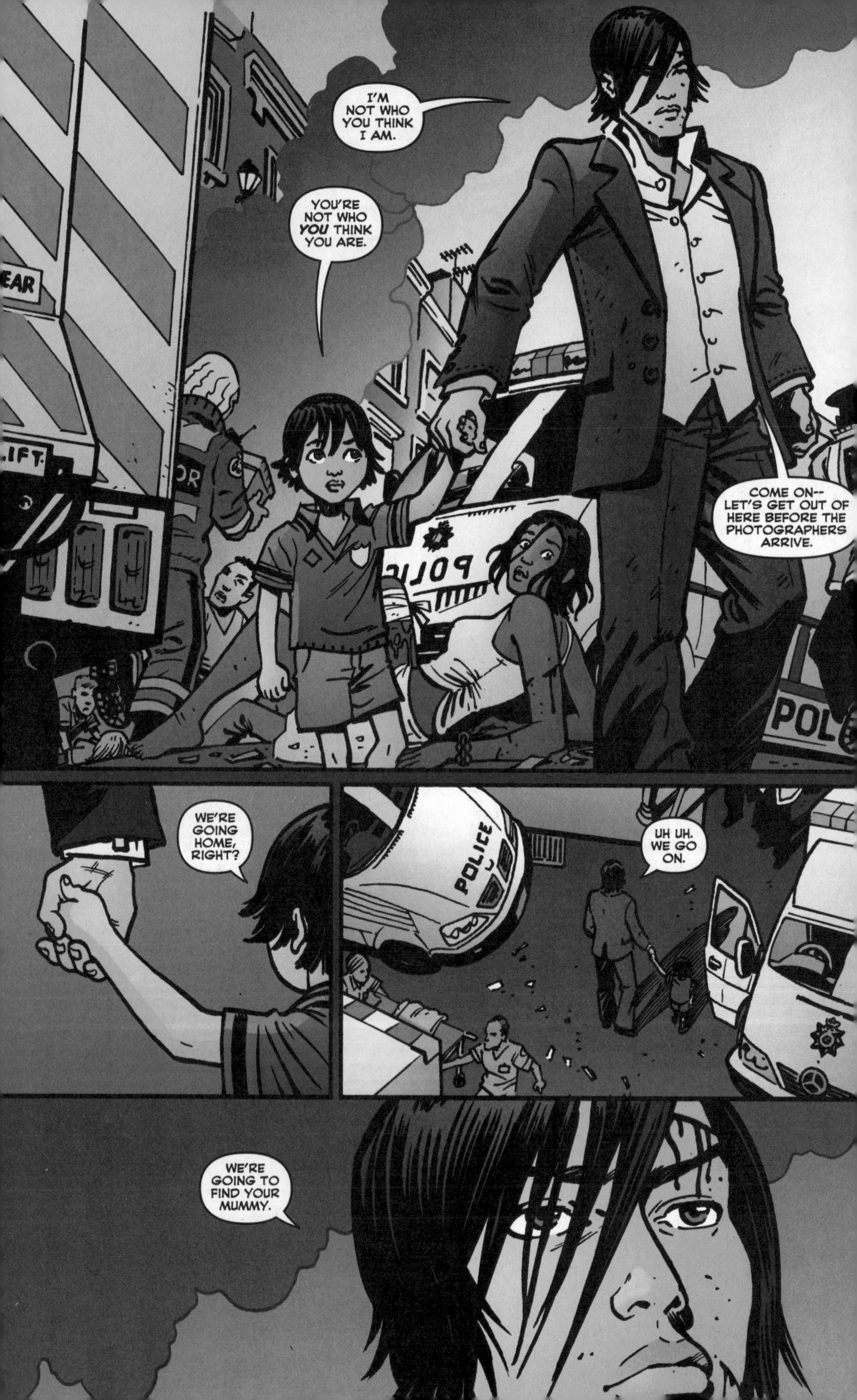
I'M NOT WHO YOU THINK I AM.
YOU'RE NOT WHO YOU THINK YOU ARE.
COME ON-- LET'S GET OUT OF HERE BEFORE THE PHOTOGRAPHERS ARRIVE.
WE'RE GOING HOME, RIGHT?
UH UH. WE GO ON.
WE'RE GOING TO FIND YOUR MUMMY.

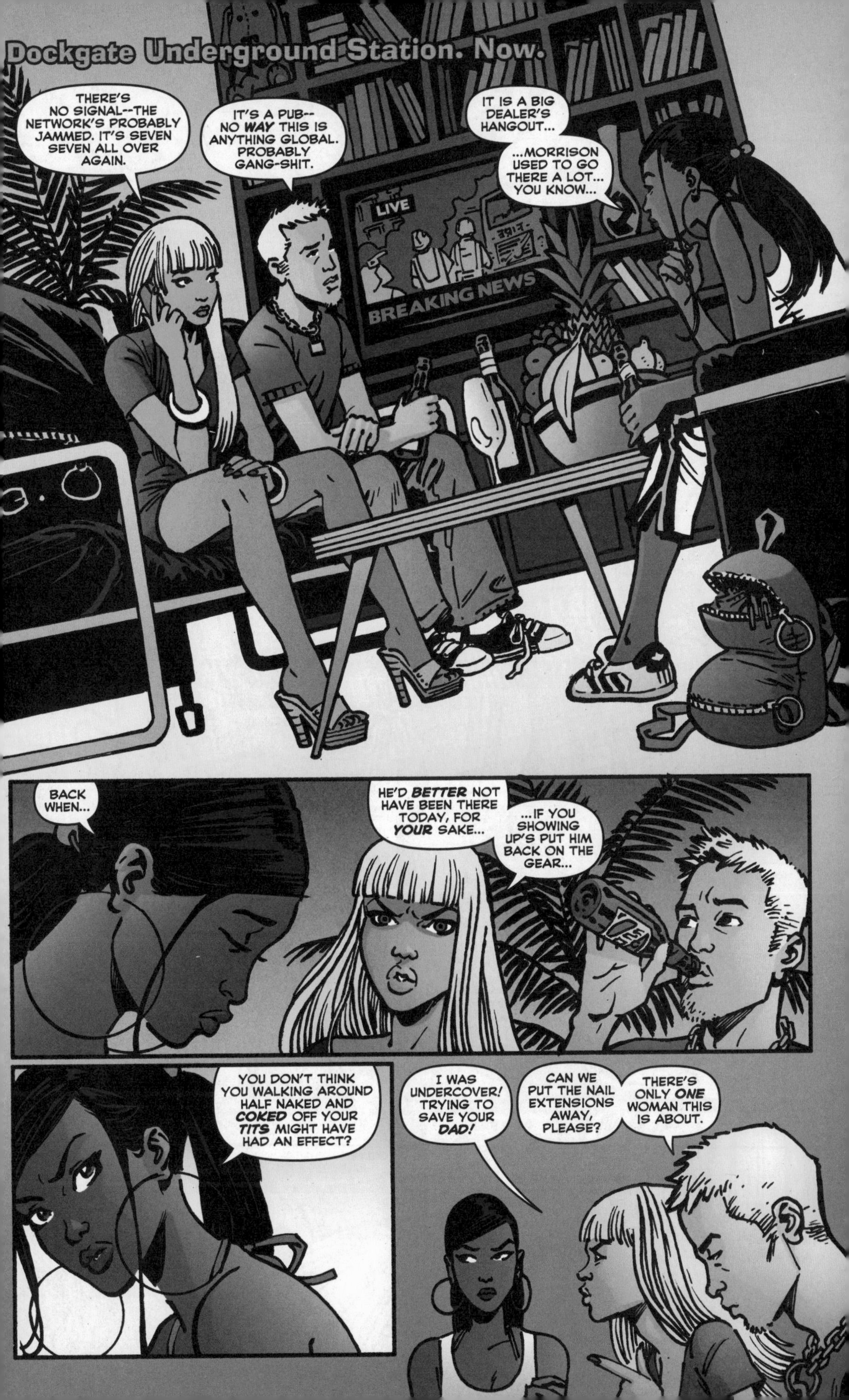
Dockgate Underground Station. Now.
THERE'S NO SIGNAL--THE NETWORK'S PROBABLY JAMMED. IT'S SEVEN SEVEN ALL OVER AGAIN.
IT'S A PUB-- NO WAY THIS IS ANYTHING GLOBAL. PROBABLY GANG-SHIT.
IT IS A BIG DEALER'S HANGOUT...
...MORRISON USED TO GO THERE A LOT... YOU KNOW...
LIVE
BREAKING NEWS
BACK WHEN...
HE'D BETTER NOT HAVE BEEN THERE TODAY, FOR YOUR SAKE...
...IF YOU SHOWING UP'S PUT HIM BACK ON THE GEAR...
YOU DON'T THINK YOU WALKING AROUND HALF NAKED AND COKED OFF YOUR TITS MIGHT HAVE HAD AN EFFECT?
I WAS UNDERCOVER! TRYING TO SAVE YOUR DAD!
CAN WE PUT THE NAIL EXTENSIONS AWAY, PLEASE?
THERE'S ONLY ONE WOMAN THIS IS ABOUT.

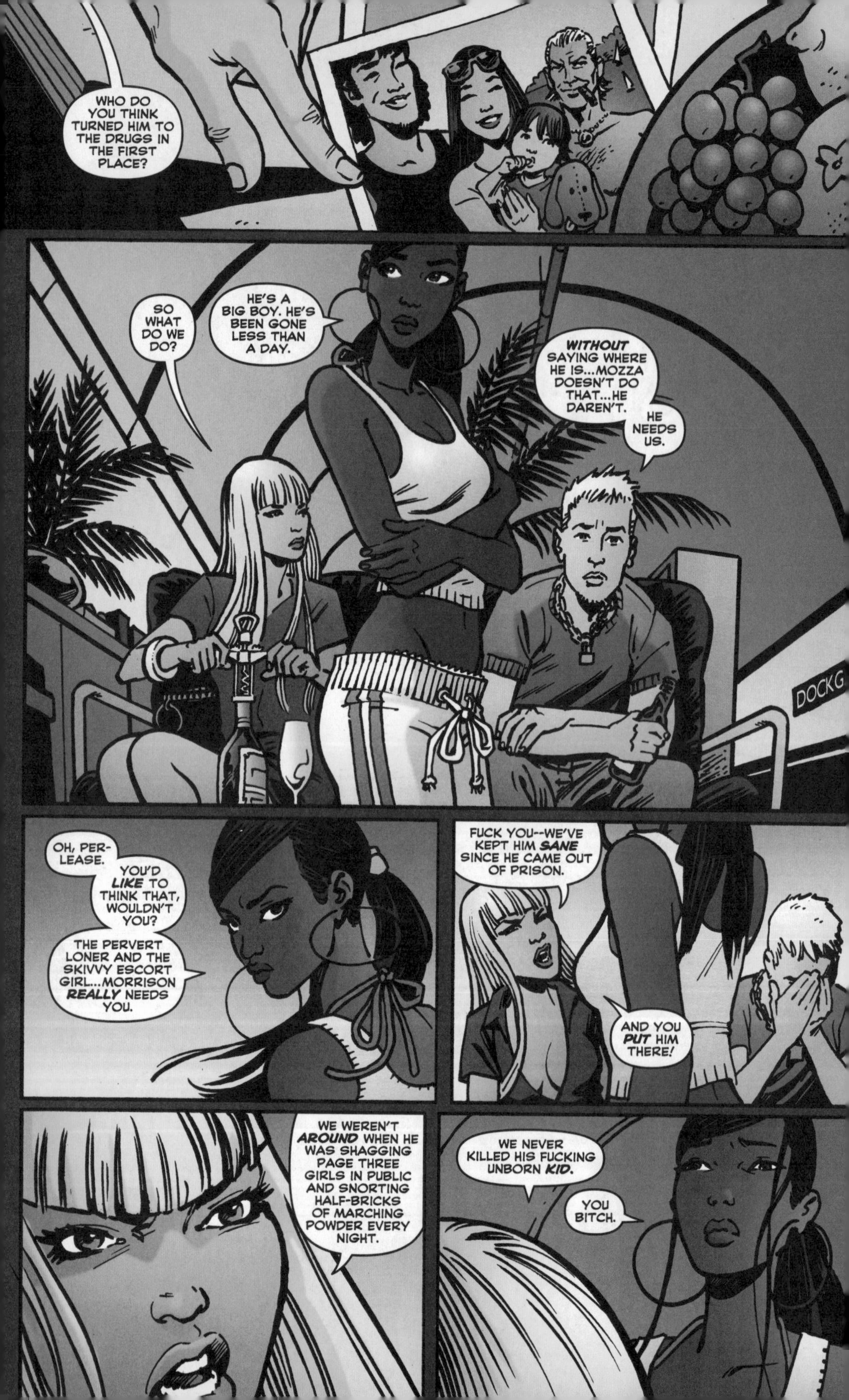
WHO DO YOU THINK TURNED HIM TO THE DRUGS IN THE FIRST PLACE?
SO WHAT DO WE DO?
HE'S A BIG BOY. HE'S BEEN GONE LESS THAN A DAY.
WITHOUT SAYING WHERE HE IS...MOZZA DOESN'T DO THAT...HE DAREN'T.
HE NEEDS US.
DOCKG
OH, PER-LEASE.
YOU'D LIKE TO THINK THAT, WOULDN'T YOU?
THE PERVERT LONER AND THE SKIVVY ESCORT GIRL...MORRISON REALLY NEEDS YOU.
FUCK YOU--WE'VE KEPT HIM SANE SINCE HE CAME OUT OF PRISON.
AND YOU PUT HIM THERE!
WE WEREN'T AROUND WHEN HE WAS SHAGGING PAGE THREE GIRLS IN PUBLIC AND SNORTING HALF-BRICKS OF MARCHING POWDER EVERY NIGHT.
WE NEVER KILLED HIS FUCKING UNBORN KID.
YOU BITCH.

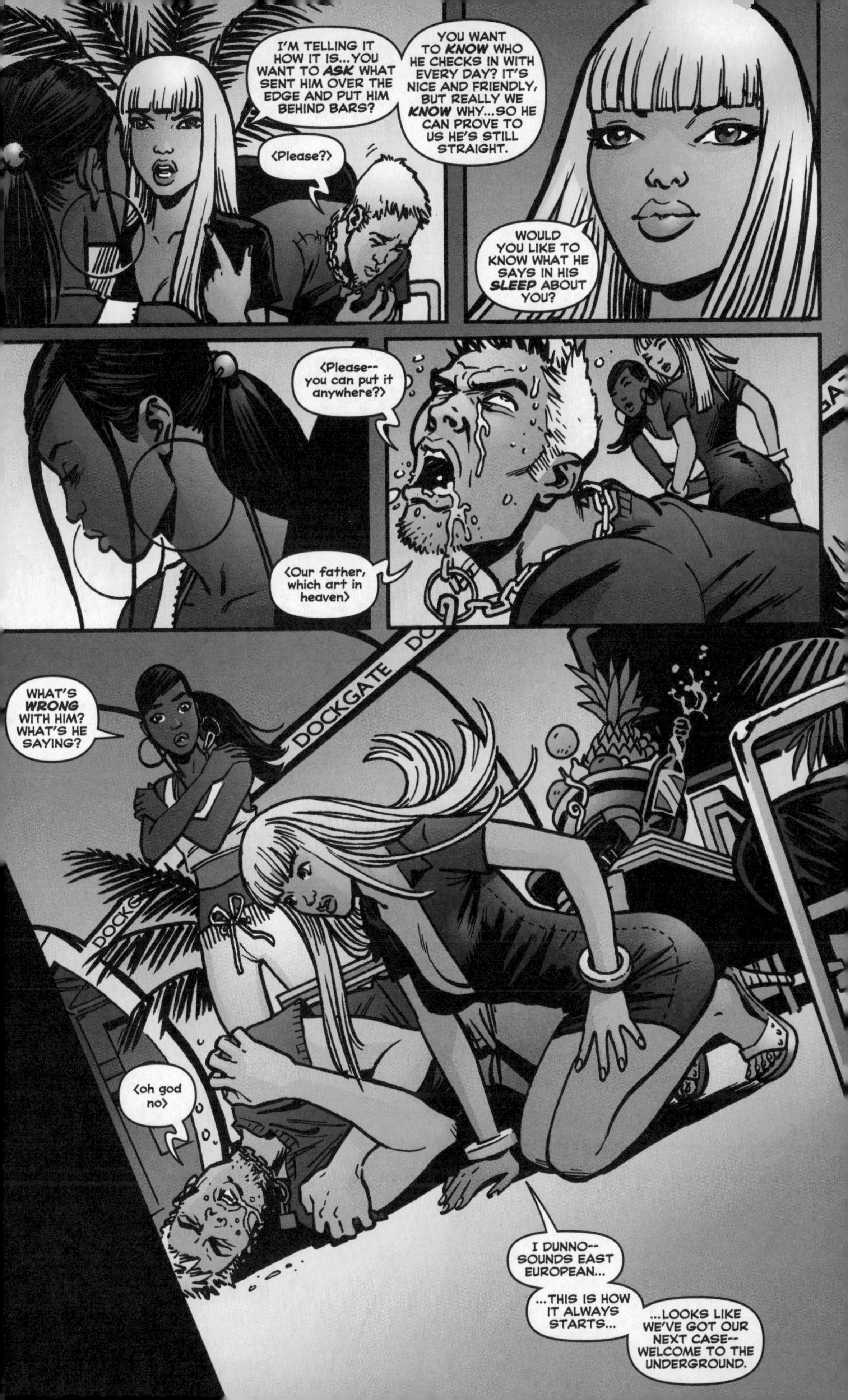
I'M TELLING IT HOW IT IS...YOU WANT TO ASK WHAT SENT HIM OVER THE EDGE AND PUT HIM BEHIND BARS?
YOU WANT TO KNOW WHO HE CHECKS IN WITH EVERY DAY? IT'S NICE AND FRIENDLY, BUT REALLY WE KNOW WHY...SO HE CAN PROVE TO US HE'S STILL STRAIGHT.
<Please?>
WOULD YOU LIKE TO KNOW WHAT HE SAYS IN HIS SLEEP ABOUT YOU?
<Please-- you can put it anywhere?>
<Our father, which art in heaven>
DOCKGATE
WHAT'S WRONG WITH HIM? WHAT'S HE SAYING?
<oh god no>
I DUNNO-- SOUNDS EAST EUROPEAN...
...THIS IS HOW IT ALWAYS STARTS...
...LOOKS LIKE WE'VE GOT OUR NEXT CASE-- WELCOME TO THE UNDERGROUND.

God forgive them for I shall not...
WHAT IS IT, PERV? WHAT CAN YOU SEE?
God forgive them for I shall not...
AND WHERE THE FUCK IS MORRISON?

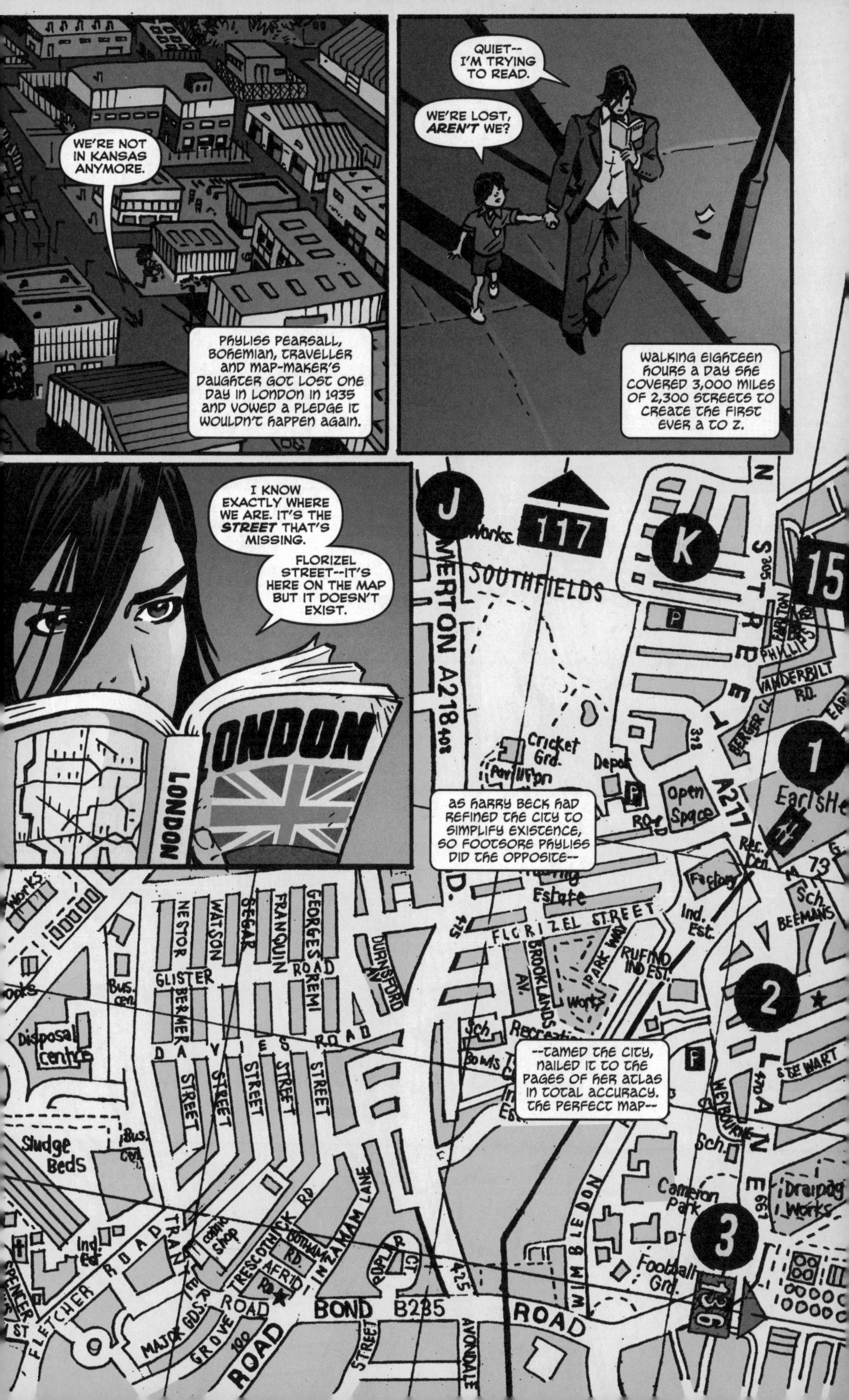
WE'RE NOT IN KANSAS ANYMORE.
PHYLISS PEARSALL, BOHEMIAN, TRAVELLER AND MAP-MAKER'S DAUGHTER GOT LOST ONE DAY IN LONDON IN 1935 AND VOWED A PLEDGE IT WOULDN'T HAPPEN AGAIN.
QUIET-- I'M TRYING TO READ.
WE'RE LOST, AREN'T WE?
WALKING EIGHTEEN HOURS A DAY SHE COVERED 3,000 MILES OF 2,300 STREETS TO CREATE THE FIRST EVER A TO Z.
I KNOW EXACTLY WHERE WE ARE. IT'S THE STREET THAT'S MISSING.
FLORIZEL STREET--IT'S HERE ON THE MAP BUT IT DOESN'T EXIST.
LONDON
AS HARRY BECK HAD REFINED THE CITY TO SIMPLIFY EXISTENCE, SO FOOTSORE PHYLISS DID THE OPPOSITE--
--TAMED THE CITY, NAILED IT TO THE PAGES OF HER ATLAS IN TOTAL ACCURACY. THE PERFECT MAP--

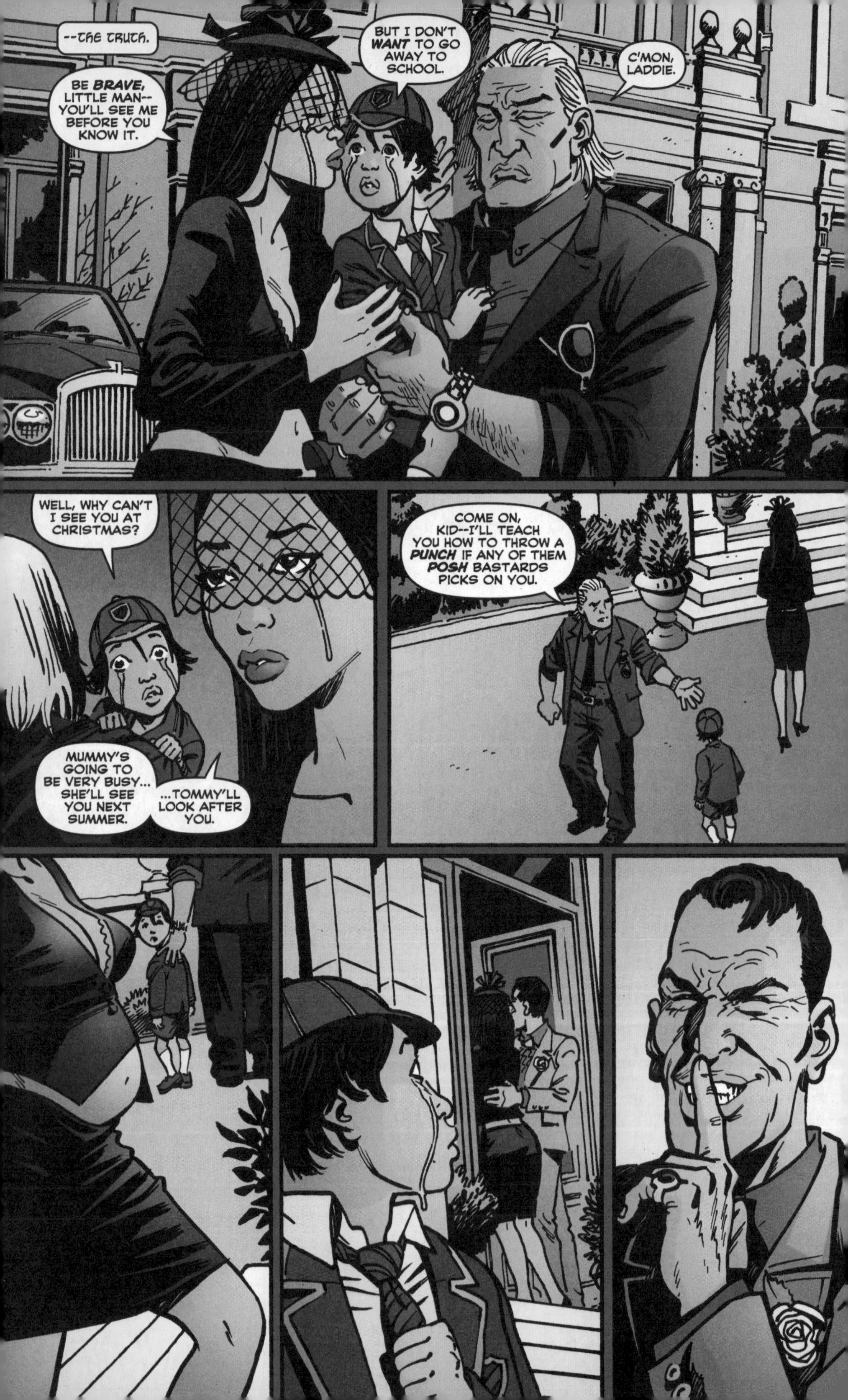
--THE TRUTH.
BE BRAVE, LITTLE MAN--YOU'LL SEE ME BEFORE YOU KNOW IT.
BUT I DON'T WANT TO GO AWAY TO SCHOOL.
C'MON, LADDIE.
WELL, WHY CAN'T I SEE YOU AT CHRISTMAS?
MUMMY'S GOING TO BE VERY BUSY... SHE'LL SEE YOU NEXT SUMMER.
...TOMMY'LL LOOK AFTER YOU.
COME ON, KID--I'LL TEACH YOU HOW TO THROW A PUNCH IF ANY OF THEM POSH BASTARDS PICKS ON YOU.

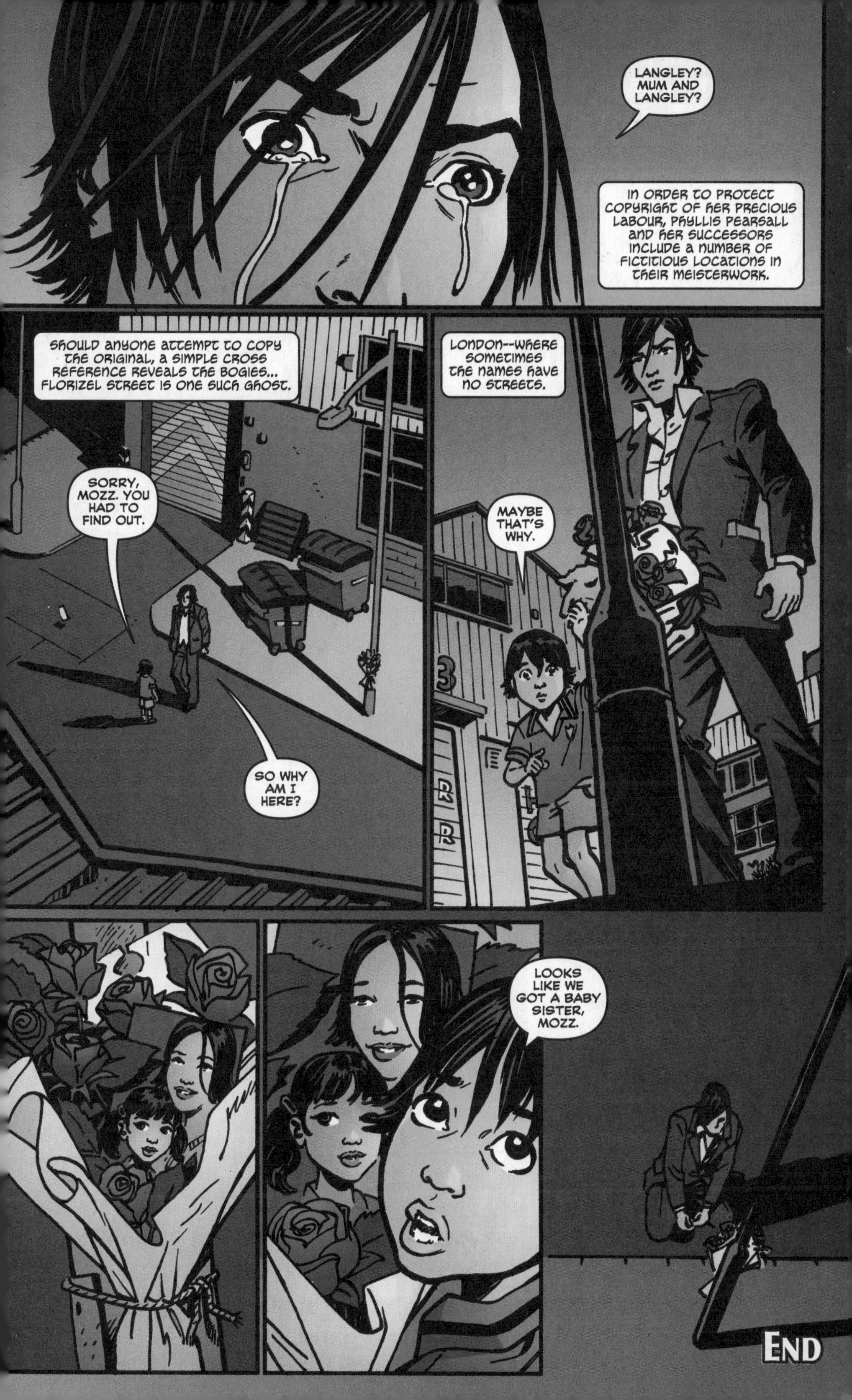
LANGLEY? MUM AND LANGLEY?
IN ORDER TO PROTECT COPYRIGHT OF HER PRECIOUS LABOUR, PHYLLIS PEARSALL AND HER SUCCESSORS INCLUDE A NUMBER OF FICTITIOUS LOCATIONS IN THEIR MEISTERWORK.
SHOULD ANYONE ATTEMPT TO COPY THE ORIGINAL, A SIMPLE CROSS REFERENCE REVEALS THE BOGIES... FLORIZEL STREET IS ONE SUCH GHOST.
SORRY, MOZZ. YOU HAD TO FIND OUT.
SO WHY AM I HERE?
LONDON--WHERE SOMETIMES THE NAMES HAVE NO STREETS.
MAYBE THAT'S WHY.
LOOKS LIKE WE GOT A BABY SISTER, MOZZ.
END

READ MORE CRITICALLY ACCLAIMED TALES
WRITTEN BY COMICS SUPERSTAR
GRANT MORRISON

Grant Morrison • Steve Yeowell • Jill Thompson • Dennis Cramer

THE INVISIBLES
SAY YOU WANT A REVOLUTION

"Watch out for Grant Morrison.
he's a regular comics apocalypse."
—Spin

THE INVISIBLES

Volume 1: SAY YOU WANT A REVOLUTION
WITH STEVE YEOWELL, JILL THOMPSON AND OTHERS

By creating self-awareness and freedom through disobedience,
a subversive group of clandestine anarchists called the
Invisibles combat a vast, existence-threatening conspiracy
which has been creating a hypnotic state of conformity and
control through their manipulation of the government,
business and entertainment.

ALSO AVAILABLE:
VOLUME 2: APOCALIPSTICK
WITH STEVE YEOWELL, JILL THOMPSON AND OTHERS

VOLUME 3: ENTROPY IN THE U.K.
WITH PHIL JIMENEZ, JOHN STOKES AND OTHERS

VOLUME 4: BLOODY HELL IN AMERICA
WITH PHIL JIMENEZ AND JOHN STOKES

VOLUME 5: COUNTING TO NONE
WITH PHIL JIMENEZ AND JOHN STOKES

VOLUME 6: KISSING MR. QUIMPER
WITH CHRIS WESTON AND OTHERS

VOLUME 7: THE INVISIBLE KINGDOM
WITH FRANK QUITELY, SEAN PHILLIPS AND OTHERS

"THE INVISIBLES... IS THAT RARE THING, A SMART,
SPOOKY, EXCITING COMIC. GRANT MORRISON IS
A MASTER OF SMART COMICS."

—*TIME OUT*

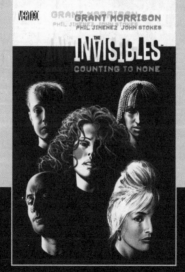

ALL TITLES ARE SUGGESTED FOR MATURE READERS.

GO TO WWW.VERTIGOBOOKS.COM
FOR FREE SAMPLES OF THE FIRST ISSUES OF OUR GRAPHIC NOVELS

© 2006 DC Comics. All rights reserved.